THE
PERFECT FIRM

Your playbook for building a perfect accounting business

Rob Nixon

DEDICATION

This book is dedicated to the tens of thousands of accountants that I have met over the last 23 years. I may have met you at a seminar, on a webinar, a coaching meeting, an industry conference or even in your office. I know I have been pushy, curious, abrahsive, opinionated and sometimes rude to you. I don't mean to offend – I am just looking for the best way. I am constantly asking questions and constantly learning from you.

Over the years, you have adopted my ideas (many times disputing them before agreeing), implemented them and ultimately achieved amazing results. As you have implemented I have learned from you.

It's your implementation (and the subsequent results that you achieve) that has inspired me to keep writing, speaking and creating solutions that help you.

Your feedback on what works and what does not work has been the inspiration for this book. It's a culmination of strategies from every great firm I have ever met. The implementation of every strategy would create "The Perfect Firm."

Thank you.

CONTENTS

Dedication iii

Introduction 9

Dear Accountant 15

The Way of the Dinosaur 27

    Cloud Changes Everything 27

    Globalization of Workforces 31

    Compliance as a Commodity 33

    Disrupting a $500B Profession 36

    Twelve Predictions of the Profession 40

It's Time to Stop Practicing 43

    The Bizarre Habits 43

    Order Takers and History Writers 51

    Steady as She Goes 52

    Build the Plane as You Fly It 54

    Sustainability Index 55

    Clients Want More 56

New Behavior Is Needed 59

    Business by Design 59

    SMAGs and BHAGs 65

    Breaking With in Order to Breakthrough 67

    Real Wealth 69

You Can't Lavish Time Unless You Have Time to Lavish 73

Toxic Relationships 78

Feeling Good about Yourself 80

The Perfect Firm 85

The New Equation 85

It's All about the Clients 95

History Makers 97

Redundant or Real Time 99

What Clients Really Want 106

Technology Makes It Too Easy 112

What to Do with the Data 115

The Intellectual Property Purveying Business 119

Sell What You Know 123

What Products Can Be Created? 125

Follow the Digit Flow 127

The Eight Nonnegotiables 128

Structuring for Success 131

The Right Numbers Matter 135

Knowing Your Numbers 135

How to Plan the Revenue and Profit of an Accounting Firm 136

The Ultimate Accountants Metrics Guide 139

The Entrepreneurial Accountant—An Oxymoron? 149

Entrepreneur: Definition 149

Why Are Partners, Partners? 150

Partner Remuneration 152

The Last Trusted Advisor 155

It's How You Think 158

Money, Money, Money 163

Improving the Profit of Your Accounting Business 163

How to Be Superefficient and Still Make Money 169

$1M Profit Per Partner 176

Time Is Not Money 179

How to Determine the Price..187

   The M Zone..187

   Charge Rates and Value Pricing................................192

   Moving to Value Pricing...193

   How to Price Based on Value 200

Delivering AWESOME Service...217

   Communicating until It Hurts...................................217

   Retaining Clients...223

   Keep a Watchful Eye on Clients Every Day.............227

   Delivering WOW Every Day......................................228

   Your Clients on Your Terms.......................................232

   Taking Control 232

   Eighteen-Step Workflow Process 235

   Finding Opportunities...237

   They Should All Be A-Class Clients.........................241

   Clients Wants or Needs...244

Let's Make Some Targeted Noise 249

   Your Marketing Objectives.......................................249

   Niche Markets—Your Best Buyer.............................253

   You . . . an Object of Interest 256

   Web Dominance 258

   Growing Your Database 263

   Marketing Must Generate Leads 265

   Measuring the Effectiveness of Marketing...............270

Accounting Is Selling..273

   Sales Is a Confidence Game......................................273

   Sales Systems...279

   Sales Is Like Workflow Management........................285

   Marketing Is Not Sales 288

   This Sounds Like You 290

   How to Be a Guru in Sales..292

   Twelve-Step Meeting Process 298

Dealing with Objections 307

Sealing the Deal in Writing 309

Template—Implementation Plan 310

Real Implementation Plan—Cash-Flow Forecasting.....................313

Real Implementation Plan—Cash Flow and Profit Improvement...............319

Real Implementation Plan—Business Development Project....................322

Some People Are Needed..329

The Current Team Might Be Short Lived 329

A Virtual Team..332

Team Engagement...334

Rewarding Your Team 337

Together Everyone Achieves More 338

A Growth Culture...342

Where the Rubber Meets the Road 347

Measuring a Well-Developed Firm 347

Getting Buy-In 351

Implementing Anything 354

It's All about You 359

Core Purpose..360

Goals and Values 361

Courage—Being Bold...363

Thirst for Learning...364

Get on a Plane 365

Live Large 366

Self-Belief...367

Fail a Lot..369

Don't Learn Stuff 370

Fun Every Day..372

Discipline...373

Leave a Legacy 376

Making an Impact...379

The Final Word 381

About Rob 383

INTRODUCTION

I am asked all the time what a perfect firm looks like. I've never met one, but I have met hundreds of firms who are doing many things right. However, I've never met one firm that does everything right. My reasoning as to why so many firms do not work well is because they are designed by default—they just happen. Most firms are started with little capital input and they just grow. No plan, limited capital at the start, and limited capital reinvested to make a real sustainable, highly profitable business.

Every person reading this has an opportunity to start again with a new sheet of paper and a new plan. You just need the desire to change and the courage to act. Sometimes the action part will never happen in the firm you are in—which might mean you need to leave the firm you're in and start anew.

If there was a perfect firm, here's what it would look like.

People and Structure

There is one owner only, unless additional partners/owners demonstrate that they can sell at least $1M in new revenue per year. If a partner cannot (or will not) sell and bring in new business (all based on value-based fees), then they are an overpaid accountant and not needed as an owner.

- ✓ Initially the owner is the chief executive officer (CEO), but as the business expands, a full-time CEO is appointed.
- ✓ From day one, the primary owner does zero chargeable time. He is heavily involved in sales from the start, but not doing any of the work that was sold. The owner is a client relationship manager, not a client doer!
- ✓ There is an external chairperson and board of directors/advisors that holds the CEO and management team accountable.

- ✓ A corporate structure is present, where every team member qualifies at some point for the employee share ownership program.
- ✓ A full-time marketing manager is locally based and builds an offshore team to market the firm. Hire immediately.
- ✓ A full-time quality controller/reviewer checks all client work before it goes out the door. (Typically, this is a partner at the start. We don't like that plan—it stinks of effort.)
- ✓ A general manager runs the day-to-day operations of the business. Hire when there are eight people in the business.
- ✓ A lead workflow manager coordinates all the work that needs to be done.
- ✓ A client service coordinator (ratio of one CSC to three professionals) interacts with the clients for all administrative work associated with the professional work. This team is based offshore.
- ✓ Offshore processing professionals work as needed. If it can be done more efficiently for $5–$10 per hour offshore, then why pay $35–$80 per hour locally?
- ✓ Local client relationship managers (CRM) deliver client work at a high level and sell new projects. All CRMs must have sales ability, otherwise they are not needed.
- ✓ A revenue manager makes sure the revenue is sold and delivered. Initially done by the CEO, but as the firm gets larger it would need a full-time person.
- ✓ Administrative functions of the business are performed by a virtual assistant team offshore.
- ✓ Locally the business is client facing (sales and advice) and everything that is administration or processing is done offshore.

Operations

The general manager is running a finely tuned instrument. Everything just works. The systems are awesome, the rules are set, and every team member and client follows the rules.

- ✓ 100 percent of internal technology is Cloud based. No server required, and the business can operate from anywhere in the world on a mobile device.

✓ 100 percent of clients' accounting systems are Cloud based. No Cloud accounting equals no client of the firm.

✓ All internal Cloud systems seamlessly interact with client Cloud systems. Client trading data is visible to the firm every day.

✓ All clients are on an annual accounting service for known regular work. They pay a monthly fixed fee for a set scope on the first day of every month in advance.

✓ If there is an additional project, then this is priced upfront and the entire fee is collected upfront before commencing work.

✓ All team members are paid 20 percent (or more) above market salaries. Attract the best people that money can buy.

✓ All team members have 5 percent of their salaries allocated to a learning and development fund for "soft skills," such as seminars, book of the month, internal speakers, etc. If your payroll is $1M, then $50K is allocated to education and training.

✓ All team members have a code of cultural ethics they live by—performance standards on culture behavior and client service.

Services Offered

Any services that are offered need to be recurring in nature. You're building a subscription business. The litmus test on services is that they are "mission critical," meaning the client must use them to protect assets, grow and develop revenue/cash, and create wealth. The clients cannot do the work themselves, and they use the services from you every week, month, or year.

✓ Bookkeeping—delivered offshore

✓ Accounting—delivered offshore

✓ Business advisory—cash flow, profit, and revenue planning—delivered locally in person

✓ Coaching—group coaching eight businesses at a time—delivered locally in person

✓ Tax planning and structuring—delivered locally and offshore

✓ Insurance—home, contents, motor vehicle, key man, life, etc.—delivered offshore

✓ Legal services—general legal services—delivered locally and offshore

✓ Financial, wealth planning, investment services—delivered locally and offshore

Audit is not mentioned in this list, because I believe accounting software will self-audit or blockchain technology will take a big chunk of it away.

Marketing

The marketing manager is driving the brand and generating leads every day.

- ✓ The firm is called a snazzy name—not "XYZ Partners" or "XYZ and Associates."
- ✓ Annual benchmarking survey completed of all clients.
- ✓ A book is written about your chosen niche market.
- ✓ Your firm is the global (national, if you want to water it down) leader in your space.
- ✓ A database of all prospective clients in your niche is acquired, curated, and nurtured—at least 50,000 names.
- ✓ Content marketing is distributed to entire database every week.
- ✓ Monthly webinar series and quarterly seminar series are offered.
- ✓ Annual conference offered for all clients.

Clients

The key to clients is that they are all A-class clients. Life is too short to work with people you'd rather not work with. Defining what an A-class client is for you to work out. Here are my thoughts.

- ✓ Clients would be only one industry type.
- ✓ Clients would be 100 percent business clients, and personal returns completed only if associated with the business.
- ✓ They would be all around the world and unless they were from the chosen niche market, then they would not be accepted as a client.
- ✓ All clients would go through a rigorous goal-setting program at the outset to help understand their personal/business goals and then match professional services to the goals. Unless they have goals, they would not be accepted as a client of the firm
- ✓ Every year a personal performance review (PPR) would be held with the client owners. It would encompass personal goals, business performance, wealth creation, and risk mitigation. New services would come off the back of this.

✓ Every client would have, as a minimum, a live working and real-time cash flow forecast and a quarterly coaching meeting on cash flow, profit, and revenue improvement.

Measurement Metrics

The business needs to perform at a suitable level to get a great return on capital employed. Here are the metrics.

✓ Average hourly rate for client work more than $500.

✓ Average hourly rate for all hours worked more than $200.

✓ Team member client productivity fewer than 1,350 hours per year.

✓ Owner(s) client productivity 0 hours per year.

✓ WIP and receivables (lock-up days) fewer than 10 combined.

✓ Average fee per client group more than $40,000.

✓ Revenue per full-time person more than $300,000.

✓ Gross profit (revenue less all salaries) more than 75 percent.

✓ Profit before owner(s) salaries more than 60 percent.

That's what a perfect firm would look like. My buddy, Michael, says, "A breakthrough often happens after a break with." What do you need to break with to breakthrough?

If you are dissatisfied with the performance (personal satisfaction and/or monetary rewards) of your current firm, then you will need to change what you are doing. Not tweak it a few percentage points in productivity, average hourly rate, write-downs, or lock-up. No!

You will need to change what you are doing dramatically if you want a different result. The good news is that the change needed is not that hard to do, once you get your motivation and mindset right.

This book is about everything I know about the accounting profession, how it works and how it can truly add value to it's clients. The implementation of the ideas (in full) will turn you into a Perfect Firm.

As you dig into this book, you'll realize it a book of best practice—a guide, textbook, blue print or a playbook. It is a detailed summary of what I have learned throughout the years about what works and what does not.

My promise is that if you apply these ideas, tactics, and strategies, you will run a better business and in turn, you will enjoy your professional and personal life more than you ever thought possible.

Enjoy *The Perfect Firm!*

Rob Nixon
April 2017, Brisbane, Australia

Contact details
Email—rob@robnixon.com
Blog—www.robnixon.com
Twitter—@therobnixon
LinkedIn—therobnixon

DEAR ACCOUNTANT

Since May 1994, I have been working exclusively with accountants and accounting firms, helping them to grow, develop themselves, and build great businesses for themselves and their clients. I am not an accountant (in fact, I finished school when I was just 16), and that gives me a distinct advantage. I tend to look at things a bit differently, and I offer a perspective from a real-world, business point of view.

There was no grand plan to start working with accountants. I literally "fell" into the accounting profession. Here's how it happened.

I was running a series of customer service seminars in 1994 (I was 24 at the time) and an accountant (Ellis) attended one of my seminars. He said, "Will you come to my town and do this seminar for my clients?" He worked in a small country town called Coonamble in New South Wales, Australia. The town had a population of 3,000. It was a two-accountant town. He told me he had 126 clients.

Never one to miss an opportunity, I jumped at the chance to apply one of my favorite marketing strategies—host beneficiary marketing. He promoted the event to his clients using my marketing materials and 56 people turned up to the seminar. I made a profit of $2,500 from the night (the most ever at the time), and Ellis did a great thing for his client base and the community. It was the largest event I had ever done and the first one that made a profit!

I realized right away that accountants had marketing leverage because of their trusted advisor status and loyalty in their client base. They had enormous **IMPACT.** I immediately stopped all other marketing activities (mail, fax, radio, print advertising, and TV) that were sending me broke and decided to concentrate 100 percent on accountants.

Initially my seminars were for the accountants' clients. Then I started working directly with firms on a training and consulting basis. I moved on to providing benchmarking services, knowledge management software, coaching, DVD products, marketing/sales and business intelligence software, and then e-learning.

I am now entering my twenty-third year working exclusively with accountants (from the micro businesses to the multinationals), and I travel the world (they do the same things everywhere) speaking, coaching, and consulting. I train accountants in all facets of business improvement, researching, benchmarking, and creating tools and products. I have written countless articles about my findings, and I have created a variety of companies that serve accountants.

Anyone would think I like accountants. I do!

The way I work is by observation. I visit firms; I observe what they are doing and speak with them on a daily basis to see what is working and what is not. I take the best bits from each firm, add my twists and insights, and then recreate it for the entire profession.

It's a wonderful profession to be working with, yet I see some massive changes happening around the world.

It's all about your profession being disrupted. It's a word (disruption) we hear a lot about these days. We live in a world of disruption. Industries all around the world are being disrupted by technological advancements, social change, and innovative thinking.

Entrepreneurial thinking is being applied to these industries that have been in existence for many decades. A new nimble player will enter the market and challenge the status quo. Typically, they will use Internet-based technology to "cut out" parts of the supply chain and give a better experience to the consumer. They will invent better ways of doing something and find cheaper labor to deliver the service or product.

All around the world, industry types that are being disrupted in a major way are as follows.

1. Intermediaries and supply chains
2. Information providers
3. Processing companies
4. "Behind a computer" companies

Sound like anyone we know? Hmmm.

Yes—it's you! The accounting profession globally is being disrupted right now, and most accountants don't even know it is happening.

There are three main areas that are being disrupted in the accounting profession.

1. Compliance is being commoditized by technology.
2. Labor is being sourced from less-expensive countries.
3. Clients are using the Internet for your advice.

These three market forces will only escalate, and if you do nothing about it, then revenue, profit, and business value will erode.

Let's look at these three disruptive areas and work out what you can do to capitalize on each one.

Disruptive Area 1—Compliance Is Being Commoditized by Technology

The adoption of Internet-based (commonly called Cloud) technology is growing at a rapid rate of knots. You can't stop this happening. There is social behavior/change in action (people want to access their information on their handheld device), and there are massive technology companies investing huge sums of money to drive the change—if they don't, they won't be in business.

The applications that are used on the Internet are sophisticated, accurate, and can connect to other Internet systems. For example, the accounting system can connect to the client management system, which can connect to the inventory control system and the distribution system. At the client end, inexpensive applications can "talk to each other" and give real-time information to the business leader.

Here's an example in action.

A customer buys a product/service by whatever means. It is scanned using the bar code and automatically registers the sale into the online accounting system. Bank accounts, income statements, and balance sheet data are automatically updated. The action also updates the inventory management system that there is one less product. The client management system (assuming the customer used a login/user name/loyalty card to identify the customer) and the buying habits of that customer are updated and now can be tracked. A real-time report/dashboard is automatically updated/sent and the leadership of the business can see the trends or reports immediately on their smartphones or tablets. They might be on a private island at the time sunning themselves, when the report comes through. They can check it then or when they choose.

This level of automation (all driven through the Internet) enables the business leader to make instant management decisions and run a better business. It's happening right now. No spreadsheets are manually updated. No paper filing and updating is done. No need for a meeting to tell me the numbers. No waiting. No people. All real time. All automated.

It's exciting and it is happening right now. In my business, I have had this level of automation for more than five years.

Let's look at the accounting process.

Previously it used to be on a spreadsheet, server, or hard drive and kept at the client's premises. A bookkeeper (or spouse of the owner) did the data entry using manual keystrokes. At the end of the year, a file was saved and sent to the accountant with supporting information. There would be questions and queries back and forth. The accountant would then prepare a "set of accounts" and present it to the client some two to nine months after the initial data was received. The preparation of the historical data was unavoidable, as it had to be done to comply with the government authorities.

However, the data was old data. It was redundant. What help is it when the accountant tells me, "You should have done this and that" nine months after the fact? No help whatsoever!

Enter Internet-based accounting systems. The available products offer real-time information that do not need people to do the data entry. With these systems, the data is more accurate (super computers are doing the processing, not people) and there are fewer mistakes. In addition, the accounting systems are offering excellent reporting and data analytics, which were only previously offered by accountants as a management accounting package. The revenue I used to spend with the accountant is now delivered by technology.

Also, because the information is more accurate and the systems only have one version, the time spent at your end to prepare annual accounts is far less. In fact, we are seeing a 30–80 percent time reduction at the accountants' end (in year two onward) for accounts preparation work. What do you do with that time saving? Do you reduce your price? Unfortunately for you, the technology companies are directly promoting that "You will be more efficient working with your accountant when you buy our product." You have been selling "hours" for all these years, and more efficiency means fewer hours, and fewer hours should mean a cheaper price. That's what the business community is thinking.

We are seeing more price pressure on compliance than ever before, and it will only escalate.

As an example, the New Zealand accounting profession is one of the world leaders in the adoption of Cloud accounting technology. The accountants have been active in the space since 2008 and at the time of writing more than 45 percent of New Zealand small businesses use a Cloud accounting product.

As a result of technology and market forces, the New Zealand accounting profession has been negatively affected. In short, it's going backwards.

Take a look at the following graph, which shows my profit per partner analysis for the past 13 years (2004–2016).

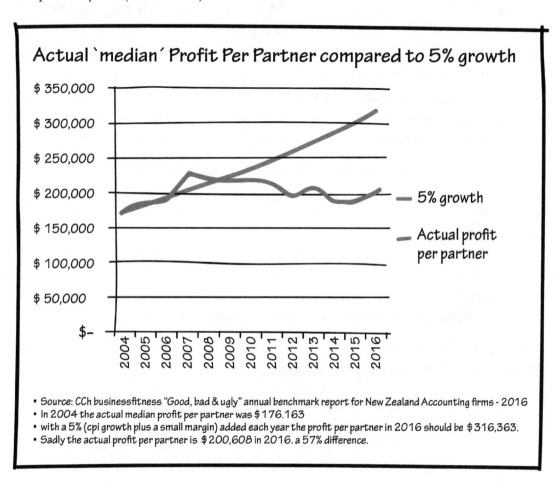

Actual `median´ Profit Per Partner compared to 5% growth

— 5% growth

— Actual profit per partner

- Source: CCh businessfitness "Good, bad & ugly" annual benchmark report for New Zealand Accounting firms - 2016
- In 2004 the actual median profit per partner was $176.163
- with a 5% (cpi growth plus a small margin) added each year the profit per partner in 2016 should be $316,363.
- Sadly the actual profit per partner is $200,608 in 2016. a 57% difference.

According to a popular benchmarking report by CCH Business Fitness (*The Good, the Bad and the Ugly*), in 2004 the actual median profit per partner was NZ$176,163. In 2016, the actual median profit per partner was NZ$200,608. Not only has the actual profit per partner declined in the past 10 years (from a high of NZ$229,646 in 2007), but when you apply "CPI plus a bit" of just 5 percent to each year since 2004, then the 2016 comparison results are staggering.

The other numbers for work in progress, receivables, write-downs/realization, average hourly rate, and productivity/utilization have gone up, down, and sideways. At the end of the day, it's the profit per partner that matters.

Every expense in a firm is increasing. Salaries and overheads are increasing, and leaders should be running a better firm each year, so applying 5 percent per year profit growth is a conservative growth target. Based on 5 percent, the median profit per partner in 2016 should have been NZ$316,363. Alas, it was only NZ$200,608. That's almost a NZ$120,000 difference per partner!

How can the average partners in New Zealand afford private school education, decent cars, reasonable holidays, and still give back to the community? Most can't.

And to make matters worse, isn't the accounting profession supposed to be the trusted advisor—the primary business advisor? Most accounting partners are making less than their clients are, yet they are advising them about business success! Hmmm.

So why is this happening? Based on my research, there are three primary reasons.

1. Cloud accounting technology is driving efficiencies in the firm, and the profession has been forced to reduce prices.

2. Savvy clients have more information than ever before, and they are asking more "price" and "value" related questions.

3. Nimble accounting firms are promoting bundled and cheaper prices than ever before and thus "commoditizing" compliance.

But it goes deeper. The majority of the New Zealand accounting profession **did not** do three things to combat the external forces.

1. They did not "price upfront" all client work. As they became more efficient with Cloud accounting (around 50 percent), they did not increase their charge rates to make up for the efficiencies gained. If you're pricing in arrears and getting 50 percent more efficient, then charge rates need to double to keep the same price.

2. They did not readjust their cost structures to combat the nimble players. They didn't outsource, offshore, or reduce their headcount fast enough.

3. They did not add value with the capacity they created. They didn't deliver additional services to clients or find new clients to fill the capacity gap.

The New Zealand profit per partner has gone backwards, because of the slowness to adapt to external forces and the lack of management of Cloud accounting.

This will happen to you, if you do not address the three points above.

As the old saying goes "if nothing changes, nothing changes." What that means is if you do nothing (strategy, process, tools, etc.), then nothing changes. In this case, doing nothing means everything changes. And a sharp decline in profit should be enough to motivate the profession to change. Let me add one more idea to the mix before we get onto solutions: **one-click filing**. With all the Internet data (which is much more accurate) already in the Internet accounting system, how long will it be before the government authorities get their systems ready and allow direct filing? The government authorities do not care about the intermediary called an accountant. All they want is their tax money on about the right time! The reason the majority of the accounting profession exists is to make sure that the government gets the correct amount of tax money it is owed.

One-click filing is not far away, and it will bypass accountants and eliminate a big chunk of their revenue.

Technology is disrupting the profession and there is more to come. Is your firm ready?

Disruptive Area 2—Labor Is Being Sourced from Less-Expensive Countries

Manufacturing companies have been using low-cost labor in developing countries for decades to produce their products. Just look at the clothes on your back. I bet few of them are made in your country!

The reality is that (because of escalating labor costs) most Western countries have priced themselves out of markets by attempting to produce the products locally.

Up until a few years ago, it was primarily "hardware" based manufacturing companies using this resource. Now we are seeing "services" companies embrace the outsourcing trend with fully resourced teams.

Most people think of this as outsourcing, where the correct term is offshoring.

Outsourcing is hiring someone to do the task who does not exclusively work for you. Accountants are a classic outsourced service. You work for many clients, and they send their work to you because you are better at it than they are.

Offshoring is where you set up a team (maybe starting with one person) in another country and they exclusively work for you. The banks and airlines have been doing this for years. They get themselves an office in a developing country, fill it with desks/chairs/computers/phones, and hire and train some people, and voila, they have an office that can support their customers.

For one-off projects, outsourcing is the way to go. However, for larger ongoing tasks, offshoring is the way to go.

Accountants have recently embraced the idea quickly and are hiring people in developing countries with some degree of vigor.

I went on an offshoring study tour (in the Philippines), and the opening speaker said two things to me that got me excited.

1. "Any job that can be done over the phone or behind a computer we can do for 50–90 percent cheaper, faster, and often better."
2. "I have been a virtual assistant for five years for a university professor in New York. I have gotten to know her job so well that I now mark her students' papers for her."

I thought WOW. There are smart, hard workers; there is an abundance of them; and they are relatively inexpensive.

If you think about an accountant's day, most of it is spent on the phone or behind a computer. Most of the day is spent dealing with client queries and processing accounting work. The technology products will take a lot of the processing work away, and the balance can be done by cheaper labor offshore.

What is left are team members who are customer facing and adding value. The accounting firm of the future has a local team who are customer facing (nurturing, sales, and advice) and everything else (back office and processing) is done offshore.

There are three compelling reasons why this makes sense.

1. An abundance of labor
2. A labor force who are supremely qualified
3. A lower cost structure

You can set this model up one of three ways.

1. Hire people directly who work from home.
2. Go through a serviced office business (called a business process outsourcing or BPO) and hire the people through the BPO.
3. Incorporate a company and set up your own office—viable if you need 30 or more people.

When hiring someone, you can conduct an interview via online videoconference (Skype, Google Hangouts, GoToMeeting, etc.), and proceed the same way you already do. Place an ad, go through a recruiter, receive résumés, cull them, and hire the best person for the job.

If you go through option two, then the BPO will help you hire the people. The training is up to you—again via videoconferencing or personally. They are your employees, and they need to be trained in your systems and your way of doing things. They become part of your team, so they need to be treated as such.

As an example, my Australian team had a cooking class one night. My team in the office in Manila did a class on the same night in their city. My Australian, USA and UK teams do daily huddles and they Skype with our team every day in the Manila office. What we do in one office, we do in another.

Some people have a problem with this idea. "We must keep the jobs in our country," I hear. "What will our accountants do if we send the work to a team elsewhere?" is also another one. "What would my clients think" is a common question. Well, most accounting firms will have different nationalities employed already in their local offices. What's the difference? You just have a team working for you in a different country in your offshore office. The teams work for you.

If you pare the comments down, often they are either racist-related comments or the person saying them has inadequacies and hang-ups that their job can be done by someone else for a tenth of their salary.

All of this is globalization and a change in social behavior. I think the concept got off to a bad start with telemarketing companies calling people at home, and the recipient could not understand what the callers were saying. It also got off to a bad start because the term "outsourcing" was created, and many accounting firms sent jobs offshore. Because the person who worked on the job was not working 100 percent for that firm, there was a lot of rework needed.

As a disruptive trend, we are seeing accountants use the available resources in the following ways.

- Hiring marketing people to do the marketing work for the firm. I know of an Australian $4M firm that has eight marketing team members offshore.

- Hiring client service coordinators to handle data collection and job setup from clients.

- Hiring bookkeepers to do bookkeeping work for clients—and charging clients $20 per hour and making a five-times margin.

- Hiring data integrity people to sort out client data before it gets to the accountant.

- Hiring technical people who can do "Cloud conversions" and other software help.

- Hiring product development people to create products for the firm.

- Hiring administrators to do document scanning, corporate secretarial, receivable collection, filing, etc.

- Hiring accountants to do the accounting work that does not involve client facing meetings.

Now here is the BIG one.

Businesses are being directly targeted by accounting firms (offshore or local that have an offshore team) offering accounting work from $8–$25 per hour. This is escalating at a great rate of knots.

As a consumer of accounting services, why would I pay $200 per hour when I can get it for $20—or less? There have to be some compelling reasons as to why I would continue paying ten times as much!

You, as a professional, must wake up and realize that you cannot maintain your current prices when technology is commoditizing compliance and global markets are offering lower cost labor direct to your clients.

To hold prices, you will have to add value, add value, and add more value to remain relevant in the future. Accountants will have to offer valuable commentary to the data in front of them and move much more into business advisory services.

My view is that as an accountant, **if you are not adding value to the data that is in front of you, then your days are numbered!** Either the computer will do the work or someone in a developing country on $5 per hour will do it for you.

This is a big disruption to the labor force of accountants in Western countries. It is also a great opportunity to capitalize on.

The world is changing fast. Are you ignoring it, embracing it, or hoping it will go away?

It won't.

Disruptive Area 3—Clients Are Using the Internet for Your Advice

It seems we use the Internet for everything we want/need to know!

Addresses, companies, people, products, concerts, store opening times, weather, golf handicap, cycling routes, finding a date, friends whereabouts (or what they are eating—yuk), and the BIG one . . . **"how to do" everything.** The Internet seems to be our first port of call for anything we want to know or find information on.

Whatever happened to the Yellow Pages phone book, asking people personally, the *Encyclopedia Britannica*, or a catalog? All are (or nearly) GONE!

Social behavior is indicating we need/want to be connected to our electronic devices. And the device rules supreme.

The world is connected, and it is getting more connected every day. Currently we go to our device (pick up a phone or tablet) and tap in the requested search. We can also talk to our device (like Siri in the iPhone, as a good example) and she/he can help us. Or we talk to our cars, and they will give us directions to our destinations.

Does this give us an enhanced human experience? Probably not. But it sure is efficient.

Mobile technology is booming. It's what consumers want. They want information at their fingertips. Tap, tap, tap (or ask it), and hey, presto—I have the answer and now I am an expert.

And that is an issue for anyone in the advice business (also known as accountants)!

Let's say I wanted to learn about borrowing money through my pension scheme to buy a property. I could search online and find the answer in a few seconds. What if I wanted to work out how to improve the profit of my winemaking business? I could go to a LinkedIn group and discuss that and get an answer. What if I needed a payroll or tax question answered? I can search it and go directly to the government portal and get the answer.

The Internet has all the answers, it seems.

Enter IBM, a global technology company that provides hardware, software, and computing services.

The IBM Watson supercomputer is an extraordinary piece of engineering. It can beat humans (really smart ones) at chess and Jeopardy (proven)! It's said that Watson is so smart, it knows what the president of any country will say next! OK . . . I made the last bit up.

You get the idea. Watson is a super smart supercomputer. Watson is based on machine learning and artificial intelligence.

IBM made a greater than $2B investment to develop Watson into a useable resource. There are more than 2,000 people on the Watson team, and their jobs are to integrate Watson into the world. One of the cool ideas is to create "Watson for business." Think of it as Siri (iPhone fame) for business. You have a business question, talk to the device, and it gives you the answer. BOOM. Great for the user—not so great for the accountant.

You see, Watson is a sponge, like a human. It can absorb, disseminate, translate, organize, and conceptualize any information, and then send it back in a usable format. Mostly all of the world's texts (as in manuals, books, and all forms of content) are accessible on the Internet. But the Internet is a bit of a mess. There is a lot of content to absorb and disseminate. Watson can sort it out and give it back to you in a useable format.

I got interested in Watson when I read the following line in a newsfeed.

"This is the start of the end of professional services as we currently know it."

WOW. WOW and more WOW!

Does that mean the supercomputer can replace the advisor? For repetitive and systematic information, absolutely YES. And there will be "an app for that" soon.

I don't mean to scare you, but I do. This is real. It is happening right now, and the accounting profession is in the firing line for massive disruption. Without notice and appropriate action, these three disrupters have the capacity to wipe out a (BIG) chunk of revenue, profit, and business value in the profession . . . QUICKLY.

How long before a business owner does not need an accountant at all? How long before billions of dollars of revenue are wiped out of the current accounting profession?

It's happening right now. To remain relevant as a profession, I think there are only three solutions.

1. Add value to what you are doing.
2. Be proactive with new services.
3. Become a real-time accountant.

This book is all about you combating the inevitable disruption to your profession. It is about you building a great business for yourself and your clients.

THE WAY OF THE DINOSAUR

Cloud Changes Everything

I have a theory as to why most clients of an accounting firm are within a driving radius of the firm. My theory is that way back when, the clients used to travel to the accountant's office with their "stuff" (cashbooks, receipts, livestock headcount, paperwork, etc.). They'd get dressed up in their Sunday best for the occasion, have a pleasant conversation about the year that was, and then leave.

The accountant would then process the stuff, communicate any queries by letter/telex/facsimile/phone or courier pigeon, then present the final paperwork to the client for signing (more pleasant conversation, unless an unsightly tax bill awaited), and then finish the annual accounts. The accountant would then file the annual return with the various government authorities, the client would pay the tax begrudgingly, and next year they'd do it all over again.

> "The only thing that has changed these days is the format of the "stuff" that arrives."

The only thing that has changed these days is the format of the stuff that arrives. These days most of the incoming information is scanned, emailed, or provided on a portable disk or memory stick.

The driving radius of the client to accountant still exists, because the data is still **heavy**. The challenge with heavy data is the version control of the software, human involvement, inconsistency, and data integrity. What happens today is that when the information finally arrives, the accountant will load the stick or the disk into the computer, check the version (damn, it's a different version), start moving information around, check the other information provided, and then realize that there is a bunch of missing information. At some point of time in the future (sometimes weeks after the client has sent the information), the accountant will contact the client with what is missing. The client will ignore the message, because it's a pain to deal with. The accountant will get frustrated and send another email to ask them to send the information. Eventually the client will send in some of the missing information—or the wrong information.

Several weeks (or months) have passed by. The accountant now has all the information. They analyze and manipulate the data and produce a draft set of accounts. They send the draft to the client for signing. The client signs, not knowing if it is right or not. The accountant then files the information with the various government authorities. The client gets a tax bill or a refund—more often than not, a bill to pay more. The client doesn't understand why there is a bill, and the accountant is not good at explaining why. The client pays the bill begrudgingly. And all is done until next year.

> "Most of an accountant's revenue is data entry, checking, and lodging historical data with the government authorities."

I'm exhausted just writing about the process. No wonder accountants take so long to do things. There are two primary reasons why it takes so long to do annual compliance work in an accounting firm.

1. Archaic systems—such as hard-drive accounting and paper
2. Human involvement—data entry and processing at the client end

The accounting profession around the world has carved out billions upon billions of dollars in annual compliance revenue (which is basically history writing) because of heavy data and human involvement.

Most of an accountant's revenue is data entry, checking, processing and filing historical data with the government authorities. We have surveyed firms, and they tell us nearly 80 percent of their compliance revenue (which is typically 80 percent of all revenue) is data entry, checking, processing and filing.

There is so much "checking and processing" going on because the data is bad, old, inconsistent and redundant.

Where's the value in historical data? Yes, a client can learn from the history lesson, but our research shows that the business community does not want an accountant who deals in redundant (history) data—they want one who is real time. We asked 411 small business owners if they would prefer a "redundant data accountant" or a "real time accountant" and 93 percent wanted a real-time accountant.

What if the entire process could be simplified? What would happen if the human element were minimized and technology took care of the data integrity?

It can. And it's happening right now. Enter light data in the form of Internet data, commonly called Cloud computing.

> "There would be much less time involved at the accountant's end because of version control and supercomputers."

With light data, there's no data. There are no files to send. No paperwork to email. No version control issues and limited human involvement. Just a login that you and the accountant has access to.

Imagine when your client transacted a purchase with a customer (point of sale) that the bar code triggered the warehouse that there was one less item available, and that updated the total inventory. At the same time, the transaction updated the customer relationship management database (often called a CRM system) that the customer had purchased the item and the accounting system also recognized the sale for the day. The accounting system would show the live inventory levels, the cash balance, the revenue, and the profit on a real-time basis. All the systems that used to be disparate, hard-drive, or heavy-data systems are now "talking to each other" via the Internet.

That would be really cool, as the accounting data would now have much more data integrity. There would be much less "checking" involved at the accountant's end, as the supercomputers would be doing the checking. There would also be much less data processing at the accountant's end, as the supercomputers would be doing the processing.

There would be much less time involved at the accountant's end because of version control and supercomputers. There would be less human intervention and better data.

Does this sound Pollyannaish, excessively optimistic? Not really. Short of robots doing all the work in the accountants' office, this is exactly what is happening with accounting firms and their clients all around the world.

You might say that this is a good thing. I think so too. You'll definitely be more efficient in dealing with clients, if you promote these sorts of systems. You'll have far less time on each and every client who has an Internet-based accounting system. However, there is a dark side.

And it has everything to do with the way you have charged your clients in the past.

The graph titled "The Effects of Cloud on Compliance" shows the real efficiency savings when you convert your clients to a Cloud accounting system. If you had 10,000 capacity hours with the annual compliance work on the old "heavy data" system and you changed them over to Cloud accounting, then for the first year about the same volume of hours is needed to produce the annual work. In year two, you will have about a 15 percent savings in time, and as the years roll on, there is up to a 60 percent savings each year after five years of having a Cloud-based accounting solution. Sometimes it takes less time than five years. Because of the data integrity, you are so much more efficient at the accountant's end.

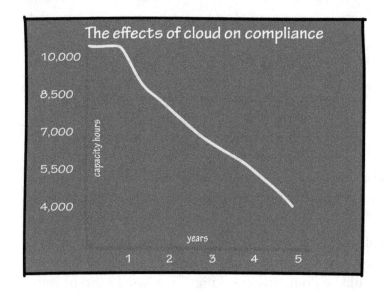

"Due to market forces; nimble, marketing-oriented, accounting firms; and social behavior; compliance will be commoditized. There is nothing you can do about it."

The challenge is what the client expects to pay based on what you deliver. For years, the accounting profession has been promoting "hourly rates" and "time." You have told us, the business community, that you have charge rates, we buy hours, and, based on the number of hours and who does the work, the price will be $X.

Because of technology, like Cloud accounting, you have created "a rod for your own back" when it comes to pricing. Not only can we see that when we use Cloud accounting that it is easier and faster to deal with you, but the technology providers are telling us "When you buy our product, you will be more efficient working with your accountant." To us, the word "efficient" means fewer hours needed to do the work. Fewer hours means reduced costs.

As such, price pressure kicks in about year two of using Cloud accounting where clients start asking questions about price and value for money. It's an awkward conversation. I know why compliance is so expensive: manual labor, labor costs, and archaic systems. It's not like you're making bongo bucks (technical term for a lot) out of compliance. I believe compliance should be value priced accordingly with the value it adds to my financial condition. That would be value priced DOWN!

> "Because of technology, like Cloud accounting, you have created "a rod for your own back" when it comes to pricing."

Due to market forces; nimble, marketing-oriented, accounting firms; and social behavior; compliance will be commoditized. There is nothing you can do about it. We see firms in well-developed Cloud accounting countries, such as New Zealand, marketing accounting services for 50–80 percent less than their competitors. They can do this because they have stripped the cost structure and are using new tools that enable them to be more efficient in their delivery.

Don't fight it. Instead embrace Cloud accounting (promote it hard to all clients) and realize that you now have access to real-time data. With the data, you can make a real-time difference—not a redundant-data difference!

Globalization of Workforces

The world is flat and getting flatter. No longer do you need to have your team in your office chained to a desk. No longer do you have to hire local labor to get things done.

Right now, there are millions of contractors around the world who will work for $3, $5, $7, or $10 per hour to do your projects. You can hire a virtual assistant for $5 per hour to do all your administrative work. Anything that can be done behind a computer or over the phone can be done for as little as $3 per hour.

So why don't you use these fabulous resources?

Some accountants have a moral issue with the world of outsourcing and offshoring. What will my children do? Let's keep the jobs in our country! We hire local! What would our clients think?

Yet what I find interesting about this is that nearly everything you wear is made offshore. Most everything you buy is made in another country. And, to top it all off, the role of an accountant is to have work outsourced to them!

So your clients are into it. Why not you?!

Here's the dilemma. With the advent of Cloud accounting technology, many of the "low-cost labor" countries are getting smart and promoting their services direct to business. They can do the work for a fraction of the cost that you can (in some Asian countries, the minimum wage is $1.50 per hour), and often they can do it better and faster.

> "With the advent of Cloud accounting technology, many of the "low-cost labor" countries are getting smart and promoting their services direct to business."

Almost every firm I meet complains about their people. "We can't get enough good quality people. The crew we have isn't good. The people are inefficient and lazy."

So, get some new employees and stop whining about it. There is an abundance of good, quality accountants and administrative team members in the world— they currently just don't work for you. Go find them and hire them. You can find accountants and other contractors on a range of contractor/freelancer websites, such as www.upwork.com, www.guru.com, www.freelancer.com, or www.99designs.com.

Here's another dilemma (wake-up call time) for those accountants who are currently employed in a firm. I'm talking to those who spend a lot of their time doing data entry and processing work. Technology is making the processing work easier and faster. The supercomputers are processing the data via massive "server farms." Low-cost labor is infiltrating the marketplace. Let me make it really clear . . .

If you are not going to *add value* to the client work you are doing, then your $70K, $90K, or $120K salary is at risk. Why does a company need to pay you large sums of money when it can get the same job done for a fifth of the price elsewhere?

Employed accountants who spend their time behind a computer and not communicating with clients will go the way of the dinosaurs. The firm of the future has a local team who is client facing and adding value. Everything else is handled by someone else in another location/country.

Technology enables globalization of workforces. The world is flat. Get used to it and use it.

Compliance as a Commodity

Statutory compliance or "have to" annual accounting is mandated by the government as a task you need to do with your clients. The main reason the government agencies want you to do this task is so you can accurately (or thereabouts) figure the right amount of money for them to collect. The government agencies are not that interested in the accounting profession. The secondary reason they want you is to check that your clients are complying with their rules.

> "The firm of the future has a local team who is client facing and adding value. Everything else is handled by someone else in another location/country."

The government is using you as an intermediary. It is outsourcing its job to you.

As a business owner, the annual compliance is a necessary evil that we don't really want to buy or really value. It's a grudge purchase. We (the business community) don't like paying for it, we know we must have it, but we just don't like it. It's like servicing the car. If we could avoid it, we would. We can't.

The old model of compliance work is to send a questionnaire to the clients at the end of year and then wait. Eventually your client sends in their "stuff" in a variety of formats (paper, scan, email, disk, memory stick, or verbal), and then you make sense of it.

If the information arrived via a file of some sort, the first step is to load the memory stick and check the version of the client's software. You then check the information received versus the information requested. Never the twain shall meet on that one!

Once you realize you do not have the information you requested, you go back to the client with an information request (typically by email), and wait. And wait and wait and W . . . A . . . I . . . T!

There is no priority to clients sending the missing information. They sort of know the answer to their finances anyway. It's a grudge purchase, so why send it back when you want?

Often the communication the clients get is not clear, when they are requested to send additional information. They procrastinate sending the information, because it has little value to them. And often when they do send it, you then ask for something else. Why couldn't you have just asked for the complete list in the first place? To make it super easy, why don't you send your administrative person to collect everything?

> "It's a grudge purchase, so why send it back when you want."

So the clients eventually get everything to you. They sign it, you file it, and the year is done. Next year we do it all over again. Rinse and repeat. Most of an accounting firm's revenue is in compliance, and it's all changing.

So what does the future of compliance look like?

There is one word to describe the future of compliance . . . commoditized. With a repetitive task, eventually systemization kicks in, and after that commoditization happens. Once a product is commoditized, then price pressure and new competition takes over. This is what is happening with statutory compliance for individuals and companies.

The reason is simple. Cloud-based accounting software. New technologies at the client's end make it far more streamlined, accurate, and thus efficient. The data received by the accountant is more accurate and better quality. There are fewer errors to make at the client's end, due to the way Cloud solutions work. With the data in better shape, that means there is less time needed at the accountant's end to finalize the work. The software applications also offer reporting that previously only external accountants would provide—such as consolidated executive summaries with key performance indicator variances, budgeting, and cash flow analysis.

I have recently seen new entrants (accountants) to the marketplace who have a low cost base and are offering 50–80 percent reduction on standard compliance work. I am also seeing a growing trend of accountants setting up teams of people in other countries and offering bookkeeping and other accounting services for $8–$20 per hour.

The next phase will be when the Cloud-based accounting systems will offer one-click filing to the government agencies. This type of technology will bypass the accountant all together for these functions. The Australian government has created standard business reporting linked to the Cloud-based accounting software. The government estimates that 12.5 percent of compliance revenue will be wiped out of the Australian marketplace in the next few years.

The reason all this is happening is due to social change and technology companies that are fighting to remain relevant. Social change says that people want to access information on their mobile devices, whenever or wherever they want—including accounting and other key business data. It is hard to do that if all the information is on a hard drive at the office!

Technology companies know this, and they are either creating new applications that are Internet based, or they are migrating their current hard-drive products to be Internet based. If they do not, then they will also go the way of the dinosaur.

> "The next phase will be when the Cloud-based accounting systems will offer one-click lodgment to the government agencies."

Because the Cloud data is more accurate and up to date, the version of the software is always up to date, and the reporting functions are more powerful, the "numbers power" is now with your clients in real time. Previously the external accountant had the numbers power. Previously your voodoo magic, hoketry poketry (hands currently waving in mysterious, mystic ways) that you did on a set of accounts was the powerful secret sauce.

Now the technology at your client site is the secret sauce!

If you want to remain relevant, you need to regain the numbers power. You need to know what is happening in your client site every day, and you need to predict issues and opportunities in advance. You need to be alerted to what is happening, so you can react in real time. You can make a massive difference, if you have the real-time data pushed to your desktop in a consolidated and simple way.

Machine learning is already here. Auto coding is already here. The apps with answers are here. The human became an app!

As an accountant, you cannot stop all this change. Social change, technology companies, and the government are creating this change. You can choose to ignore it or embrace it. Ignore at your peril, I say.

Disrupting a $500B Profession

The global accounting business is extremely large. According to global business intelligence research company IBISWorld, the 2015 revenue was US$464B in revenue and growing by 4 percent per year. Call it $500B. To put that into perspective, that number is one-third of the Australian gross domestic product (GDP), one-third of the state of Texas and three times the GDP of New Zealand.

The vast majority of revenue for most accounting firms is locked up in audit, tax, and compliance. Another way to put that is the revenue is generated from historical data checking. It's making sure everything is accounted for, in the correct column and place.

Sadly (and perhaps surprisingly), most of an accountant's day in most firms is spent looking at historical data (sometimes more than one year old), making sense of it, and going back and forth with the client to collect missing pieces of information until they are entirely happy they have received everything. Accountants spend most of their day **checking and processing data.**

"Accountants spend most of their day **checking and processing data.**"

Then they use software to process the client work, prepare a report, send it to the client, and then file it with the government agencies. The outcome of the work is that the client pays more or less tax.

If the client is lucky (it's rare), a full review is delivered to them with why they have to pay the amount of tax listed, what the numbers mean, and how to improve the numbers in the future. This does not happen with most clients. That sounds like it is trivializing the work of accountants. It's not. There is certainly a lot of "human smarts" needed to make all that happen.

Of the more than 1.27M firms in the world, it is estimated that there are a total of approximately 6M people employed in the accounting profession. It is estimated (from accountants themselves) that about 80 percent of their time is spent checking and processing data.

That's a lot of people doing a lot of "checking and processing" work!

The reason there are so many people involved is because of three types of inefficient (read archaic) information systems.

1. Inefficient systems at the **client** side
2. Inefficient systems at the **accountants'** side
3. Inefficient systems at the **government** side

All three have paper, scanned documents, hard-drive systems, and human involvement. All three are using archaic systems to deliver a historical report.

Let's look at the "interests" of everyone involved.

The business owners/individuals are interested in earning more money and improving their lifestyles. They need to make a profit to support their lifestyles, and legally they must pay tax. However, they are interested in paying the least amount of tax possible.

The government is not interested in you. It is only interested in one thing—tax paid. The agencies want to make sure that the **tax** collected at the business end is correctly accounted for and paid on time. They want to make sure that the **income** earned at the business end is correctly taxed and paid on time. They want to make sure that the **payroll** paid to employees is correctly paid and the tax is paid on time. Tax, tax, tax!

> "The government is not interested in you. It is only interested in one thing—tax paid."

They might say they are interested in improving the profitability of the business so the business owner can pay more tax, but deep down they just want what is being processed now—accurately and on time. Nothing more, nothing less.

The accountants are the **intermediaries** in the process. They sit between the business owners/individuals (they are there to support them) and the government. They make money from the clients, so that's who they'll support. Their objective is to check that every deduction is accounted for and to "move things around" and "restructure" so the clients pay the least amount of tax necessary and protect their assets.

So the accountant is the "go-between"—literally the person in the middle. And just like other "intermediary industries," the compliance accountant could well be sidelined and possibly eliminated.

As an example, we used to go to the travel agent (a real human in an office or shop) to have our airline tickets booked and processed. They were in the middle between the airline and the passenger. Now we interact directly with the airline online, or if we do go through a booking service, it's an online service with limited human interaction. The travel agencies that did not add value have vanished.

And therein is the key point ... **"Those that did not add value have vanished."**

Take Uber and Taxi transportation services, as another example. Uber adds value in the simplest of ways with an app and by making payment simple. It's just more convenient. It's friendlier. It's more comfortable. It's often faster and is less expensive. And the Uber driver cares a little more. And yet, just with those simple changes, Uber disrupts. On a recent trip to London, I learned that revenues in London taxis were down as much as 40 percent.

The following question needs to be asked.

Could the accounting profession be significantly disrupted? Or, more pointedly, will those who don't add value be doomed . . . UNLESS they add more value or quickly find new business models and new ways of delivering services?

The accounting profession is centuries old. It has $500B in revenue, employing about 6M people. Could it be disrupted where 50–80 percent of the current revenue is completely eliminated?

What do you think?

If you go back to the reasons why there is so much revenue in the accounting profession—paper, scanned documents, hard-drive systems, and human involvement—then (if you wanted to disrupt) what you would do is attack these areas, thus eliminating the "go-between." Here's what I think would need to happen to have the vast majority of $500B in revenue disrupted.

> "Cash flow forecasting is automatic because all the systems interact with one another and predict the future cash flow. Happening now."

1. Businesses owners would need to use Cloud accounting systems to streamline accounting processing at their end. Happening **now** at a great speed.
2. Point of sale, inventory control, payroll, and customer data systems (all in the Cloud) would need to integrate with the accounting system to give an accurate income statement, cash flow analysis, and balance sheet analysis. Happening **now.**
3. Cash flow forecasting is automatic because all the systems interact with one another and predict the future cash flow. Happening **now.**
4. Manual bookkeeping (with humans) could be eliminated if every transaction had a barcode or source code so it automatically updated the accounting and other systems. Can happen **now.**

5. To avoid total human interaction, checks and cash would need to be eliminated. All transactions were digital—by credit or debit card, electronic funds transfer (EFT), BPAY (bill payment service in Australia), PayPal, direct debit, or other electronic processes. Can happen **now.**

6. Paper receipts were eliminated and coding of credit card statements happens automatically. Can happen **now.**

7. The Cloud accounting system used "digital accountants' who used artificial intelligence (maybe an offshore human at first) to answer complex accounting questions. **Soon.**

8. The audit was done automatically by the software system as frequently as required. **Predicted.**

9. Business owners go to a range of "chat" forums or networks to interact with other business owners for experienced-based advice. Happening **now.**

10. For complex business advice, the business owner uses "Ask Alec" on their computer or smartphone. Alec is a virtual accountant, a supercomputer that uses artificial intelligence (think Siri on the iPhone for business) and can answer any complex question about business. **Soon.**

11. To complete the loop and make sure the government gets their appropriate amount of tax, it needs to upgrade its computer systems, the receiving systems of the data. All the agencies need to do is take their systems to the Cloud, so they can seamlessly interact with the business owners' systems. Happening **now.**

If all these technologies came together, then a big part of the accounting professions revenue could be totally sidelined. Maybe even wiped out.

In countries where Cloud accounting is heavily used (at the small business end), we've seen accounting firm profits decline in Australia and New Zealand during the past few years. Could this happen to you?

Disruption is real. It's happening right now. And it's happening with a faster pace each and every day.

> "Disruption is real. It's happening right now. And it's happening with a faster pace each and every day."

Twelve Predictions of the Profession

The last time I made 12 predictions about the future of the accounting profession was in 2010. They were bold predictions, and I am happy to report that 66 percent (eight) are done and the other four are works in progress, but happening. The profession has changed a lot, mainly due to the new threat and opportunity with Cloud computing. So, it's time to make another 12 predictions . . .

1. **Compliance will be completely commoditized.** Statutory compliance is a repetitive task where supercomputers are taking over the processing and checking of data. Soon enough, the tax departments will install standard business reporting and one-click tax filing into Internet accounting systems. The accountant will be bypassed for standard annual reporting in the future.

2. **Cloud accounting will be installed in more than 90 percent of small to medium businesses.** No one can stop social change. People want their data and information on their mobile devices. No one can stop huge technology companies from heavily promoting their solutions to businesses. It's time to embrace the change.

    > "No one can stop huge technology companies from heavily promoting their solutions to businesses. It's time to embrace the change."

3. **Cloud practice management will be in more than 90 percent of accounting firms.** The benefits are clear with improved efficiency, cheaper operating costs, and mobility. At some point in time, the hard-drive providers who also provide Cloud solutions will turn off the hard-drive updates. It's time to embrace the benefits of change.

4. **Coaches and consultants will take more clients.** The one who has access to the financial data owns the long-term relationship. It is easy for a non-accountant to help a client get onto Cloud accounting and other add-on products. Accountants should not let someone else get more financially intimate with their clients.

5. **Clients will be more transient.** One thing that hard-drive systems did was make it harder for the client to move accountants. They had to physically deliver or courier the data and thus felt compelled to stay with an accountant. With Cloud accounting the data is light data. There is no data

to deliver—just a login. The data can be manipulated anywhere. Tighter and more enduring relationships will be needed.

6. **Offshore teams will be more prevalent.** With Cloud computing, why do accountants need a team of people in the office? Why not look for labor in other countries? Often the labor is cheaper, more accessible, and more willing to work. Accounting firms already work with full-time teams in other countries serving clients around the world.

> "If there was ever a system that denigrated self-esteem and the value of one's knowledge, it is time-based billing."

7. **Compliance prices will plummet by 50 percent or more.** Let's face it. Where is the value in a financial report that is 6, 12, or 18 months old? The labor costs and archaic systems cause the cost of annual compliance to escalate. With new systems, the costs will come down to where they should be. Compliance should be value priced . . . down.

8. **Traditional valuations will change.** With commoditized services comes price pressure and new low-cost entrants into the market. That means it'll be a race to the bottom on price and broken client relationships. That means (along with an aging partner population) that traditional valuations will drop. Those who have moved to a subscription model will see their valuations increase.

9. **Young people will not buy-in to staid and boring.** The old models of "commander control" management and hierarchical office-bound seniors are not what the 20-somethings want to sign up for. They are not interested in old-fashioned systems, equipment, furniture, offices, and boring restrictions. Loosen up, partners—the next partners are tech savvy and want to progress faster than ever before. Accounting firms need to accommodate this. Maybe we need a reality TV show about accountants. Maybe we need to "sex" the profession up a bit. I think so.

10. **No more time-based billing.** If there were ever a system that denigrated self-esteem and the value of one's knowledge, it is time-based billing. It suggests that the time taken was correct and the rate per hour was correct (based on a silly salary multiple formula) to determine the value of the intellectual property. The profession needs to stop this archaic behavior and start valuing the intellect that has taken many years to develop and hone. Price upfront, based on value created, not time taken in arrears.

11. **Business advisory services to be more than 50 percent of revenue.**
    Accountants can add a huge amount of value when they know the facts. If a client is in trouble, they can "swing into gear" and sort out the situation with the bank or tax department. The problem is that most accountants are swamped by compliance services and don't have time to add value. That's all changing and with new technologies that alert accountants as to what is going on with their clients, accountants can truly live up to the trusted advisor status they so richly deserve.

> "With accurate real-time data, accountants can add value like never before."

12. **Clients are finally served properly.** It always amazes me that when we give an income statement and balance sheet (of a client) to accountants and get them to brainstorm (in small groups), they come up with loads of ideas on what the client can do to improve. Isn't that what it's all about? Helping the clients. With accurate real-time data, accountants can add value like never before. At the end of the day, the client is why most accountants got into this profession in the first place. I think it's a duty of care, a legal obligation, to serve them well.

These predictions are my predictions. They are based on more than 20 years of advising just one profession in many countries around the world. I am privileged to be independent from all vendors and associations, and my views are based on observations, facts, and what works.

My belief is that if you do not step up, be proactive, and add value, then many in the accounting profession will go the way of the dinosaurs.

That's it for the doom and gloom. The rest of the book is all about the solutions. Accounting doesn't have to be a profession that is marginalized or made extinct.

It's Time to Stop Practicing

The Bizarre Habits

I am convinced that the inventor of the current profit model of an accounting practice was not good at strategy or business development.

I am certain that the creators of this model had charity in mind. I am also convinced that the current model will bring in a decent income (and maybe a reasonable lifestyle, if you are frugal), but it will not make you wealthy.

Now that I have your attention, let me share with you what is right and wrong with the traditional model.

The current model just does not add up—it's flawed from the start. Take a look at the following graph to see how the vast majority of accounting practices around the world make a profit.

> "I am convinced that the inventor of the current profit model of an accounting practice was not good at strategy or business development."

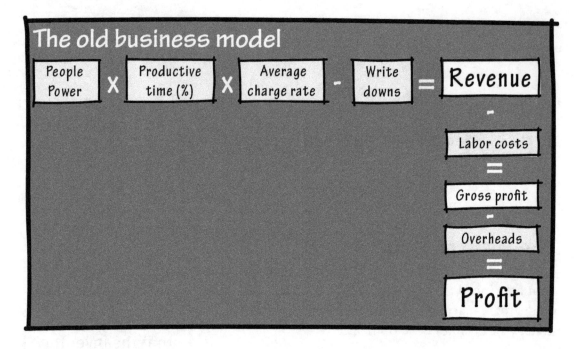

Most partners of most accounting practices earn $200K–$400K per annum. However, that's before taxation and working capital. You can build a reasonable lifestyle, but it won't make you wealthy!

This model truly is bizarre. The success of the revenue model is predicated on . . .

1. A volume of people to do the work—who always seem to be in short supply.

2. Squeezing maximum chargeable hours out of the accounting team. (In a Scottish accent the partners rant, "We want more billable hours out of you, laddy").

3. Increasing charge rates. However, they are typically linked to salary levels so you get marginal profit improvement.

4. Reducing write-downs, which is discounting before billing. While you price in arrears, you will never ethically reduce write-downs.

5. Reducing labor costs. Since when has that strategy worked?

6. Reducing overhead and being extremely frugal. See point above!

> "While you price in arrears, you will never ethically reduce write-downs."

What's wrong with all that, you say?

The entire model is based on "labor for hire," and that is not what you sell. You sell what you know; you sell intellectual capital turned into intellectual property, which is disguised as letters, reports, statements of advice, meetings, and recommendations. You DO NOT sell labor—yet that is what your business model says you sell.

Around the world at various partner retreats (why they are called a retreat is beyond me—I thought you were supposed to be "advancing" at these things—not "retreating"), I am sure at pontification time the following discussions have taken place . . .

Partner A

"If we could only find another five qualified accountants and get 1,250 hours out of each of them at an average charge rate of $200 net of 10 percent write-downs, then we can grow our revenue by $1.25M."

Partner B

"Or another way to do this is to try to squeeze more productivity out of our current 15 accountants, from 1,200 hours to 1,400 hours and increase their charge rates from an average of $150 to $165. That would increase our profit by $45,000."

Partner C

"I think we need to reduce our write-downs from 15 percent to 5 percent. We have been targeting 15 percent for years—why don't we target 5 percent write-downs? We have been writing-down $300,000 and the new target would only be $100,000."

> "We have been targeting 15 percent for years—why don't we target 5 percent write-downs?"

Partner D

"But what about our labor and overhead costs? We were planning to give the team a 5 percent pay increase this year—one of them even asked me for 20 percent, for goodness sake—why don't we just give them a 3 percent increase. Our information technology (IT) costs are out of control, I think if we spend some time renegotiating our contract, we could save at least $15,000 per annum."

What is wrong with the discussion?

☒ Increasing the head count—Labor costs and general overheads just went up also.

☒ Squeezing chargeable time—Just go slower and make more mistakes that will increase chargeable time.

☒ Increasing charge rates—The team members will expect to be paid more.

☒ Still budgeting for write-downs—What a strategy that is.

☒ Paying people less than they are worth—Well, that's going to work.

☒ Spending an inordinate amount of time scrutinizing reducing expenses for little return.

In my career I have met many firms who have grown their headcount by 5 times yet their profit per partner has not grown by 5 times.

Write-Downs

Another bizarre habit that accountants get involved in is "writing-down." Write-downs (discounting before billing) occur in three distinct areas.

1. **At the time of setting the annual budget.** Line one on the budget says, "Expected fees charged to WIP (work in progress)." Line two says, "Expected write-downs." How bizarre—expecting to fail before you start. I visited a six-partner firm in Melbourne. They had fees charged to WIP of $9.7M and write-downs of $2.6M, with net fees billed of $7.1M. They wrote-off nearly 27 percent! Or another way to look at it, they set fire to a luxury home every year—and that would have been more enjoyable. Anyway, I asked the six partners if they budgeted for write-downs. "Yes, we do," they said. I asked, "What's your budgeted number?" They proudly stated, "25 percent." I said, "Well, you nearly hit it." Bizarre behavior—budgeting for write-downs. What would happen if you budgeted for write-ups? You might just hit them.

2. **At the time of doing the work.** In workshops, I ask accountants to honestly answer how much time they put on the clock while doing the work. The accountants in

> "A staggering 15 percent of the time taken does not hit the clock in the first place."

question all use an archaic method of time-based billing in arrears—what's on the clock is multiplied by the charge rate and should be billed to clients. How much time hits the clock? The average is 85 percent. A staggering 15 percent of the time taken does not hit the clock in the first place. The team members are discounting before the gutless partners have a chance to do so!

3. **At the time of billing.** With all the pride in the world, the accountant who did the work typically presents it to the partner for review to determine the size of the bill the client will receive. The partner looks at the work and says, "The client will never pay that," and promptly wipes off 5, 10, 15, or 20 percent of the value of the project.

So, if you budget for write-downs, expect to get them. If you use time and rate as your billing method, expect to get them. If you have gutless partners at the time of billing, expect to get them. You get what you expect.

You might think that write-downs are a behavior issue. They're actually a system issue. If you want to change the behavior you have to change the system.

To fix write-downs, you price up front, you get super efficient and take the value of the write-up. The price is fixed, the time reduces. You wll always have write-downs if you price in arrears.

You might be setting fire (figuratively) to the value of a luxury home, a condo, car or motor cycle. Stop it. Write-downs are the easiest thing to fix. You just need to change the system.

Pricing Methods

A client comes to you for business advice. The client specifically wants some ideas about how much she should charge her customers for a new product. With as much sage advice as you can muster, you say, "What you should do is work out how much time it will take to make the product. Then work out a charge rate for each person who is making the product. You work out the charge rate by taking the annual salary and dividing by the time they are at work for the year—say 1,800 hours—then multiply that number by four times and you have a charge rate. Multiply the time taken by the charge rate, and you have the price for the product. That's what we do here, and it has worked for decades."

> "Follow the magic formula, and it will lead you to the correct price."

Your client says, "I haven't made the product yet." "It doesn't matter," you say. "Follow the magic formula and it will lead you to the correct price."

Or what about this way to set a price? Let's say (gentlemen), you want to buy a suit. You go to your favorite tailor on Savile Row in London, England. You enter the shop and the following dialogue takes place.

You: "How much for a suit?"

Tailor: "That depends."

You: "Depends on what?"

Tailor: "It depends on the type of fabric I use to make the suit."

You: "OK, I'll select that one there—how much for the suit?"

Tailor: "That depends."

You: "Depends on what?"

Tailor: "It depends on how much of the fabric we use for your suit (under breath—'fatso')."

You: "OK, measure me up—I'm a 42-inch chest and a 30-inch waist (yeah, right)."

You: "Now, how much for the suit?"

Tailor: "That depends."

You: (getting frustrated) "Depends on what?"

Tailor: "It depends on the quality of the thread, number of buttons, and patches that we use."

You: "OK, I'll go with these. Right then. Now, how much for the suit?"

Tailor: "That depends."

You: (getting mad now) "Depends on what?"

Tailor: "Well, it depends on how much time it takes me to make it for you."

You: "You mean to tell me that the longer you take, the more I will have to pay?"

Tailor: "Precisely, sir."

And that is how usual accounting practices work out the price for their services: hours times rate plus disbursements. That is no way to price a product.

> "You just test different packaging and price every project upfront. The price for intellectual property is based on just three factors."

The only way to set a price is to have the marketplace (clients) set the price. You just test different packaging and price every project upfront. The price for intellectual property is based on just three factors.

1. Your personal value belief
2. Your value contribution
3. Your client's value perception

You will know that the price is wrong when your client says yes, without hesitation. If your clients keep saying YES, then the price is WRONG.

Partner Habits

As I mentioned, since 1994, I have been working exclusively with accounting firms. I am constantly bemused at what the owners (partners) of the firms do with their time. If I visit a four-partner firm, I will ask their roles.

The first partner says, "I am the marketing partner."

The second one says, "I am the information technology (IT) partner."

The third one says, "I am the human resources (HR) partner."

And the fourth one so proudly says, "And I am the operations partner."

> "Partners should only be doing three key things with their time."

Yet not one of them knows "diddly squat" (technical term for very little) about these four important topics. Have a look at how partners (you) spend their time. Keep a time log of everything you do. When the time log starts to repeat itself, stop keeping the log. Go back over the list and work out the "highest dollar productive activity" that you do and highlight that one. Then work out the second and third highest dollar productive activity. Get rid of the rest. They'll mainly be administrative tasks. Delegate them, don't do them, and get focused on three only.

Partners should be following my 30:60:10 rule and only be doing three key things with their time.

1. **High-end chargeable work.** Advisory, cash flow, profit improvement, and structuring-type work for the percentage of time that keeps you interested. No charge rates with this sort of work—all value-based fees. No more than 30 percent of time.

2. **Sales activity.** Visiting prospects and clients, phoning them and getting to know them—finding out what they need and then selling additional services to them. About 60 percent or more of time.

3. **Leadership.** Driving performance of the business, searching for new ideas. New products to sell, new clients. About 10 percent of time.

Everything else is administration. Hire a business manager to do it—not you.

Partner meetings can be interesting and bizarre things to watch. In addition to looking over the previous month's numbers and chastising whatever under-performance needs, they get into discussions about costs and petty details. I have seen partners debate (kid you not) what color the receptionist's chair needs to be and which model to select for him/her. "I saw a chair that would be perfect at the wholesale office store for $99. It was $23 cheaper than where we normally buy chairs."

Majoring on the minors and management by committee. Bizarre. Can someone (not the committee) please make a decision? Empower people and trust them.

Also at partner meetings, the topic of marketing might come up (by the marketing partner, no less), and there might be a seminar to invite clients to. "None of my clients will be interested," says one of the partners. "I think I have only five or six who might want to go," says another.

I have even met partners who debate if they should send the electronic newsletter to some clients. "They'll never read it."

> "Majoring on the minors and management by committee. Bizarre. Can someone (not the committee) please make a decision?"

How bizarre. Prejudging what clients will buy, how they will act, what they will respond to, and what they are interested in. I think prejudging has to be one of the most arrogant activities. For the sake of your clients, stop prejudging. Let your clients know about everything you do, and see who responds. Simple.

I remember a three-partner firm joined one of our coachingclub programs (revolutionary group coaching method that creates outstanding results—when the clients follow the advice). Their lock-up (work in progress and receivables combined) was running about $900K. For a $2M firm, this was out of control. There was about $750K in WIP and $150K in receivables. By the time we met again, the WIP balance was down $50K and receivables were about $125K. "Good result," I said. "How did you do it?" Answer—one of the partners decided to write-down $650K! I hit the roof. Before even giving it a chance to be collected, it was written off. I hasten to say that partnership no longer exists. Bizarre behavior.

What bizarre behavior exists in your firm?

Order Takers and History Writers

Unbeknownst to those who work in accounting practices, the favorite word (and often it seems the firm's mantra and culture) is to **wait.** Here is some dialogue you might have heard before.

Q. "Why can't we get that job out?"

A. "I sent the client an email and I'm now waiting for them to send the missing bank statement in."

Q. "Why is your productivity so low?"

A. "I was waiting for the graduate to finish his/her part of the work."

Q. "When can we grow the revenue?"

A. "We'll have to wait until the government changes the rules. Then we write our clients and tell them we need to do . . . ."

Q. "Why haven't we sold more budget and cash flow forecasts?"

A. "We've been waiting for the banks to tell the clients that they need one."

Q. "What have you been doing all day?"

A. "I have been waiting for the phone to ring, the email to ping, the client to come in, and the team members to complain about being paid so poorly."

> "Reactive accountants wait, wait, and wait."

Reactive accountants **wait, wait, and wait.**

It was once said that some people make things happen, some people wait for things to happen, and some people wonder what happened. Which one are you? What is the culture of your firm?

This waiting mentality creates "order taker" mentality. Constantly on the back foot, dealing with client issues (putting out fires), and never getting on the front foot and being proactive.

Clients want you to be proactive. They do not know, what they do not know. They want advice. They want help. They want someone to tell them what to do.

> "Instead of waiting to write your clients' history . . . **help them to make history."**

Among other things, you are the expert on finance, cash flow management, and structuring—not your clients. If you see an opportunity where your clients could use your services, then you owe it to them to tell them. If you do not promote all your services, then you are doing your clients a complete disservice.

If you continue down the "order taker" route for compliance, then you are basically a history writer. Primarily writing the past. If you continue down this track, then you will be a slave to the government and a post office for the taxation department.

Do your clients want you to be a history writer who waits for history to happen? I think not. Do *you* want to be a history writer?

By way of actions, many accountants say yes, that's it—history writing and waiting is for me. They assume that they know what the client wants, so they just give them what they ask for. Accountants constantly prejudge what the clients want and never give them what they really need. As I said earlier, I think prejudging is one of the most arrogant actions possible.

No doubt, you've heard the phrase—"ready, aim, fire!" The challenge with the accountants' mentality is that without coaching, you will spend most of the time "getting ready." Most accountants spend their whole life getting "ready" (the spreadsheet or the system will never be right). They rarely aim and hardly every fire.

By getting ready, they WAIT. You have a disclaimer on everything (I suppose that means you don't even think the numbers are right), so what do you have to lose? Start aiming and start firing.

Instead of waiting to write your clients' history . . . **help them to make history.**

Steady as She Goes

The traditional growth model is a slow and steady path to moderate success. Most years, an accounting firm grows by revenue. It's a simple equation. Put the charge rates up each year (unfortunately, salaries go up also), accept a few new clients by referral, retain the clients you already have, and, voila, the revenue increases.

But does the profit increase? Typically not.

This reactive "steady as she goes" approach causes two critical issues that hold back the performance of the firm—and ultimately your clients being delighted to deal with you.

> "I want you to have a BIG problem. I want you to have a high self-esteem problem."

1. Apathy
2. Self-esteem

It is relatively easy to make money in an accounting practice. Seriously, you do not have to try that hard to make a decent profit. You know that about 90 percent of revenue will come in each year. You can write the budget on the 90 percent. It's effectively recurring revenue—you know it's there; you just have to bring in the work. You know that the government will change the rules, and you'll need to introduce something new to your clients. You know that some of your clients will get in financial trouble, and you'll need to help them out with a refinance or similar. You know you can get away with paying your people 50–100 percent less than they are worth, because everyone does that. You know that you will get some new clients by referral—not many, but there will be some.

This reactive, steady-as-she-goes approach is comfortable. However, this comfort zone breeds **apathy,** it creates laziness, and you start to believe that all you are going to get is all you are going to get. Your dreams and aspirations all but disappear. And because your life is all about reacting, all day, every day, your **self-esteem** declines. You start to talk a lot in client meetings; you constantly give the answer to clients in detail (and quickly); and you write long, arduous, and verbose letters, statements of advice, and invoices. You do not listen attentively to people, and you start being a bully to others—all are sure-fire signs of low self-esteem.

You are strong when the client comes to you, but not so strong when you go to the client with an idea.

If the steady-as-she-goes approach breeds apathy and low self-esteem, then the knock-on effect is that you do not help your clients fully and you do not reach your business potential.

You end up with minimal business value, minimal assets or savings in your superannuation or pension program, and you settle for less than you should at retirement.

I want you to have a BIG problem. I want you to have a high self-esteem problem. I want you to enjoy the life you deserve. I want you to realize your business and personal potential.

To do that you MUST do something different. Your decisions and actions of the past got you the results you achieve today.

Another way to look at this is that you are where you are because you choose to be!

Will the same strategies of the past realize your success of tomorrow?

> "What I like to do is 'write the brochure first' before I create any new product."

Build the Plane as You Fly It

I have noticed that accountants can be fairly good procrastinators. Really, you say! I think it's because they think they need to get it right before getting started. If you take that attitude, then you'll never get anything off the ground.

There was a dog food company that invented the "world's best dog food." It had everything perfect—the texture, the smell, the protein and fat content, etc. It even had amazing packaging, and the dog food company was able to get onto the supermarket shelves at eye level. After a massive marketing campaign, dog owners bought the product with hope and enthusiasm. They fed the product to their beloved dogs; however, **the dogs didn't like it.** The company went broke, because they let perfect get in the way of success.

What I like to do is "write the brochure first" before I create any new product. What I mean by that is I will draft the promise, the website, or the sales letter, and then do some marketing to see if my market wants to buy it. Then I'll create the product. I don't want to waste my resources creating something, if no one is going to buy it. I like to build the plane as we fly it.

Creating products and productizing your accounting firm need not be difficult. There are eight questions to ask and implement.

1. What do you know?
2. Who is it applicable to?
3. How will it be packaged?
4. What technology is needed?

5. How will it be marketed?
6. How will it be sold?
7. How will be implemented?
8. How will it be supported?

On a nimble, low-cost model, we implement new product ideas all the time. They don't always work. Sometimes the dogs don't like it. A great example of that was the "Rob doll" action figure—not a big seller!

You have to be prepared to cut your losses fast when you start creating and promoting products. Not everything will work as planned. Just because you like it doesn't mean your market will. You can't prejudge who will buy and who will not. With your best marketing, give everyone the chance to buy what you have.

> "You can't prejudge who will buy and who will not. With your best marketing, give everyone the chance to buy what you have."

If you're onto something that is working, then get testimonials or case studies from happy clients (we call them WHAMs—written happy accountant moments) and leverage those so you can sell more. Keep testing different methods of explaining, promoting, packaging, and pricing until you get it close to being right.

Then rinse and repeat. Over and over and over again!

Sustainability Index

How sustainable is your firm? Meaning, if the partners were not there, how would it perform? Would it make money? Would it lose money? Could it continue to grow without you?

Here's a simple but sobering equation.

Take partner revenue delivered (your personal billable time/dollars) away from your profit (before partner salaries) and see what is left.

The reason I say take it away from the profit is because partner revenue is nearly all profit. If the answer is a loss, then the question needs to be asked, "Why do I need the rest of the team and infrastructure?"

You could work from home, look after your clients, have less hassle, and make more money. If the answer is a small profit, then the observation is the same.

If you want to get really critical, take partner billed time away (revenue delivery) AND take partner sales (revenue production) away and see what you've got left. Hmmm. Time for a rethink.

I once heard that the purpose of a business is to sell it—whether you want to or not. That means it's always ready to sell. That means it works without any key people. Or if the key people departed, they could be quickly replaced and the business would continue regardless.

If you have a firm that is heavily reliant on you (low sustainability), then you don't have a business but a paid job—hopefully a well-paid job. Now that might be OK, if that is your strategy. If that's your strategy, you have to realize that there is ZERO business value in a well-paid job—just cash value.

If your objective is to build an accounting business, then you need to think leverage. You need people and/or machines doing the work, not you as the business owner. You'll need marketing people and salespeople. You'll need to have a systemized business that follows process. You'll need a recurring revenue model that ticks along and grows every month. You'll need a leadership team who powers on with or without you.

The ultimate goal is that you could take three months (or longer) vacation and the business still performs. You're not missed at all. I think financial retirement is the goal. That means that you have assets that produce cash to support your ideal lifestyle and going to work is a choice—not a must. Your accounting business could be one of those assets. You probably have clients who own a share in multiple businesses, and they produce a return yet they spend little or no time in the businesses.

Why can't you be that person? You've built your accounting business, systematized it, leveraged yourself out of it, and you keep it as an asset. Now that's sustainability.

Clients Want More

I **know** that many (not all) of your clients want more help than you currently give them. I have asked them directly what they want—and so have many others.

There have been two significant, personal surveys done to prove that your clients want more.

> "As a customer of an accounting firm, I am not buying time from you—I am buying what you know."

1. I personally interviewed 1,077 business clients on behalf of 126 accounting firms in a "Client Advisory Board" format. There were about eight business clients at a time in a meeting room, and I asked them what they wanted from their accounting firms. They all said basically the same thing, "We want them to be more proactive with us. We know they know more than we get. We want to them to tell us in advance what we need to do."

2. My business partner of 10 years, Colin Dunn, surveyed 1,500 small-to-medium businesses over the Web. The main question was, "What else do you want from your accountant that you are not getting now?" The primary answers were cash flow, profit, and management accounting help.

The evidence stacks up. Clients want more help. Are you in a position to offer it? If you do not offer it, then someone else will—and you might lose the client.

Mostly you do not react until the client calls you (sometimes late on a Friday afternoon) and says, "HELP, the bank has just called. We hit our overdraft limit, and the bank is going to start bouncing checks and credit cards. The bank wants us to have a budget, cash flow, and refinance plan by Tuesday—HELP, HELP, HELP!"

You say (or think), "Why didn't you call me sooner?"

Did the clients know they were trading insolvent? Did they know they had a cash flow issue? To many businesses, they think cash flow management is Internet banking.

If you are the expert in finance, cash flow management, and structuring, then why didn't you build strong relationships, keep in touch, and inform them of the pending issues?

All good in theory, you say. The biggest objection I get is that you think there is no money to pay for these much-needed additional services. Let me tell you—**there is always money available**. The client is paying the rent, mortgage, school fees, car lease, salaries, and overhead. It's not a case of not having any money—it's the prioritization of the money.

> "They all said basically the same thing, 'We want them to be more proactive with us.'"

At the time of this writing (I switched accounting firms eight years ago), I was your typical $4K–$5K per year compliance client. With the new firm, I have so far paid them more than $300,000. By the way, you do not want me as a client—I know too much about what goes on!

As I finish this chapter on what's wrong and right with the current model, I am intrigued by the word "practice." You call it an accounting practice. Are you a practitioner practicing your craft, constantly practicing before getting it right?

I think it's time to stop "practicing." You should be good at it by now. You have a business to run! Let's change the model and get a vastly different result.

New Behavior Is Needed

Business by Design

Most accounting firms are operating their **business by default**—not operating their **business by design**.

Most accounting firms just seem to exist. They get through the years with a limited plan; they seem to "acquire" a bunch of clients who are a hodgepodge of makes, models, and sizes. They do not typically run the firm like a business, and worst of all the partners typically operate the firm based on learnings from the partners of the firms where they used to be employees.

This beast that you own is a business—not a practice. You own it. You take all the risk. Your name is on legal documents. Your name is on the insurance policies, the credit cards, the loans, and the leases. Your entire team will leave one day (they eventually do), and you'll still be there. Your clients are in the deal for their annual fee and their work done. Your team members are in it for their salaries and career progression. You are in this thing for millions!

> "Most accounting firms are operating their **business by default**—not operating their **business by design**."

This thing that you own is not a community service or a charity. However, many firms operate just like that. They operate like a not-for-profit, community-serving establishment, taking on clients they don't like, doing work they don't like, and dealing with people they don't particularly like either.

Remember, it's your business and no one else's. You should be the benefactor of the spoils and the one enjoying it the most. One of the key purposes of a business is to create wealth for the owners. How's that going for you?

My definition of success is **"doing what you want, when you want, with whom you want, in a manner you want."** That's my life success formula. In a business sense ...

1. Are you doing the sort of work (100 percent) you want to do?

2. Are you doing the work when you want to do it? On your terms?

3. Are you working with people (team and clients) who are inspiring, challenging, and fun?

4. Are you operating the business in a manner (style) that you want?

My business structure allows me to do all the above, all the time. It's my business; I designed it my way with what I want to do. You shouldn't be a slave to your business—it should be a slave to you.

It's not too late to take charge and remodel it. The clock of business existence is ticking. If you have 10 years left in your business, that's only 2,000 days. If you have 20 years left, that's only 4,000 days. It's not much time.

> "To build a business by design, new rules need to be made. Sometimes tough decisions need to be made."

To build a business by design, new rules need to be made. Sometimes tough decisions need to be made. New strategies need to be implemented and often new people need to be involved.

As you are remodeling, there are five key areas (in order of priority) that need to be focused on.

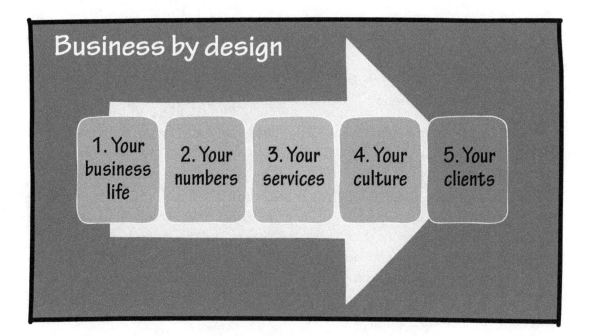

It starts with you designing (or redesigning) **your business life**. If you had a fresh start, how would you operate on a day-to-day basis? Would you do so many personal chargeable hours? Would you work such long hours? Would you schedule more holidays? Would you be selective with the clients you are serving? Would you have the operational responsibility that you currently have?

It's your business and it starts with you. Toward the end of every year, I schedule the year ahead. I block out all known activities, such as . . .

"I think partners of accounting businesses should be doing three things and three things only in their business life."

- ✓ Gym sessions
- ✓ Date nights
- ✓ Bike riding
- ✓ Blog post writing
- ✓ Kids drop off
- ✓ School holidays
- ✓ Man-cations
- ✓ Rob and Nat holidays

- ✓ Unavailable time
- ✓ Golf—practice and play
- ✓ Meetings—team, board, forum
- ✓ Conferences to attend

I then work around what is left. If a client wants me to do something on a Wednesday, then I politely decline because that's golf day. How can I do proper work when I am playing golf?

I hired a general manager to run the day-to-day operations of my software company. I am not that good at day-to-day operations and, more important, I don't like doing it. I only do work that I want to do for a fee that I think is acceptable. I only speak at events I want to speak at. I work when I want to work. And I work where I want to work. It's my business.

I think partners of accounting businesses should be doing three things and three things only in their business life.

1. High end chargeable work for the percentage (hopefully low) that lights your fire
2. Sales and nurturing meetings with existing or prospective clients
3. Leadership to drive the performance of the firm, develop new ideas, and keep people accountable

What do you need to change in your business life?

Next come **your numbers.** What do you want them to look like? If you are totally happy with the financial performance of your business, then skip this part. Most are not happy with the numbers.

The cool thing about the accounting profession is that you can create wealth from it. I know of many partners who make more than $2M per year. Not that profit is the most important thing—but hey, it's right up there with breathing!

> "If you had a fresh start, how would you operate on a day-to-day basis?"

If you want one location or five locations, make it happen. If you want your profit before partners' salaries to be more than 60 percent, then make it happen. If you want a $5M, $10M, or $100M firm, then build it. If you want negative work in progress or receivables, then do it. If you want high or low productivity/utilization, then make it happen. If you want fewer clients but more revenue per client, then do it. If you want revenue per full-time person (including administration) to be $200K, $300K, or $500K, then do it.

The neat thing is that all the strategies already exist on how to improve any number in any accounting business. The numbers can be whatever you want them to be. It starts with a decision.

So, you've worked out what your business life and your numbers need to look like. Now you need to focus on **your services** that you want to deliver.

Your government tells you what you **must** deliver, but is that what you **want** to deliver? I sell the same thing you do, which is intellectual property. We both sell what we know. What do you know and what do you want to sell? How do you want to package that? How do you want to price it?

Studies consistently show that your clients need (and are prepared to pay accordingly if the value is articulated correctly) additional services from you. Your clients do not need more compliance work. They need help with revenue, profit, cash flow, asset protection, succession planning, financial retirement, and tax minimization. The compliance work is unavoidable and a grudge purchase. The business advisory work really helps improve the financial condition of your clients. It's more fulfilling for you and also more lucrative.

> "If you don't like doing compliance work, but think you have to deliver it, then systemize it, delegate it, or send it offshore for someone else to do."

If you don't like doing compliance work, but think you have to deliver it, then systemize it, delegate it, or send it offshore for someone else to do it. If you want to have more business advisory work in your revenue mix, then make that decision and implement what you need to make it happen.

Selfishly, the first three are about you. Your life, your numbers, and your services. Now you need to develop your **operating culture** that suits your style, and then find team members who want to operate within that culture.

In 2010, I had my "annus horribilis" of a year when it came to team members. I had 27 people movements in a team of 16! Some of the roles were like a revolving door. The culture was bad and I was at fault. As you can imagine, it wasn't a great year for team performance. So, I decided to do something about it. What I did was write 15 culture standards and 15 service standards. They were standards of behavior. I documented the behavior I wanted. I documented my culture.

I wrote them all first and then I rolled them out via email every three days and at the weekly team meeting. I included a description of what each one meant. At the team meeting, we did a small workshop on each standard. I included them in employment agreements. I got giant banners made; we emphasized them every week; we made them crucial to new team member induction process; and slowly the culture started to change.

> "Throughout the years, I have had to fire people because they did not live up to the culture standards."

And we called people on them. Throughout the years, I have had to fire people because they did not live up to the culture standards. We make decisions based on the standards and we live by them every day.

What do you need to do to design your culture?

Your business life, your numbers, your services, your culture, and last comes **your clients.** They don't come first. You come first. Your team is second, and your clients are last. I think it is wrong to put the clients first. You're the one taking all the risk— you come first.

I am not saying that you should be arrogant toward your clients or treat them poorly. What I am saying is that you design the business the way you want it to be designed, and then find clients to fit that design. Not the other way around!

Most accounting firms start getting clients by default—and more clients and more clients and more clients. Then one day, you ask, "Where did they all come from?"

If you're going to build a business by design, then you need to understand who your ideal clients are. What do they look like? Where do they hang out? What is their profile? What fees are they paying? What services are they buying? Are they on Cloud accounting or can they be moved to Cloud accounting? Are they part of your niche focus? Who are your best buyers?

Now the challenge is that many of your current clients are not your best buyers. Many might have been suitable when you started the firm. Are they suitable now? It is certainly difficult to "right" your client base in a short space of time. It can be done, however. If you make the decision to sell off some of your less-than-desirable clients, then do it. If you make the decision to fire (compassionately) some of your less-than-desirable clients, then do it.

> "If you're going to build a business by design, then you need to understand who your ideal clients are."

Whatever you do, make sure the next client you accept into your firm is the right client for what you want in the future. If you have an abundance mentality, rather than a scarcity mentality, then you'll make the tough calls. If you believe that you have the capabilities to gain more clients, then why not let a few go?

Business by design is all about designing (or redesigning) the business the way you want it done. If you need to redesign the business, then it will take time; however, it is worth it in the end.

Your clients will be happier, your team will be happier, your family will be happier, and most important, you will be happier.

SMAGs and BHAGs

Most accounting firms set no goals or, at best, they set small goals. If they do set any goals, they set **small-minded, adequate goals—SMAGs.**

If you go back to my success formula (doing what you want, when you want, with whom you want, in a manner you want) then a SMAG might be appropriate for your style. At least it's a goal—albeit a goal that doesn't fill your potential.

In my opinion (and this entire book is based on my opinion—plus a lot of research), we're only here once, so let's do something purposeful. Let's do something grand. Let's do something that lives beyond us.

Let's set some **big, hairy, audacious goals— BHAGs.**

From the seminal work of US business consultant Jim Collins, in his landmark book *Good to Great,* the term BHAG was first used. A BHAG can inspire you, your team, and your clients. The great US president, John F. Kennedy, had an awesome BHAG that inspired the nation and many parts of the world.

"I believe that this nation should commit itself to achieving the goal, before this decade is out, of landing a man on the moon and returning him safely to the Earth" **(May 25, 1961, Speech to US Congress).**

Now that's a BHAG, and it did happen! It got people excited and hundreds of millions of people watched in excitement in July 1969 as astronauts Neil Armstrong and Buzz Aldrin walked on the Moon and then returned safely to this planet.

What then followed was space exploration, new research, new industries, and now there are wealthy entrepreneurs building and testing spacecraft to take the regular public to suborbital space. I am one of those "future astronauts"—in the future I will be flying on Virgin Galactic into space. My wife bought me my ticket in 2009 for my fortieth birthday. Pretty cool gift and pretty cool wife!

BHAGs for an accounting firm come in many shapes and sizes. The BHAG could be internally related, such as "$10M in revenue in 10 years." It could be team member related, such as "100 of the best, brightest, and most creative accountants on the planet." Or it could be client (externally) related, such as "All of our 500 clients are financially retired."

Whatever the BHAG is, it needs to be bold; it needs to inspiring; and it needs be easily communicated. It needs to get you excited, and it needs to get the team excited.

Before the BHAG is your purpose and your mission. Why is it you do what you do? What's your purpose for being? Why do you go to work every day? Why do you care so much about your clients? As bestselling author and technology, entertainment, and design (TED) star Simon Sinek would say, "People don't buy what you do; they buy why you do it."

> "Whatever the BHAG is, it needs to be bold; it needs to inspiring; and it needs be easily communicated."

Here are two examples you might want to duplicate and use.

Purpose: Make a massive difference to clients' financial performance.

Mission: Help all our clients to be financially retired.

BHAG: By [insert date], 100 percent of our current clients are financially retired.

Or ...

Purpose: Help all clients achieve all their goals.

Mission: Provide every service to every client that helps them achieve their goals.

BHAG: $10M in revenue from 400 awesome clients.

I particularly like a client-focused purpose, mission, and BHAG. And the reason for that is you can promote it to the clients. You can use it in your marketing. Let's say you're talking to a new prospective client. The conversation might go something like this.

"At our firm, we help our clients achieve all their goals. We make sure that every single client is only buying what they need from us to help them achieve their goals. We're only looking for 400 awesome clients who want our help to achieve their goals. Tell me, Bob, what are you looking for in an accounting firm?"

Unless Bob is a complete "nuff nuff" (technical term for not a good client), then he's probably going to answer with something like this: "I want an accounting firm that helps me achieve my goals." Sale made. Rinse and repeat.

Get creative with this. Start with what you (the owner) want, and then involve your team. Some of your team members have some super ideas. Ask them individually why they became accountants. Ask them what "juices" them up. Ask them what they want from their careers. Ask them what they would do if they were running the firm. Get to a consensus. Then do a reality check and see where you are today with your purpose, mission, and BHAG. After that, it's action time. If you want a different result (BHAG), then you have to make some different decisions, and then action those decisions.

> "Ask them what 'juices' them up. Ask them what they want from their careers. Ask them what they would do if they were running the firm."

Decision + Action = Result

What's your purpose, mission, and BHAG?

Breaking With in Order to Breakthrough

My good buddy, global real estate coach Michael Sheargold, has a fabulous saying: "Often a breakthrough happens after a break with."

I love it. If you look at making progress, often there is something in the way of achieving that progress. So, if you want the result bad enough, "break with" whatever is in the path.

Throughout the years, I have seen many firms break with many things. I have seen firms break with people who are unwilling to change. I have seen firms break with clients who are just downright rude, obtuse, and hard to work with. I have seen firms break with systems, processes, technology, methods, furniture, workflow procedures, and pricing models. And I have seen firms break with business partners!

> "If you look at making progress, often there is something in the way of achieving that progress."

I once did a TEDx talks about success, and one of the points was on toxic relationships. Why put up with toxic, energy-sucking, demoralizing, uninspiring people was the essence of it. Get rid of them, I said. Life is too short.

I was hosting my annual conference. A partner of a firm who I hadn't seen for a while approached me the minute he got there and said, "I listened to your TEDx talk three weeks ago, and what you were saying about toxic relationships really hit home. So I left my wife the next day!"

Whatever it is that is holding you back, break with it. You'll be happier when you do. When you do break with it, consider having some fun by having a "breaking with ceremony."

Recently I was operating two brands in the accounting profession. There was confusion in the office and confusion in the marketplace. I was confused sometimes. We decided to do something about it. On October 17, 2014, we got rid of one brand. But we didn't do it quietly. We **burned** the brand we didn't want to keep. When I say burned, I mean burned. We had a burning ceremony with a fire drum and burned the old brand . . . literally. We had the entire team plus 35 clients watching. I gave a short speech, everyone had champagne in hand, and then I set fire to anything that had the old brand on it. There was black, billowing smoke coming out of the fire drum, and it lasted for close to two hours in our office car park. It's a wonder the fire department wasn't called.

To make some more noise, we sent out media releases. We sent out emails and letters to announce the burning. We had the national press pick up on the story, and it featured the following Wednesday covering a third of the page in the most prestigious financial newspaper in Australia. Let's face it, it was a brand makeover. Brand makeovers are not exciting reading and don't make the press often. We were picked up online and even had a number of interviews.

If you're going to go to the trouble of breaking with something, make some noise about it.

The issue with all of this is you and your motivation. Do you want the result bad enough? If you have business partners, do they want the result bad enough? People are generally motivated by fixing pain or achieving pleasure. What pain do you want to fix and what pleasure do you want to achieve?

I heard a saying at a seminar once, "If the dream is big enough, the facts don't count." I don't entirely agree with everything regarding the facts—we need facts. However, the context of the saying is that if your reasons are big enough, then you'll do whatever it takes to make your dreams happen.

When it comes to breaking with, are your reasons strong enough? Do they motivate you? Are you prepared to do what it takes? Hopefully, everything you read in my Dear Accountant letter and in the first chapter is enough to motivate you to action.

Real Wealth

If you ask people about the definition of wealth, most will say that it's lots of money, lots of free time, great health, or enjoyable relationships. Is it one of those or all of those?

Some people think being wealthy is just having a lot of money. Many people who have a lot of money do not have the free time to enjoy it and often they are overweight and unhealthy.

Others think that real wealth is having loads of free time. Unfortunately, most people with a lot of free time do not have much money—although they do have the time to be healthy and work on relationships.

As this is an opinion-based book, and it's my opinion, my definition of being wealthy is this.

"Doing what you want, when you want, with whom you want, in a manner you want."

To get to the bottom of my definition, let's break it down.

> "The audience (all accountants, remember) came back buzzing. We had some of the audience share what they had written down—applause and tears followed."

What's Your Ferrari?

Doing what you want means you need to be living *your* dreams. Whatever they might be. You must first work out what you want from your life.

Ferrari—Part 1

I was in Naples, Florida, at a worldwide consultants' conference. At dinner one night, our host (Alan) told a story of how a friend of his always wanted to buy a Ferrari but never did. The friend was severely injured in a barbecue explosion and the friend's wife said to Alan, "You know, he never did buy that Ferrari." At that point in time, another dinner guest (Mark) said to the table, "So what's your Ferrari?" And around the table, one at a time, we were engrossed in stories of everyone's inner-most dreams and ambitions. It was an electrifying discussion.

> "**Doing what you want** means you need to be living your dreams. Whatever they might be."

Fast forward to our annual conference (Queenstown, New Zealand), and we had a special presenter's dinner with all the speakers and accountants who were presenting on stage during the four-day event. We were in a private room at an upmarket restaurant and Alan (being one of our guest speakers) was there. Alan told the story again, and again we went around the table asking each accountant (and other speakers) what their Ferrari was. It was amazing that deep down there were dreams not yet fulfilled and goals not yet met. One of the guest speakers (a business manager of a successful firm, Sean) leaned over to me and said, "This is the best night of my life."

Ferrari—Part 2

At our next conference (Hawaii), I decided to do something more elaborate with this Ferrari story. In my opening keynote address, the room was dark and I appeared on the big screen driving a racing Ferrari in full racing suit. Once the film was over, smoke appeared and I came through the haze in my racing suit and helmet. The conference room had a Ferrari theme to it, and I told the Ferrari story, complete with a slide show of potential dreams that the audience might be interested in. I covered housing, travel, charity, sports, health, toys, and overall lifestyle improvement.

Once I was finished, I gave the audience members instructions to leave the conference room (this was only 15 minutes into a four-day conference) with pad and pen and go write every conceivable dream, goal, aspiration, and ambition they had and then come back in one hour. The audience (all accountants, remember) came back buzzing. We had some of the audience members share what they had written down—applause and tears followed. Then each person wrote a detailed plan, to achieve their goals.

Each and every accountant in that room has a much higher propensity of achieving their dreams because they have committed to writing them down and coming up with a plan to achieve them. They are also held accountable to their plans through our coachingclub process.

What is your Ferrari?

Spend some time working out what you want to achieve in your life. Write everything down. Let your mind run free. Be creative and remember all the things you wanted to achieve when you were younger. If you need some inspiration, look at some magazines or lifestyle books. There is a plethora of books available on goal setting—go and absorb them and come up with a definitive list.

I am goal oriented—diligently writing my goals since I was 17. After years of goal setting, I have worked out a number of personal systems that work for me. This system keeps me on track and focused on living the life I want to live.

> "What is your Ferrari? Spend some time working out what you want to achieve in your life. Write everything down."

- ✓ My life **mission** and **purpose**—this is a statement like a company mission statement.
- ✓ My **eulogy**—I have a written statement that I want people to say about me after I am gone.
- ✓ My **inspiration**—I look for inspiration through magazines, TV programs, and dreaming.
- ✓ My **people**—I only associate with positive, goal-oriented, forward-thinking people.
- ✓ My **electronic** goals—I type my goal list into an electronic file.
- ✓ My **written** goals—I physically write every goal into my special "dreams and ideas" book.
- ✓ My **dream board**—I have a corkboard where I stick pictures of what I want to achieve.
- ✓ My **focus**—I have broken down my goals to life, three years, one year, and 90 days.
- ✓ My **accountability**—Each month I meet with my mastermind buddies to keep me on track.
- ✓ My **achievement**—As I fulfill a goal, I cross it off and put it on the achieved list.

With all my goals, I follow the tried and tested SMART formula—with a twist.

Specific—the goal must be specifically stated.

Measurable—the goal must be able to be measured somehow.

Audacious—the goal must stretch you and excite you.

Realistic—the goal must be realistic at the same time.

Timebound—the goal must have a completion date.

One of my favorite achievement models is this formula: **goals + vehicle + decisions + actions = results.**

The model says that if you want a different result, make some different decisions, and then follow through with the appropriate actions. Sounds simple enough. You set a result that you want to achieve; you decide what needs to happen or change; and then you go about implementing the action.

Here is what typically happens—YOU DON'T IMPLEMENT!

Why is that? When all the planning took place, you did the painstaking process of decision making and then you didn't follow through. The "action" part is definitely the tough part, and most people get distracted during the implementation process.

Here's my theory as to why the action bit doesn't happen. Action does not happen because the **result** you wanted to achieve was not **big** enough or **inspiring** enough to motivate you into action.

If you have bigger, more audacious goals, you will be more motivated to implement them.

A correctly structured accounting business that is run well is a vehicle to achieve whatever result you want to achieve in your life. As one of our coachingclub members said to me one day, "I know of a four-partner firm in Asia where one of the partners is a billionaire through the accounting firm."

> "The model says that if you want a different result, make some different decisions, and then follow through with the appropriate actions."

You have the right business vehicle. The questions are these: "Do you have the motivation? Do you have the dreams and goals to drive you forward?"

You Can't Lavish Time Unless You Have Time to Lavish

Doing what you want, when you want, with whom you want, in a manner you want means you need to MAKE time available to do what you want to do.

There are many excuses that people make for not doing something. The poorest, weakest excuse that has no meaning is, "I didn't have the time." How can anyone not have the time, when we all have the identical same amount of time to use? We all have 24 hours in a day, 168 hours in a week, and 52 weeks in a year. No one gets one second more or one second less.

It's not how much time we have; it's what we do with our time that counts. **It's never a time issue; it's a priority issue.**

So what do you do with your time? Does the day just go so fast and you wonder what you have done that day? Do you constantly get interrupted by emails, phone calls, clients, suppliers, and team members? Do you get home tired, kick the dog (not literally), have a drink, watch some TV, go to bed, and then wake up and do the same thing the next day? Do you feel unfulfilled and dissatisfied?

> "It's not how much time we have; it's what we do with our time that counts. It's never a time issue; it's a priority issue."

Or do you feel fulfilled every day because you were in charge of your time, and you only did things that were uplifting, exciting, and energizing?

How do you get to the point where you only do what you want to do and you are super effective on a daily basis? Here are some ideas that have helped me and many accountants I have worked with to become effective with their time.

Your Top Three

Work out what you actually do by initially keeping a log of what you do on a daily basis. When the list starts to repeat itself, stop keeping the log. Go back through the list and work out the number one highest dollar productive activity that you do—the one that you enjoy the most that is the best use of your time. Highlight that one.

Then work out the number two highest dollar productive activity. Highlight that one. Find the number three highest dollar productive activity and highlight that one.

Get rid of the rest. Delegate them, don't do them, or create a system so they do not need to be done at all. Get focused on just three things that are the best use of your time on a daily basis. You will find that a lot of your list is administration focused. You might need to hire an assistant to help you—if you do not have a personal assistant, then you are one. What are your top three?

Years ago, I was relocating my family from Sydney to Brisbane. I asked the mover if he owned a lawn mower. He did not. I said, "Now you do," and I gave him my lawn mower. I have never mowed a lawn since.

> "When the list starts to repeat itself, stop keeping the log."

The moral to this story is that if you do not want to do the task, then do not learn how to use the equipment to do the task. There are people more qualified, cheaper, and faster than you to do most tasks.

Time Blocking

Think of your week as 14 half days. You can achieve a lot in half a day, if you have uninterrupted time. If you block time out to do the important things in your life (for example, working "ON" time, sport, family, hobbies) and you are not interrupted, then you have a good chance of achieving them. I block out kids sports and school events, writing time, annual holidays (10 weeks, set a year in advance), exercise time, golf practice and play, date night, and short breaks. I then deal with clients and other work matters around the blocked-out time. I have taught many accountants how to use a strategy called **"lockdown."** Lockdown is where you commit to (say) two hours of uninterrupted time, shut the door, put a sign up, notify the team, and get on and do whatever you need to do.

The more time you spend working "ON" your business will mean the less time you need to spend working "IN" your business.

It's Your Calendar

If you feel out of control with your day and you are constantly interrupted, then it is no one's fault but your own. You have to remember it is your calendar—not your clients, suppliers, team members, or anyone else's schedule. Because it is MY calendar, I take control and have some strict rules regarding my calendar and phone calls. I do not return phone calls in the typical way, which is where you engage in telephone tag—you call me, leave a message, I call you, leave a message, and at some point in time (usually an inconvenient time) we finally connect. No way do I do this—it's a complete waste of everyone's time.

> "Lockdown is where you commit to (say) two hours of uninterrupted time, shut the door, put a sign up, notify the team, and get on and do whatever you need to do."

Instead, I have telephone appointments for every phone call. If you want to speak with me (and I'll speak with anyone), then book a 10 or 15-minute telephone appointment with me. I do the same thing if I want to speak with someone—I have some neat scripts about this. I typically have these calls booked on the 10, 15, 20, or 45 minute of the hour. Even if I want to speak with someone, I will book the calls at this time. The reason for the odd time is that most meetings start or finish on the hour—and meetings (not mine) are always late. It is also a bit different. I ALWAYS make the call precisely at the allotted time—I do not let the other person call me—even if they have made the appointment. Why? It's my calendar, and I am in control of my schedule.

I always remember signing up a new client (Damian) one year after I initially spoke with him. He said he joined because I called him precisely the time I said I would—one year after the call was initially booked!

Managing Email

I get as many emails as the next senior executive. I have an executive assistant (EA), but she does not manage my emails—I manage every single one of them. To manage them, my golden rule is that on any single day, I will not have a scroll bar on my inbox. To have only a few emails at a time in my inbox, I use some daily techniques that you might find useful. I do not deal with emails as they come in—I deal with them in chunks throughout the day. I might dedicate 30 minutes to replying to emails. When I reply, I reply quickly and succinctly. My email responses are short and succinct because my view on email is that it is a short messaging tool and file-sharing tool—not a conversation tool. Come and see me or call me if you want to have a conversation.

I file (if need be) emails quickly into a file folder for later. I delete junk and other useless emails quickly. I turn the email into a task—if needed—to be actioned later. I never reply if I am copied on an email. I rarely reply if there is not a question in the email. I do not have the email alert that tells me I have a new email—what a distraction that is. Before email there was an inbox filing tray that housed the letters, papers, phone call reminders, and other files. Imagine if you had an old-style filing tray that looked like your current email inbox.

Meeting Effectiveness

Meetings can be such a waste of time. Especially meetings that are unstructured and with an unfocused agenda. I will meet with anyone as long as I know what the meeting is about. Here are some of my rules about meetings that will enable you to have fewer but more effective meetings.

To get the agenda out of someone I have my EA ask callers, "What would you like to meet with Rob about—can you put it in an email, please?" The agenda comes through and then we determine how much time is needed to deal with the agenda—normally much less than the person initially thought. In many cases, I will have a telephone meeting before a face-to-face meeting. I love "stand up" meetings, "walk and talk" meetings, "breakfast" meetings, and "coffee" meetings. These meeting styles are shorter in nature because they are not as comfortable as a nice office chair with endless coffee. Although a keen golfer, I do not like "golf" meetings. They are too long and besides, I am there to play golf not talk business.

> "I will do a time check before the end of the meeting (say 15 minutes left) and we will wrap up next steps. I always finish meetings on time"

When a team member comes into my office, I always stand up to talk (I do not want to have them get too comfortable), and we have a shorter conversation. At the start of every meeting (I learned this from my accountant) I always ask, "What do you want to get out of today's meeting?" I write the agenda. I always have time allotted to each meeting and at the start of the meeting, we determine the time and I always finish before the allotted time—I will do a time check before the end of the meeting (say 15 minutes left), and we will wrap up with the next steps. I always finish meetings before or on time.

To get you focused on succinct meetings, remember the following saying, "Tell them what they need to know, not everything that you know."

Self-Imposed Deadlines

What is the most efficient week of your year? That's right—the week before you go on a holiday. You are going to be offline for three weeks and the week leading up to it you are happening. You are succinct in your communication (your email response might be simply "no" instead of a long, drawn-out answer), and you are able to get things done much faster than normal. The reason you are so efficient is that you created a self-imposed deadline. In the accounting business, there are few real deadlines that must be adhered to. Because there are few deadlines, you get quite sloppy with getting things done. Getting back to clients takes longer than need be. You get workflow blowouts, and there is a mad rush at the end of every month.

> "I create self-imposed deadlines for everything. I take my laptop to the café to do some writing, and my deadline is the battery life."

If you were to have a self-imposed deadline on every task, then this would not be an issue. Instead of saying to a client, "I'll get back to you," say, "I'll send you the engagement letter by close of business Tuesday." Instead of saying to a team member, "Come back to me when you have finished the job," say, "When will you be coming back to me?" You need to have some fun with this and trick your mind into changing gears—hyper gear! I create self-imposed deadlines for everything. I take my laptop to the café to do some writing, and my deadline is the battery life. I use the airline seat belt sign (on and off) as my deadline for writing. I say to myself, "I am going to get this finished in this time," and then I reward myself somehow. Sometimes my reward is golf, a coffee, a swim, a walk, or maybe even some shopping.

If it is a BIG deadline (like when I ran the London Marathon, or my goal to be a "scratch" golfer, or even finishing this book), I will tell many others about my deadline. That way I am accountable to more than myself.

My friend, Michael, tells a wonderful story of when he was coaching a large homebuilder. The average time to build a house was 120 days, and the contractors thought (because they were the second biggest builder in the land) that they were really good. Michael was in front of the executive team members, and he challenged them on their building time frames. He said to them, "How can you do it in 10 days?" They thought he was from another planet or on drugs. They protested about the exercise, but Michael stayed firm. He asked them to brainstorm how they could hypothetically build their houses in 10 days. Michael said in a perfect and hypothetical world, **"What would you need to start doing, stop doing, continue doing, have a different process, run a different system, use different materials, or any other changes to make it close to being built in 10 days?"**

He broke the group into small teams and off they went and brainstormed for 30 minutes. They came up with dozens of ideas, which were transferred to a series of flip chart paper. At the end of the exercise, Michael simply said, **"Just go and do that"**—while pointing to the flip chart paper. And they did. They didn't hit 10 days, but they did hit 40 days. From 120 days to 40 days meant a massive upgrade on cash flow, a massive upgrade on customer service, and a massive upgrade on new referrals.

You can't make any more time. You can be more effective with your time. Work out what you have to stop doing, start doing, and continue doing to **make the time you have count.**

Toxic Relationships

Doing what you want, when you want, **with whom you want,** in a manner you want means you need to get rid of toxic relationships and only associate with people you want to associate with. If the people around you are miserable, snarly, sarcastic, negative, or just downright nasty—get rid of them.

Do not associate with these people. Only associate with people who are uplifting, have similar ideals to you, and are challenging and energizing at the same time. Find some new friends, and don't associate with any relatives who are like this.

You need to have the right people around you who will support you. You should not need to "suffer fools" or have anyone around you who has an ulterior motive. Sometimes these people are on your payroll, and they tend to act like terrorists where they

> "You need to get rid of toxic relationships and only associate with people you want to associate with."

recruit other terrorists. Eventually, it's like a cancer spreading quickly through your organization. Get rid of the lot of them. Make the hard decision and fire them or force them out—you'll be glad you did.

If you decide to go on a holiday with another family, then make sure the family has similar "spending ideals" to you. If you are generous with your money on holidays (you like dining out, drinking good wine, and generally enjoy the finer things in life) and the other family is not generous (they prefer buying groceries and cooking at your villa, cask wine, and are generally "tight"), then neither of you is in for a fun time. Both parties will be miserable and want the holiday to end. Message to self—never go anywhere with these people again!

If you go out for dinner and you decide to "split the bill," be wary of your dinner friends who want a different (always lesser) amount, because they only had the soup, the salad, and one glass of wine versus your steak and three glasses of wine. Message to self—never go to dinner with these people again!

> "Both parties will be miserable and want the holiday to end. Message to self—never go anywhere with these people again."

Perhaps you have a dinner party or barbecue at your home and the people you invite promise, "We will have you over next time," but they never do. Message to self—never invite them back to your home again for a function.

For as long as I can remember, I have been running or participating in a mastermind group. This is a group of likeminded businesspeople who are doing different things than me. We meet each month (normally over a long breakfast), brainstorm ideas, and we keep each other accountable.

Maybe you need to join a network of like-minded entrepreneurial accountants—where everyone is striving for the same thing as you.

If you need help or support, then someone in the world has more than likely done what you want to do. Seek them out and ask for their help. It's my experience that people who are truly successful give back and lend a hand to others.

It's your choice who you associate with. Make some decisions and take action.

Feeling Good about Yourself

Doing what you want, when you want, with whom you want, **in a manner you want** means you'll start feeling good about yourself. If you do not feel good about yourself, then you will probably hate your clients.

You need to be happy with what you see in the mirror. You need to be fulfilled and you need to be excited about life. You need to be happy with the way that you execute your goals.

> "Do not be a cheapskate when it comes to the way you look. If you want to be a success, start looking like a success."

It might mean you need to change some of your dietary and exercise habits to get into shape. The healthier you are, the more energy you have and the better you feel about yourself.

It might mean you need to upgrade your wardrobe to feel better about yourself. There is a lot of truth in the saying, "clothes make the man [or woman]." Do not be a cheapskate when it comes to the way you look. If you want to be a success, start looking like a success.

It might mean you need to upgrade your travel style. Substantially better accommodations does not cost that much more. Having a driver pick you up does not cost much more than a taxi. Upgrading your airline ticket to business or first class makes a world of difference in how you arrive. My wife and I always travel in business or first class (depending on what is available), and we put the kids in economy. Much to their disgust, we tell them they have to earn better travel themselves—just like we had to.

It might mean you need to become an object of interest. To become an object of interest, you need to be interesting to be around. You need interesting stories, worldly experiences, good social skills, and to be seen as someone who is achieving something.

Feeling good about yourself is about looking after yourself. It is more important than looking after your clients.

Marathon—Part 1

Two weeks after my fortieth birthday (where I received a ticket to space on Virgin Galactic as my present), my wife Nat casually said, "By the way, I have also signed you up to run in the London Marathon on Richard Branson's team." A space trip and now a marathon—I was wondering if she was trying to kill me. I had never run more than 2 kilometers (km), so always up for a challenge, I said yes without hesitation. The Virgin Group was the primary sponsor of the 2010 London Marathon, so there was a detailed training plan that came out. Just to be safe, I verified the Virgin training plan with a four-time marathon winner—he added some ideas and gave me some support along the way, which was great. I had no idea what it meant to run a

> "Feeling good about yourself is about looking after yourself. It is more important than looking after your clients."

marathon, so I set three goals. The first was to **finish without stopping.** The second was to **finish without walking.** The third was to complete it in **less than four hours, 30 minutes**—the average was four hours, 41 minutes. I told everyone I met my three goals—even all my clients and I announced it on my forum.

Marathon—Part 2

To help me, and keep me accountable, I enlisted my personal trainer, Craig, to train with me—except on Sundays, when I did the long runs on my own. After six weeks, I was up to 8km in distance, and I got a bad knee injury. It turns out the knee injury (which actually occurred playing golf in New Zealand) was aggravated the week before while I was trekking up a mountain in the Caribbean. I was out of action for seven weeks while I had 15 physiotherapy sessions. Time to restart my training program. I had a 26-week program with only 17 weeks to do it in. For the next 17 weeks, I grinded away, meeting my trainer at 5:00 a.m. each weekday morning for a one-hour session. I averaged 40km per week, running the 17-week time frame. I was training six days a week to get at least partially ready for this event. My last big run was 33km (this is what the plan said) before I headed off to London to run 42.2 grueling kilometers. Nat was trekking the Himalayas for a charity the week prior, so we met in Singapore and traveled together to London.

Marathon—Part 3

Time for the day of reckoning—race day. I was as ready as I would ever be. I was up bright and early to get the train to the starting line. It was about 90 minutes away. I was told to go to the green start, which I found out was reserved for celebrities, potential record breakers, and people wearing crazy costumes—even Sir Richard was dressed as a butterfly with 2-meter wings! I thought I was the celebrity, however, I subsequently found out that I was not on a celebrity team. There were 37,000 competitors and 750,000 spectators lining the streets to cheer me on. The atmosphere was brilliant and motivating. There were 80 pubs along the way, and each one had a theme and a party going on. There were people drinking, singing, and partying while I was slogging it out step by step. Every few pubs, the partygoers would thrust a beer out and shout, "Do you want a beer?" I thought I would love a beer, however, if I had a beer, then I would need to stop or walk and my goals would not be achieved.

> "There were 37,000 competitors and 750,000 spectators lining the streets to cheer me on. The atmosphere was brilliant and motivating."

The halfway mark was the Tower Bridge over the River Thames. I was feeling good and energetic and crossed the halfway marker in exactly two hours. Full of confidence, I was thinking maybe four hours was realistic. I was pounding away, as I listened to my four and a half hour, motivational playlist on my iPod, when at the 30km mark, the battery went flat—right in the middle of Kenny Loggins "Footloose" song. I said to myself—"The crowd will have to bring me home." More partygoers were thrusting beer at me, and I started to dream about having a beer—you think crazy thoughts when you run a marathon.

Nat gave me two affirmations to help me when things got tough. She told me these affirmations got her through childbirth and trekking the Himalayas the week before. I said to myself, "There's only one way home, Rob," and "It's only two hours of your life, Rob," and then, as the finish got closer, "It's only 45 minutes of your life, Rob." These affirmations helped me enormously. The crowds got thicker and thicker as we neared the finish line, and my pace got slower and slower. The last 5km or so was just exhausting but the crowd, my determination, and my goals got me through. My name was on my shirt and the crowds were cheering for me.

The end was in sight. I knew that once I could see Buckingham Palace, there was one corner and a few hundred meters to go. Exhausted as I crossed the finish line (I was practicing my stylish photo finish for weeks but could not muster the strength to do it), I completed my marathon **without walking, without stopping, and in four hours, 20 minutes, and 57 seconds**. Woohoo—I achieved all three goals. I collapsed in a heap, then got myself together and went and celebrated my greatness.

Did I feel good about myself after running a marathon? You bet! It was a life achievement that I will remember for a long, long time. I also learned some powerful lessons during the process. I call this "marathon success."

Set goals and tell others about them.

Someone else has done what you want to do; follow the leaders.

If you want something bad enough, often you have to sacrifice.

Create a plan and stick to it.

Avoid temptations that might derail you.

If the dream is big enough, the facts don't count.

My favorite Māori (an indigenous New Zealander) word is "mana"—pronounced **mah**-nah. It means presence. When you feel good about yourself, you will increase your mana and you will attract much more success.

> "Did I feel good about myself after running a marathon? You bet!"

THE PERFECT FIRM

The New Equation

If the old equation is internally focused, then the new model is externally focused. It is based on marketing, sales, building relationships, value pricing, and customer service. This equation in the following graphic is a mathematical equation, which, when you know and adjust the numbers, becomes a powerful formula.

"Just like you know your numbers in the old equation, you must know your numbers in your new equation. What you can measure you can manage."

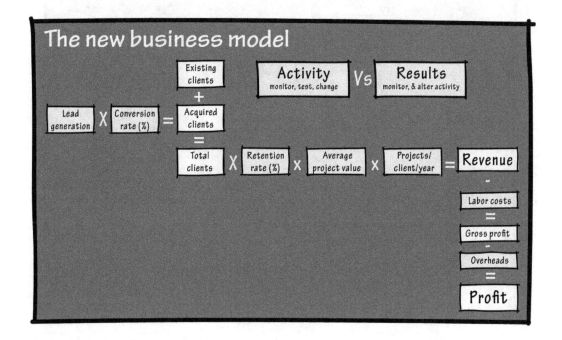

Knowing Your New Numbers

Just like you know your numbers in the old equation, you must know your numbers in your new equation. What you can measure you can manage.

- ✓ You need to know how many (exactly) existing clients you currently have.
- ✓ You need to know how many (exactly) leads you get from each marketing campaign.
- ✓ You need to know your conversion rate (exactly) from inquiry to sale.
- ✓ You need to know your retention rate (exactly) of existing clients.
- ✓ You need to know the average sale value (exactly) of each project.
- ✓ You need to know how many projects (exactly) your clients buy from you each year.

What business can exist without knowing the numbers? Work out what your numbers are, and then you can apply strategy to improve each one of them. After your analysis, your numbers might look something like the following graph.

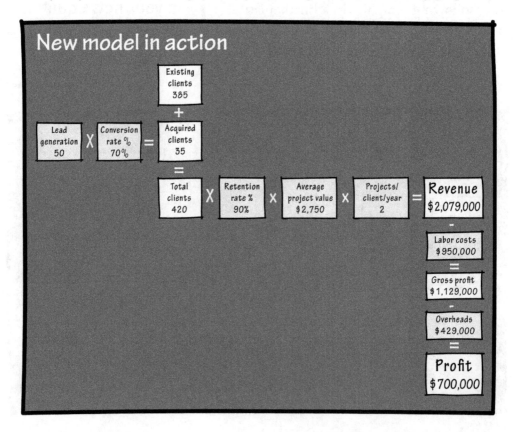

Your Brand

Before we break the equation down into bite-size bits, you need to determine what makes you unique and different. Are you in the "sea of sameness," like every other accounting firm, or are you different? What is your unique position in your marketplace? Do you want to be different? Do you want to stand out?

> "Before we break the equation down into bite-size bits, you need to determine what makes you unique and different."

Once you answer these questions (hopefully positively in so far as you want to be unique), you can position your firm in any way you choose. As my team and I coach, visit, and observe firms, we notice that their "brands" are often tired and, to put it bluntly, boring. The firms' websites (if they have one) was created some years ago and the partners' photographs do not represent what they look like now. Your new clients might not say it, but they might think, *Hmmm, you seem to have less hair now, and you look like you are larger around your middle than you are on your website.*

The colors on the website are often bland and there is no modern style to anything. I went to a firm one day and the owner showed me the company letterhead. I asked, "Why is it in black and white?" Answer, "So we can print right out of the printer—it saves on printing costs." You can't make this up! Your brand is every aspect of your firm—from the way you dress, to your building, to your colors, your collateral, your work, your style, your furniture, and especially the paperwork you send to your clients.

Tired, traditional, cheap, and boring—that's what most firms' "brands" looks like.

It's time for a brand makeover. Employ a branding consultant to do a complete overhaul of the entire look and feel of the firm.

This is called "positioning." It's how you are positioned in the marketplace before or while the client does business with you. Here is a checklist of positioning tactics (many cost zero money) that you can apply, so you are positioned differently to what you are now.

- ✓ High prices
- ✓ Articles
- ✓ Media releases

- ✓ E-newsletters
- ✓ Website, blog, social media
- ✓ Testimonials and case studies
- ✓ Free reports, tools, videos, and audio
- ✓ Speeches—paid and free
- ✓ Other people's newsletters
- ✓ Reference list of existing clients
- ✓ Competitions and awards ceremonies
- ✓ Being controversial

There are many ways to be positioned differently. Implement something.

Lead Generation

Most accounting practices have a zero-based lead generation (or new inquiries) strategy, which means they do nothing. New clients just "appear," typically via referral. There's nothing wrong with getting referrals from existing clients. In fact, they are the best quality leads you can get—free and credible. The challenge with a referral is that it is typically reactive, and you have no control of how many you will get and when. So just having a referral-only strategy is a path to slow growth. To be proactive in lead generation, you need multiple methods to attract the clients you want to attract. It starts with a database of your target market (niche, geographic, service focus). Then with proactive and persistent marketing (with the focus on generating leads), you attract potential clients to your firm.

> "To be proactive in lead generation, you need multiple methods to attract the clients you want to attract."

Here are some examples of proactive marketing tactics that you can apply.

- ✓ Direct mail and email
- ✓ E-newsletters
- ✓ Paper newsletter, magazine
- ✓ Seminars and workshops
- ✓ Boardroom briefings

- ✓ Teleseminars and webinars
- ✓ Referrals from clients or spheres of influence
- ✓ Host beneficiary relationships

People buy from people, and if you want to get my attention as a business owner (assuming that's your target market), then you have to remember one word—**experience.** Not your years of experience, but the ways that I **experience** your smarts. You need to create multiple points of **experience** in your marketing campaigns. Mix it up with voice, video, meetings, presentation, words written, tools downloaded, etc.

Conversion Rate

> "You need to know what your current conversion rate is over a reasonable time frame."

If lead generation is about getting people to come to you and make an inquiry, then conversion rate is about converting that inquiry to business. Typically, the conversion rate from quality referrals is relatively high. However, when you start proactive marketing (using additional lead generation methods), your conversion rate might drop.

You need to know what your current conversion rate is over a reasonable time frame (we call this the opportunity open days), and you need to acquire new skills and methods to increase your conversion rate.

Here is a list of skills, techniques, and tactics you can apply to increase your conversion rate.

- ✓ Your conviction, self-belief, and self-esteem
- ✓ Finding your prospects'/clients' objectives and motivation
- ✓ Follow up, follow up
- ✓ Activity levels—number of calls, number of meetings
- ✓ Nurturing during sales—points of experience
- ✓ Time and scarcity-based offers
- ✓ Sales aids—collateral
- ✓ Scripts, dialogues, language
- ✓ Needs analysis
- ✓ Role plays and practice

- ✓ Presentation style
- ✓ Educating prospects
- ✓ Closing techniques
- ✓ Consultative selling
- ✓ "What if" based selling
- ✓ Testimonial and case studies
- ✓ Objections and answer list
- ✓ Asking for the business

With new skills (in this sales area), you will reduce the days the opportunity is open, increase your conversion rate, increase your average project value, increase the number of projects each of your clients buys from you, and also increase the margin (average hourly rate recovered) on each project.

Retention Rate

The retention rate of existing clients is typically high. As I will explain in more detail in later chapters, it is high because you have the clients "bluffed" that it's hard to change accountants. By the time the client thinks about leaving the firm, you have completed most of this years' work. When you start pricing upfront, you might lose a small number of clients. It's an out for them. That's a good thing, because typically you will lose the types of clients you wanted to lose.

> "That's a good thing, because typically you will lose the types of clients you wanted to lose."

Increasing (or maintaining) retention rate is about building closer relationships with clients and increasing the customer service levels.

Following our theme, here is a checklist of tactics you can apply to improve retention rate.

- ✓ Create a client-nurturing program.
- ✓ Provide outstanding client service.
- ✓ Call clients and ask, "How's it going?"
- ✓ Visit clients at their places of business.
- ✓ Invite clients to social and business events/seminars.

✓ Send personal cards, letters, emails, and items of interest.

✓ Build a community of clients.

✓ Run client advisory boards.

✓ Refer business to the clients.

✓ Offer additional and new services.

✓ Send business newsletters and updates.

✓ Ask the clients how they want to be served.

Increasing loyalty in relationships is about being proactive and communicating more.

Average Project Value

The average project value is not the average fee per client. The average project value is where you average all your invoices over the year. If you have three invoices for the one project, then that is one invoice only. You might call a project a "job" or "task" for the client. For example, annual compliance is one project. A budget/cash flow forecast is a project. A restructure is a project. A company due diligence is a project. What is the average for you?

Once you know your average (and you do want to increase it), you can use some or all (or others) of the checklist below to increase the average project value.

> "The average project value is where you average all your invoices over the year."

✓ Realize your services are worth more.

✓ Find the courage to charge more.

✓ Increase all prices immediately.

✓ Offer additional services at the time of buying.

✓ Have a standard menu of services and price list.

✓ Price in advance, not arrears.

✓ Articulate the value of each project eloquently.

✓ Get rid of low-margin services and low-margin clients.

✓ Improve your language and sales skills.

✓ Target more profitable clients and services.

✓ Use value-based fees—not hours times rate!

You are doing the project anyway, so if you can get more "margin" out of it, then the new margin is free and clear profit.

Projects Per Year

As you work out the average project value, you also work out how many projects your clients are buying each year. Or another way to think of it is how many **products** they buy from you each year. I remember having lunch with the CEO of a major bank. We were talking about retention of customers for the bank. He said something that really resonated with me. He said, *"If we can get a customer to buy four products from us, then we will keep the customer for a long time. If they only buy one or two products, then it is easier for them to leave."*

> "Another way to think of it is how many products do they buy from you each year."

It's the same for your business. If the client only buys one product from you (say, annual compliance), then they are not really "wedded" to you. In Internet speak—the **stickiness** is just not there.

The vast majority of your clients have unmet needs, and your job is to find out what they really need and offer it to them. Your objective is to have all of your clients buying everything they need that helps them achieve their goals!

When I shifted accounting firms, I went from an average of one-and-a-half projects per year to six per year with the new firm.

There are many ways to do this—here is yet another checklist.

- ✓ Productize your existing services into a definitive list—with prices.
- ✓ Create new services—leverage off other firms.
- ✓ Lower the barriers to doing business—free phone calls, emails.
- ✓ Build relationships by having a communication schedule.
- ✓ Educate your team to find opportunities.
- ✓ Think a minimum of four products per client.
- ✓ Work out what they haven't got on your client/service matrix.
- ✓ Constantly market services through all channels.
- ✓ Have a service theme for the month/quarter.
- ✓ Have your "intellectual property selling opportunities" radar on at all times.

✓ Find out what the clients really need—do not prejudge.

✓ Offer your services—they can only say no!

The simplest business model in the world is "find the need and fill it." I think it is your duty of care to offer every service you have to every client you have. Who knows, some might buy the additional service. I also think you should continually innovate and invent new products and services.

The number of projects a client buys from you is one of the easiest in the new growth equation. There is already a high level of client loyalty and trust, and they have unmet needs. You just have to ask the right questions!

> "The vast majority of your clients have unmet needs, and your job is to find out what they really need and offer it to them."

Rob's Rule of 38:43

If you were to work out your numbers using my equation and then focus on strategies to improve each key area (I just gave you 74 separate strategies in the checklists), then you would have a vastly different result. Consider the numbers of the equation in the previous graph.

It was 420 clients x 90 percent retention rate x $2,750 per project x two projects per client = $2,079,000 revenue.

If you were to apply "Rob's rule of 38:43" (5 + 3 + 10 + 20 = 38), then you would have a 43 percent increase in revenue. Let me explain . . .

✓ A 5 percent increase in clients.

✓ A 3 percent improvement in retention rate.

✓ A 10 percent increase in the price per project that you sell.

✓ A 20 percent increase in the number of projects per year per client (which means only 20 percent of clients buy one more service per year).

This equates to 441 clients x 92.7 percent retention rate x $3,025 per project x 2.4 projects per client = $2,967,938 or a 43 percent increase in revenue.

Apply the same process two years in a row, and you will **double the size of your current revenue.**

With a focus on value pricing (not pricing in arrears on hours times rate) and being more efficient (reducing labor intensity), you will not need as many people as you think to deliver the new revenue. Even if you added $200,000 in additional salary expenses (if you follow our efficiency model, you will not need too much in the way of labor) and you added $100,000 in additional overheads, you will still be better off by a whopping 84 percent increase in profit. See the following graph.

> "If you were to apply "Rob's rule of 38:43" (5 + 3 + 10 + 20 = 38), then you would have a 43 percent increase in revenue."

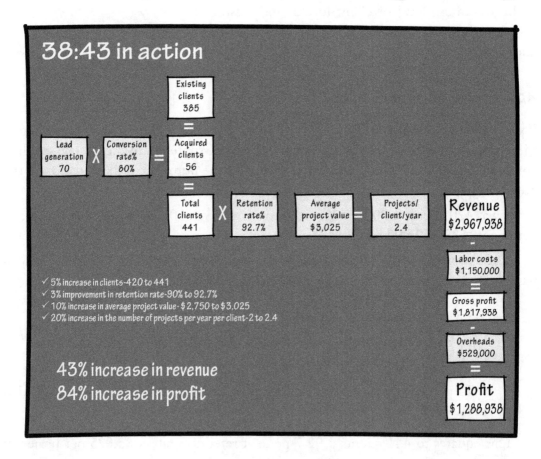

38:43 in action

		Existing clients 385

Lead generation 70 **X** Conversion rate% 80% **=** Acquired clients 56

Total clients 441 **X** Retention rate% 92.7% Average project value $3,025 **=** Projects/ client/year 2.4 **Revenue $2,967,938**

−
Labor costs $1,150,000
=
Gross profit $1,817,938
−
Overheads $529,000
=
Profit $1,288,938

✓ 5% increase in clients-420 to 441
✓ 3% improvement in retention rate-90% to 92.7%
✓ 10% increase in average project value- $2,750 to $3,025
✓ 20% increase in the number of projects per year per client-2 to 2.4

43% increase in revenue
84% increase in profit

Break down the entire model to bite-size bits, and it becomes more achievable.

It's All about the Clients

The old (traditional) growth model is all internally focused. Nowhere in it is the client mentioned. The new business model is all about the clients. It's about marketing to get additional clients from firms who are not giving legendary service (hopefully, like you do). It's about serving them well to keep them delighted, loyal, and referring others. It's about offering all services to them, and it's about you receiving fair compensation for the value that you create for the client.

> "The old (traditional) growth model is all internally focused. Nowhere in it is the client mentioned."

Yes, you need to be efficient and track job turnaround times and productivity. And you need to monitor the average hourly rate and other measures, so you know if you are on track. These are all important things to quantify, but they should not be the primary focus.

The primary focus should be your clients. In our coachingclub meetings, we are constantly discussing "sales visits" that each partner or client-facing team member is doing each month. We are asking (and keeping accountable) how many were completed, how many projects eventuated from the visits, and what was the new revenue that was created as a result. Yes, I want you to drive top-line revenue, and I also want you to drive customer service and loyalty.

If it's all about the clients, then you need to be into the clients. You need to think creatively about how you can help them, and you need to constantly meet with them and discuss ideas and opportunities with them.

Consider this model when it comes to clients and services.

The ranking system says that the easiest thing is to have existing clients buy existing products and services. You have client loyalty and you have already done the project with another client, so there is limited research and product creation to do.

The second easiest thing is to have existing clients buy brand new services that have just been created. Again, you have brand loyalty and the conversion rate is extremely high, so the cost of sale is dramatically reduced.

"Let's focus on the easiest thing to do (box 1), which is existing clients buying existing products services from you."

The third easiest thing is to have a service you have done before with another client and you perform that service with a completely new client. You do not have to spend much effort creating the service, and the new clients will be quite receptive to it because they typically want additional services from the previous accountant.

And the fourth easiest (or hardest) thing is to win new clients and offer them something you have never done before.

Let's focus on the easiest thing to do (box 1), which is existing clients buying existing products services from you.

In my live seminars, I have a three-part quiz in relation to box 1. Remember, it's the easiest thing to do, so I assume it has already been done!

> "Your clients need to know what all the services are and so do you and your team. Start right there."

1. How many of your existing clients have **purchased** every single product or service that you can currently deliver?

2. How many of your existing clients **know** that all these products and services exist? They could read the services list back to you, verbatim. They might not need the services now, but they could need them in the future or they could refer someone who needs them.

3. How many of your existing team members (and this includes the partners) **know** about every product and service that exists within the firm's capabilities?

OK, question one was a trick question. The answer will be close to zero, because not every client needs every product or service that you have to deliver.

The real questions and opportunities are in questions two and three, because the answers to those questions will be similar to question one. Your clients need to know what all the services are and so do you and your team. Start right there.

If you focus on your clients and you make sure that the price you charge is based on the value you contribute, then you cannot go wrong—unless, of course, you grossly underpriced the service or you take too long to complete each project.

History Makers

The old model suggests that most of the work that accountants do is history writing. Writing the past and presenting it is a time frame that it is not relevant any more. Clients want additional help, and if you take the view that by being proactive and really helping your clients, you can become a **history maker**.

Accountants have so much to offer, if they just get proactive. After surveying thousands of clients of all types of industries, I have narrowed it to eight key areas (over and above compliance services) where clients want help. I call them The Awesome 8.

The Awesome 8

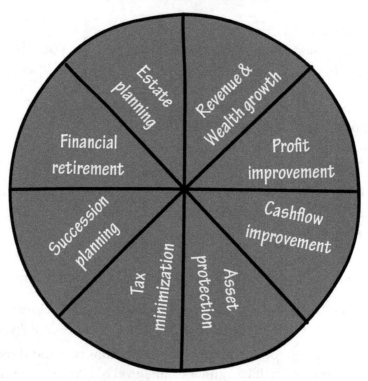

If you just ask the right questions and listen carefully, you'll hear your clients saying—

"Help me to grow my revenue and my wealth."

"Help me to improve my profitability."

"Help me to understand and free up my cash flow."

"Help me to protect my assets for future generations."

"Help me to minimize tax."

"Help me with succession planning or with the sale of my business."

"Help me to be financially retired."

"Help me to structure my business so I can leave a legacy."

Your skills and services (that clients have not bought yet) can do these things.

> "By just offering history writing services, which (although important and must be done) is a grudge purchase, you are not really helping your clients at all."

Offering The Awesome 8 services really does help your clients to define their futures, create wealth, build a better lifestyle, and create a legacy.

By just offering history writing services, which (although important and must be done) is a grudge purchase, you are not really helping your clients at all.

To get your firm into a position to offer additional value-added services to clients and prospects, I see five distinct steps to make it happen.

1. Get specialized coaching to guide you on how to do it—this is new territory and you should only follow those who have already done it with others.

2. Get better with what you have—sort out workflow, WIP, receivables, write-downs, pricing, people, systems, etc.

3. Free up capacity—hire more people or reduce labor intensity by being more efficient.

4. Develop your product/service offering—look at your range of services and productize them or seek external help to do so.

5. Market and sell your services—get active by marketing and selling to existing and prospective clients.

Start making history today. Call all your clients and go visit them. Offer something new. Your clients will be better off for it, and you'll be rewarded accordingly—unless you price your services the old way—hours times rate.

Redundant or Real Time

The vast majority of accountants I meet are offering "redundant data" services and advice. They are offering information based on old data. Clients don't want services that are late. They want real-time services that are on time, relevant, and preemptive.

Where is the value offering advice that is late? Picture the scene. You are doing your client's annual accounting and you spot some anomalies or issues from the previous year. You finish the work and then write a letter to the client explaining what she should do to fix it!

What she should do! Seriously, it's typically too late.

I know you have a duty of care to tell the client the issue—and you did that. Well done, you. But it's still too late.

With today's accounting technology (on the Internet), you can know what is going on all the time. You don't need to know all the details, just enough to spot issues and opportunities. Your clients are not accountants, and you have an uncanny knack of seeing financial data and helping to make sense of it for them.

You can even have the data consolidated into single dashboards, so you can get a summary of all your clients' affairs on one page. Then the technology can alert you to the good and the bad issues only. With this sort of technology, you can preempt issues and advise the clients accordingly. Now that's adding value.

> "You can even have the data consolidated into single dashboards, so you can get a summary of all your client's affairs on one page."

It's all about becoming a real-time accountant, not a redundant-data accountant. It's all about being proactive and not reactive. Real-time accountants behave differently, and they are much more client focused. The following table highlights some of the behaviors.

Redundant or real time

Redundant Data Accountants	Real Time Accountants
Offers advice late or not at all	Offers advice before it happens
Processes work and administration	Value added services that help
Waits for things to happen	On front foot making it happen
Majority of revenue in compliance	Majority of rev in Business Advisory
Prices in arrears	Prices in every project upfront
Doesn't visit / call me	Visits and calls on systematic basis
Doesn't follow up	Follows up in every opportunity
Doesn't promote the latest thing	Always promoting
Most clients on 'hard drive' accounting	Most clients on 'cloud' accounting
Numbers power with the client	Numbers power with the Accountant

Let's break down each one and see what they mean.

Offers Advice Late or Not at All Versus Offers Advice before It Happens

Offering advice after the fact and late really does not help anyone. Conversations that start with "What you should have done is . . ." or "Next time, do this . . ." or "Can you tell me what this means?" are conversations that are about to offer little or no value. Instead, why not preempt what is going on with the client. Be on the front foot, spotting trends and anomalies before they happen. Let your client know that you have noticed (for example) that receivables are up, payables are up, and inventory is too high. Let them know that they are probably in for a cash flow grind. Let them know that you can help fix it. Now that's being proactive. With Cloud accounting and predicative analytical software, you can do this. Real-time accountants are analyzing data as it happens and offering real-time advice.

Processes Work and Administration Versus Value-Added Services That Help

There is a lot of administrative work in compliance. A lot of data entry, checking data, and ultimately filing. I know that the filing of tax returns and annual financial statements is mandated by governments around the world. It's unavoidable that people have to buy. They don't want to buy it, yet they have to buy it. A bit like fuel for your car, it's a grudge purchase. There is a lot of processing work to be done, yet there is little value in it for your clients. It is all based on historical data that the clients cannot change. As a business owner, clients want the "good stuff." They want the help that actually helps improve their financial conditions. They want services that create a tangible return. Real-time accountants are always finding new services that offer more value to the clients.

> "Real-time accountants are analyzing data as it happens and offering real-time advice."

Waits for Things to Happen Versus On Front Foot Making It Happen

Accountants are world leaders in waiting. If there were an Olympic gold medal for the profession that waited for things to happen, then most accountants would probably win every year with no competitors! Redundant-data accountants wait for the government to change the rules, and then they offer more services. They wait for the phone to ring, the email to ping. They wait for the bank to tell them that their client is in trouble. They wait for team members to complain. They wait and wait and wait for missing information to be sent back from their clients. They spend most of their professional waking hours . . . WAITING. Real-time accountants are on the front foot making it happen. They are creating their own stories, their own futures. They are not waiting for clients to send back missing information when they are ready. They are not waiting for the government to marginalize their services by developing standard business reporting (SBR). This is happening in Australia, where it's estimated that $500M of annual compliance will be eliminated because of SBR. Real-time accountants are proactive, making things happen and not waiting for things to happen.

Majority of Revenue in Compliance Versus Majority of Revenue in Advisory

Having 60 percent, 70 percent, or 80 percent or more of your revenue tied up in compliance is your choice. No one's decisions or actions except your own have given you the burden of a great amount of your revenue tied up in redundant-data accounting services. If you truly believe that your clients want to buy business advisory services, then do something about it. Many firms have systemized the function of compliance so that they can be more efficient and create capacity. Many firms have automated the compliance process so that they have capacity to deliver business advisory. Many firms are actively promoting business advisory services to their clients. Many firms are offshoring compliance work so they have the capacity with the current team to deliver business advisory. It starts with the will to change, then the decisions to be made, and the actions to be taken. The true real-time accountants are making business model decisions and turning the percentage around (of compliance to business advisory), so they have much more revenue in business advisory versus compliance.

"The ONLY legitimate way to price a product or service is to see what the market is prepared to pay for it."

Prices in Arrears Versus Prices Every Project Upfront

The old way of pricing was to work out how much time was spent on the client job and apply an hourly rate to the time and then multiply hours times rate. And hey, presto, a price is derived. Imagine if a client came to you and said, "Oh, wise accountant, I have a new product idea, and I would like some advice on how much I should charge for it." And you respond with, "Here at the accounting firm, this is how we would price it. We would take the total salary of the person creating the product and divide that number by 1,700 working hours. That would give us salary price per hour. We would take that number and multiply it by four times and that would give us a charge rate for the person doing the work. Then we would divide that number by 10, so we had a unit price for every six minutes of work. Then, as the person is creating the product, we would have him record how many units of time it took to create the product. At the end, we would multiply the units (hours taken) by the unit price and voila, we would have the price."

At this point, your client is logically wondering if the marketplace would pay that price, if the person doing the work is efficient, or if the salary level is correct in the first place. The ONLY legitimate way to price a product or service is to see what the market is prepared to pay for it. You do that by putting your offering to the market (with a fixed price upfront) and see how readily people buy it at your offered price. If they say "yes" without hesitation, then your price is too low. Real-time accountants know this. They price every project in advance and notify the client at the outset the scope and the price of the project.

Doesn't Visit/Call Versus Visits and Calls on a Systematic Basis

Your clients are not accountants. Your clients are typically businesspeople who know how to run their businesses. They know how to make a product, sell a product, and service a product. They do not understand all the ebbs and flows of cash flow. And they're so busy doing what they do, that they do not call you. Most people think you charge for every phone call, so they don't call or communicate nearly as much as they should. What if you called us and visited us from time to time? I remember vividly I was running a client advisory board meeting for a firm in regional New Zealand. The partners were not in the room, and I was interviewing 10 of the firm's best clients in a group meeting. I asked the question, "What else could your accountant do for you?" A paint retailer, Barry, said, "I would love it if (partner name) would call me from time to time and simply ask, 'How's it going?'" Simple stuff—yet so powerful. If you did call and visit your clients

> "I would love it if (partner name) would call me up from time to time and simply ask, 'How's it going?'"

on a systematic basis, then they will love you for it, and you will pick up a lot more work. Real-time accountants know this and are doing it.

Doesn't Follow Up Versus Follows Up on Every Opportunity

It has been a pleasure serving the accounting profession since 1994. There are so many positives that I continue inventing, reinventing, and offering new methods and ideas. One thing that does annoy me a lot is that most accountants do not follow up on opportunities. They might get a lead or an inquiry or even conduct a seminar and have people wanting to buy. Yet they do not follow up. I am not sure why (maybe they think it's too tacky) they don't follow up. In this day and age, you cannot wait any longer. You need to create opportunities and follow up on them. Real-time accountants have a special nose on them. They can sniff out opportunities and they know how to follow up on them.

Doesn't Promote the Latest Thing Versus Always Promoting

The ultimate goal for an accounting firm is to have every client buying every service they need that helps them achieve their goals. If that is the case, then real-time accountants are constantly on the lookout for the next idea/method/product that will help their clients. Sadly, redundant-data accountants are not on the lookout for the latest thing. They are happy to sit in their offices, go to technical tax sessions to get their continuing professional development hours, or do nothing. Same old, same old. Real-time accountants are constantly attending different types of workshops and seminars. They are reading all the time. They are networking and they have a thirst for learning. They don't see the service or the idea they are promoting to their clients as selling. They see it as servicing. They are always promoting something to their clients that helps them achieve their goals.

> "The minute the client saves the accounting data to the USB stick or emails it to you, it is out of date."

Most Clients on Hard-Drive Accounting Versus Most Clients on Cloud Accounting

It is almost impossible to be a real-time accountant if your client's accounting system is on a hard drive rather than the Internet—the Cloud. The minute the client saves the accounting data to the USB stick or emails it to you, it is out of date. You will always be a redundant-data accountant when the accounting system is not on the Internet. With Internet-based accounting technology, you truly can be real time. You have access to the data as it is happening at the client site. You can predict what is going to happen as the trend lines appear. You can advise your client based on real-time data. Real-time accountants are heavily promoting Cloud accounting to their clients. Their future relies on it.

Numbers Power with the Client Versus Numbers Power with the Accountant

Back in the day (whenever that was), your clients used to bring their financial information for you to interpret, prepare, manipulate, and file. They would physically bring in bank statements, invoices, receipts, inventory lists, contracts, equipment details, and so on. You would prepare the accounting information based on the data presented. You would then present the financial information back to them and tell them their profit, revenue, and other key numbers. The numbers power used to rest with the accountant. These days, the accounting software applications are so powerful that reports are generated with the click of a button (we used to buy those from you) and the analysis is so rich that I can make management decisions based on what a software application tells me. The numbers power is now with the client. Real-time accountants are bringing the numbers power back to them. They are formally connecting their clients to them through software (not accounting software, but business advisory software), and they are monitoring the performance in real time. It's time to bring the numbers power back to the accountant.

Recently we surveyed 428 business owners about what they wanted from their accountant. One of the questions was about the type of accountant the client would like to work with—a redundant-data accountant or a real-time accountant. An explanation was given and, as you can see by the following graph, an overwhelming 93 percent said they wanted a real-time accountant.

"The real-time accountants are bringing the numbers power back to them."

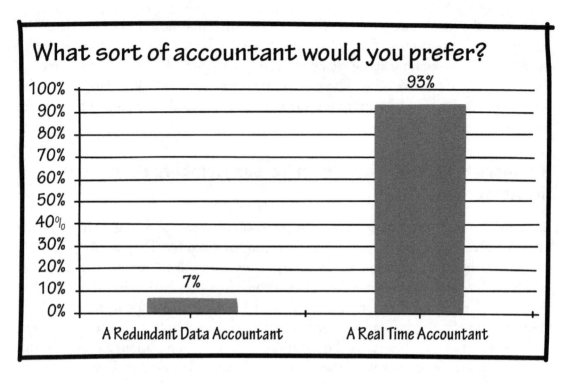

What sort of accountant would you prefer?

It's your choice to become a real-time accountant or remain a redundant-data accountant. The future of the accounting profession is real time! I hope you choose to be part of the future.

What Clients Really Want

There are two schools of thought on finding out what a customer wants and what they are prepared to pay for.

The first I'll call the Henry Ford way. Mr. Ford (who founded the Ford Motor Company) famously said that if he asked his customers what they wanted, they would have said "a faster horse." He didn't ask his customers what they wanted. Instead he designed something that they needed. However, the customer didn't know that they needed it yet.

A modern example is the late Steve Jobs (who cofounded Apple Inc.). Mr. Jobs didn't ask us if we thought having "a thousand songs in our pocket" was

> "Many hundreds of billions of dollars in sales later would indicate we liked his company's inventions."

a good idea. He built the iPod anyway. He didn't ask us if we thought blending music, phone, calendar, Internet, navigation, and so on into one device was a good idea. He built the iPhone anyway. He didn't ask us if we wanted to carry around yet another device so we could consume content and do quick work on the fly. He built the iPad anyway. Many hundreds of billions of dollars in sales later would indicate we liked his company's inventions.

So, the first way is to be an extraordinary visionary and tell the marketplace what it needs. Then create services and products that don't exist yet. Educate the people why they need this new cool thing and hope like crazy that they buy it. You have to back yourself!

The second school of thought is to ask. Seeing how most accountants are not visionaries, then this is probably a safer option.

Asking can take many formats. You could send out a survey. You could run a client advisory board where you have 8–10 of your best clients in a room and an independent facilitator asks what they like, don't like, and what they would like to see improved or added if they were the owners. You could ask every client one-on-one at a "coffee" meeting.

Or you could do all three.

Whichever way you ask, you have to be prepared for the brutal truth coming out. You have to be prepared to take action and make some changes. You have to listen.

Many years ago I was facilitating a series of three client advisory boards for the new owner of a company he had just bought. I arranged 30 of the best clients into three separate meetings. Some of the clients traveled a long way to get to the meeting and they were honored to be invited to give their candid feedback. The feedback from the first meeting was amazing. The clients shared many insights for improvement, innovation, and service. It was fabulous. After the first meeting, on the way to the restaurant, the new owner said to me, "What did you think of that?" I told him I thought it was brilliant feedback and we should act on many of the ideas. He said, "They have no (insert expletive here) idea what they are talking about." I was gobsmacked. The next two meetings he did not give the clients a chance to speak. He simply told them what he was going to do with his new company. They didn't like it. He made the changes

> "He said, 'They have no (insert expletive here) idea what they are talking about.' I was gobsmacked."

anyway without feedback. The business went from $25M in revenue to a disastrous $5M in revenue in 12 months.

To help accountants, my company did a bit of asking for you. We had about 50 accountants send out a survey request to their clients. We had a cross section of firms and 428 business clients respond. It was all anonymous and the following results tell the story.

One of the early set of questions was about communication. We were specifically looking for how well accountants communicate now and what their clients want. With face-to-face communication, you can see by the following graph that 62 percent want more face-to-face contact. Of course, provided there is value in the meeting.

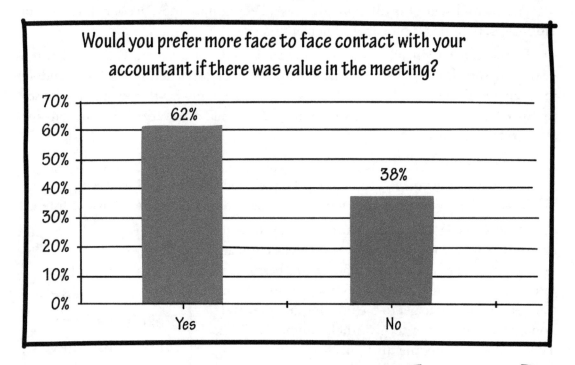

The key is that there is value in the meeting. You are busy and your clients are busy. If there is value, then (judging by 428 responses) your clients are receptive to meeting you more frequently. To create value, why don't you do a brainstorm meeting in your office on the client? Come up with some ideas for improvement and take those ideas to the client.

Face-to-face meetings take time. A phone call does not. A touch base "how's it going call" is seriously

> "To create value, why don't you do a brainstorm meeting in your office on the client?"

valuable and shows that you are interested in their business affairs. As you can see in the following graph, a staggering 40 percent of clients NEVER get a call from their accountants. What a wasted opportunity to add value and maybe find a new project. More than half got a call never or once per year.

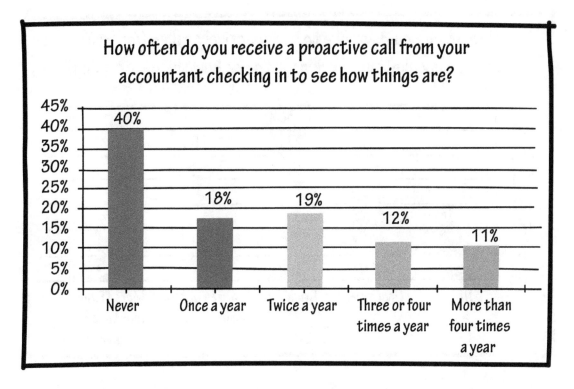

I ask accountants all the time if they have good relationships with their clients. An overwhelming YES is the response. To create a relationship requires communication. How can you honestly have a good relationship with someone if you only meet with them one or two times per year and speak with them once a year? Just imagine if you only spoke to your life partner (assuming you have one) at home once or twice a year. How would the relationship be? For some of you . . . better!

So how much communication is too much? Just by asking the target market, some (12 percent) say that they do not want any phone communication from you. It's interesting that 40 percent do not get a call, yet 12 percent do not want a

> "How can you honestly have a good relationship with somone if you only meet with them one or two times per year and speak with them once a year?"

call. So, I am thinking that 28 percent of the "I don't get a call" group do actually want a call. The vast majority (78 percent) in our survey think a proactive call anything from one to four times per year would be a good idea. So, I'd call it as two or three times per year.

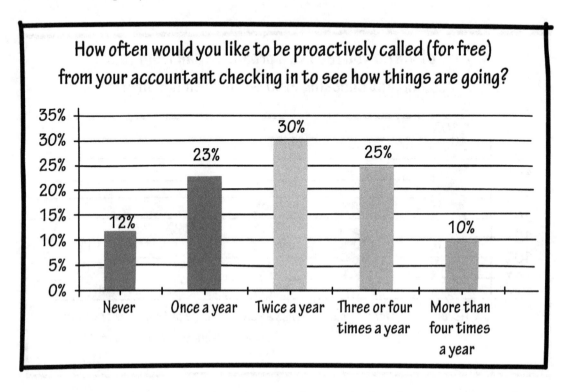

This is not rocket science. The service levels are so bad in the accounting profession that anything simple like a proactive phone call to "check in" can make the world of difference to the perception of you, your business, and your services.

"We asked 428 business owners, 'If you had to choose one thing, what should your accountant do?'"

Our research indicates a client will leave an accountant for either "service" or "services." They are either unhappy with the customer service (speed of communication, turnaround time, etc.) or with the services they are buying or not buying from you. Under the services banner, it includes value for money, pricing, mistakes, or something else they think they need but are not getting.

We asked 428 business owners, "If you had to choose one thing, what should your accountant do?" We gave them five possible answers.

1. Do more marketing.
2. Lift your service levels.
3. Be more transparent with your pricing.
4. Focus more on the future rather than the past.
5. Offer more services that help me improve my business.

As displayed in the following graph, if we bunch numbers two and three together (service levels and pricing), then we get 31 percent. I am going to call those the "service" answers. If we bunch numbers four and five together (better advice and valuable services) we get 61 percent. This would be the "services" answers. A staggering 92 percent said they want more from you, and they want to improve your customer service.

> "You have financial intimacy right now with your clients. That's why they stay with you."

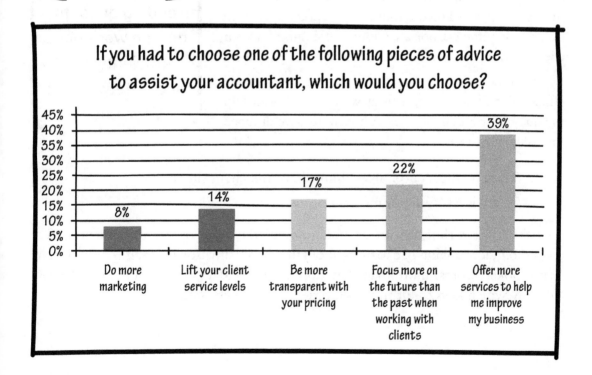

If you had to choose one of the following pieces of advice to assist your accountant, which would you choose?

The business community has spoken loud and clear. Your clients want more help, more communication, and better customer service. I know you're busy (doing compliance) and that can no longer be an excuse. We're all busy and time allocation is a priority, not a resource. You must get a systematic program in place for contacting your clients. You must offer more services that really help your clients' financial conditions.

You have financial intimacy right now with your clients. That's why they stay with you. You know things about them that few people do. If you want to keep them, then you need to increase the level of financial intimacy. You need to improve the customer service, and you need to broaden your service offerings. Since I started in this profession in 1994, I have been saying the same thing in many different ways. Be proactive and add value. If you don't, someone else will.

Technology Makes It Too Easy

Accountants have been in the "pursuit of efficiency" for as long as I can remember. You have electronic working papers, email, document management, knowledge management, social media, multiple computer screens on every desk, intranets, portals, Cloud accounting for your clients, and super-fast computers! The list goes on and on.

> "It's a never-ending quest to get the work done efficiently and accurately. But at what cost?"

It's a never-ending quest to get the work done efficiently and accurately. But at what cost? Because of the quest to drive efficiencies, you seem to have dropped the ball in two areas.

1. Team members no longer think about the client situation.
2. There is less real communication with your clients.

I think the technology is "dumbing down" the value of the accountant. Before technology, accountants had to think about the client's situation more and communicate (with spoken words) more than they do now. These days, the accountant just needs to know which keys to hit in which order on the keyboard.

It seems accountants would rather send an email and think their job is done rather than give the client a call. It seems accountants would rather send work via email or courier rather than present the work to the client. I think most of the value created is in the conversation and the presentation.

Take a look at what 428 business owners told us when it comes to annual accounts. More than half (52 percent) said they got their year-end work either emailed, posted, or couriered to them for signing.

This is disgraceful. Most of the profession's revenue is in compliance right now. This is your primary product, and you email it to your clients for signing! Save me, please. No wonder clients do not value compliance! You don't value it. You downplay the value of it by emailing it. I (and your clients) have two primary questions when it comes to our year-end financials.

1. How much tax do I have to pay and why?
2. Where did the money go?

How will I know those answers if you email me your primary product? I do also wonder what happens in the face-to-face (45 percent) meetings. I bet they are not structured, nor do they offer a huge amount of value.

Stop sending your primary product for signing via courier post or email. You are wasting an opportunity to add value, ask questions, and maybe find another project.

"The real-time accountants are bringing the numbers power back to them."

Make sure when you do meet with your client to present the year-end accounts that you actually explain what they mean. Make sure you do a three-year historical business performance review at least once per year to add value to the history. Make sure that you ask (in this meeting) what their goals are, and then you can start to match services that help them achieve their goals.

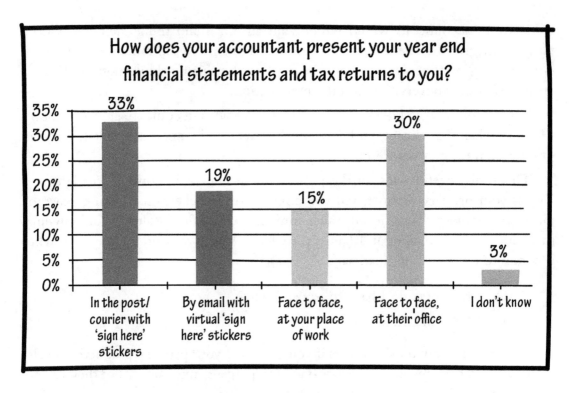

Technology can certainly make our lives easier and more efficient. Technology should enhance a client experience not diminish it.

Without a doubt, the number one technology thing that you can do in your firm is to suggest/encourage/cajole/insist your clients move to a Cloud accounting product. Although there are issues (outlined in my Dear Accountant letter and the first chapter about dinosaurs) associated with Cloud accounting, I think it is the most important thing you can do with your clients. The issues are only issues if you do nothing about the efficiency gains you get from using Cloud-based accounting.

With your clients on a desktop product, you have redundant data. With your clients on Cloud accounting, you can be so much more real time. You can add value now, not later. You can get the heartbeats of your clients every day. You can make a massive difference to their financial conditions. You can take the financial intimacy up a number of levels.

Many firms are insisting that 100 percent of their clients move to a Cloud-based accounting system. It

"With the data being so up to date, there is an amazing opportunity for you to add value with new services."

just makes sense to do so. The vast majority of firms will have two or three products in their client base. Most accountants will not align themselves with just one provider. I think that is the right thing to do. You match the product to the clients' needs.

There are many firms who are going further than just promoting a Cloud-based accounting system. The ultimate solution at the client's site is where every aspect of the technology "talks" to one another. The accounting data is integrated with the customer data. The accounting and customer data is integrated with the inventory control data, and all that integrates with the distribution system. So, the entire supply chain is covered. All that data is consolidated into daily dashboards, so the business owners can see what is going on in every aspect of their businesses. This sort of technology used to cost millions of dollars to buy and implement. Because of the massive development in Cloud computing, you can get it for a few hundred dollars per month.

> "With the right technology and the right data, you truly can become a real-time accountant."

The right technology can give the business owner better data to make better management decisions. You can be at the center of all the technology by recommending systems that will help.

You are the expert in financial coaching. With better data, you can be a better financial coach. With the right technology and the right data, you truly can become a real-time accountant.

What to Do with the Data

As you become a real-time accountant, one of the key steps is to strongly recommend that your clients migrate to a Cloud accounting solution. That'll take 12–36 months to systematically help your clients change. Let's assume you have done that. You have spent the time training them. You have helped them to get good data in, so good data can come out. You have got them active in checking their financial situation on a more regular basis. Your clients love the new reporting, and they are able to make better management decisions.

What about you? You used to sell management reporting. Now the computer is doing it for free.

As I have said a number of times so far, with Cloud accounting implemented with your clients, you have access to more real-time financial data than ever before.

With the data being so up to date, there is an amazing opportunity for you to add value with new services.

You can even take it up a notch and get daily and automatic key performance indicators (KPI) direct to your device (Web browser and/or email) that will tell you the story as to what is going on—good and bad. We asked 428 business owners if they were interested in you having direct access to their data in real time, and then you would send alerts and advice if something untoward is happening. As you can see in the following graph, 21 percent are not interested at all, yet 79 percent said they were interested in this, said it was worth exploring, or suggested that is what you should be doing in the first place!

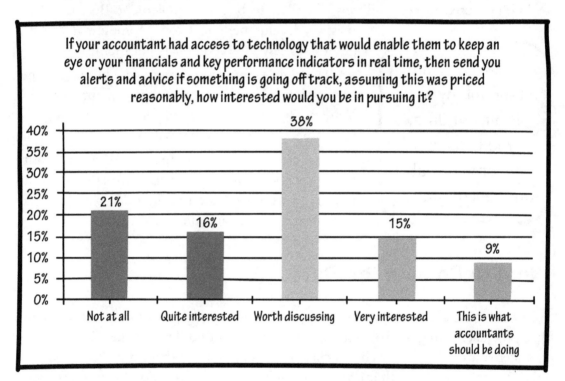

With real-time data consolidated into one location, you can interpret the numbers, be alerted to what is going on, and then advise your clients accordingly.

With all this data at your fingertips, what are you going to do with it? I think you have a duty of care and obligation to advise the clients how to improve their numbers. If you are living by the mantra to "provide every service to every client that helps them achieve their goals," then it's not selling new services—it's servicing your clients properly.

Here is a list of 14 services that you could offer.

1. Cash flow forecasting and analysis
2. Profit improvement program
3. Monitoring and accountability program
4. Debt restructuring
5. Capital raising
6. Interest reduction service
7. Waste audit
8. Revenue improvement strategies
9. Creditor analysis and negotiation
10. Product profitability analysis
11. Receivable management service
12. Tax planning and tax minimization
13. Business planning
14. Inventory management system

> "The number one issue in businesses around the world right now is cash flow management. We all know it, and the accounting profession is uniquely placed to help improve it."

All are valuable services that will make a significant impact to your client's financial future. By "staying close to the numbers," you have a better chance of the client buying the service. With good systemization of the services, you can have accountants of all levels deliver the service—not just the partners.

You will need to learn some sales skills about how to have your clients buy the services. You will also need some new tools (get rid of the spreadsheets, please) so you can systemize the services.

Now here's the big one. We all know that cash flow (lack thereof) is the main reason businesses fail. The number one issue in businesses around the world right now is cash flow management.

We all know it, and the accounting profession is uniquely placed to help improve it.

Your clients also want it. Well, not all clients want it. In our survey, 21 percent said they did not. However, 79 percent said that if the service was reasonably priced and they could see value in it, then they would be interested in exploring the idea.

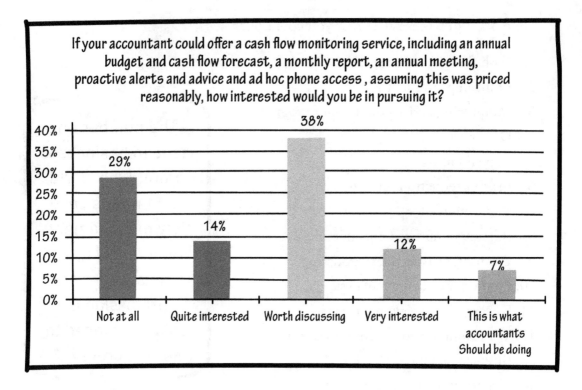

It's a no-brainer. I ask accountants what's the most valuable service they can offer to their business clients. No surprises. It is cash flow monitoring and forecasting. So, if it's the most valuable, then how many of your business clients have a live, working, accurate, and real-time cash flow forecast? "Few" is always the answer. Yet this is the most valuable thing you can do. Here's what the business community wants when it comes to cash flow.

"Your clients are not financial analysts like you. You can help them in this area."

The owners want to know how much free cash they have each month to spend on whatever they want to spend it on. They want to know how they are tracking and what they can do to improve it. Your clients are not financial analysts like you. You can help them in this area.

The service you provide is a cash flow forecasting and monitoring service. In your definition, you call it a "three way rolling cash flow." It covers the cash flow forecast, the profit and loss, and the balance sheet. If your client is borrowing money from a bank, then the bank wants it. Even if your client is not borrowing money, then it is a good thing to have. The problem with hard-drive based systems (or heaven forbid, spreadsheets) is that once they are created, they are out of date. By using old technology, you cannot monitor the cash flow unless it is manually entered.

With Cloud accounting and add-on partners, you can do this automatically. You can prepare the forecast based on historical data plus some planning. You can "normalize" the numbers month to month with the client. You can consolidate the data as it is transacted at the client's end. And because the accounting data is linked to the bank feeds, the cash flow, the forecast, and the balance sheet are kept up to date every single day. Now that's real-time accounting!

> "The owners want to know how much free cash they have each month to spend on whatever they want to spend it on."

If the bank needs an update, then you can provide it quickly. If your client wants it, then you can provide it quickly. If you have your client on a monitoring service, then you can be immensely valuable.

The Intellectual Property Purveying Business

Every time I do a seminar and ask the question, "What do you sell?" the answers are always the same. The responders either say knowledge, solutions, me, or ideas. I completely agree that this is what you sell. However, the vast majority of business models of accounting firms suggest they sell "time." Keeping an accurate check on time and making sure every minute is recorded and hopefully charged to clients. The business model suggests that you own a "labor hire" business rather than an intellectual property purveying business.

If you persist with the labor hire business model, then you need more people, bigger offices, and more hassles. **All of that stinks of effort**!

A far better way is to package what you know in different ways and sell what you know over and over again—with the least amount of labor possible. As a customer of an accounting firm, I am not buying time from you—I am buying what you know.

You and I are no different. I know things that you don't know and you know things that I don't know. I just choose to package and sell what I know in different and highly leveraged ways. I have been in the intellectual property purveying business since 1993. I have always taken what I know and packaged it so it could be delivered in a leveraged way. There is only one me, so I have to. Since 1993, I worked as an employee for six years and the rest of the time I have owned my own businesses.

Since 1993, I have been directly involved in creating, marketing, selling, and delivering more than $200M of productized and packaged knowledge. I wish it was all profit!

Here is a list of the types of products I have created and/or delivered throughout the years (I am not including free giveaways, just the products that were sold).

> "You and I are no different. I know things that you don't know and you know things that I don't know. I just choose to package and sell what I know in different and highly leveraged ways."

- ✓ Seminars and small workshops
- ✓ Multiday workshops
- ✓ Multiday conferences
- ✓ Client advisory board meetings
- ✓ Team advisory board meetings
- ✓ Round table briefing sessions
- ✓ Keynote speeches
- ✓ Audiotapes in a box
- ✓ VHS videos in a box
- ✓ CD audio recordings in a box
- ✓ DVD training programs in a box
- ✓ Books, manuals, and reports—hard copy and e-copy
- ✓ Group-based coaching and mentoring
- ✓ Group-based consulting
- ✓ Franchise system
- ✓ Phone and Web-based business performance review
- ✓ In-office training sessions
- ✓ E-learning platforms
- ✓ Posters and wall charts
- ✓ 90-day business challenges
- ✓ Webinar series
- ✓ Conference call series
- ✓ Software – hard-drive and cloud

Every one of these products was delivered with leverage in mind. Some required a little labor and many required no labor at all to deliver them. Labor-based delivery products stink of effort.

Every single one of these products could have been delivered "one on one," but I chose not to do that. I am in the intellectual property purveying business, just like you are. I am not in the time-selling business. The time-selling business stinks of effort.

Did all of the products work? Not at all. Some are still active today and many are not. I take what we (my business partner, Colin, and our team) know and we look to use it over and over again in different delivery mediums. If it works, we keep doing it in that format. If it doesn't work, we pull the product and do something else.

To come up with ideas for products, we look at three areas.

1. The situation (why create a product in the first place)
2. What we know (our knowledge base)
3. The innovation (the actual product)

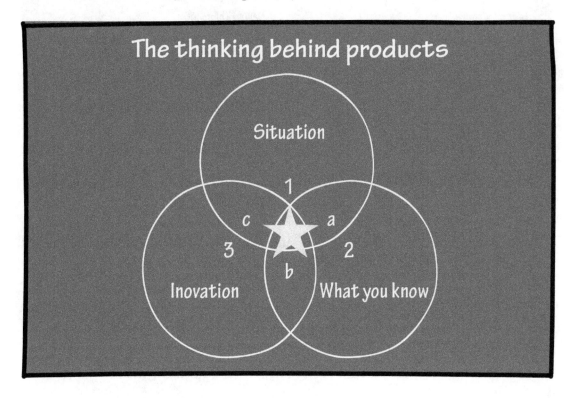

When all three are in sync, the product works. Points two and three will be dealt with later in this chapter. For now, I want to talk about the situation. The situation (that forces you to create a product in the first place) could be negative based or opportunistic based.

You could have a negative situation that was out of your control and you want to recover from that. You could have an opportunistic situation that you see and you want to capitalize on.

> "For the profession to remain relevant, it needs to realize that it is in the intellectual property creating, marketing, selling, and delivery business."

Negative	Opportunistic
Rising salary costs	Government legislation change
Cashflow problems (yours)	Technology (cloud) movement
Lost clients	New tax changes
Recessionary or hard times	Niche markets you want to target
Clients cashflow problems	Trends in an industry
Revenue declining	Offshore labor availability
Team members leaving	Selling your business
Increased expenses	Client demands / needs
Competition	Capitalism

The situation is what forces you to act. There needs to be a trigger of some sort as to why you want to make changes. Sometimes the situation is survival based and sometimes it is purely an idea that you think the market might need.

The accounting profession is being threatened by many outside forces. For the profession to remain relevant, it needs to realize that it is in the intellectual property creating, marketing, selling, and delivery business. With labor rates increasing every year and new nimble players appearing daily (who do realize this) it is a nonnegotiable.

Just realizing it is not enough, the business model needs to change to capitalize on the future.

Sell What You Know

What you currently know is the starting point. What knowledge do you have and what knowledge does your team have?

This is an interesting exercise. To create this segment, I spent 20 minutes coming up with a list of what my team and I know. It is not a definitive list, but it is a decent one.

How to Improve/Develop/Implement/Create . . .

- ✓ Cash flow
- ✓ Profit
- ✓ Team
- ✓ Lower attrition
- ✓ Higher morale
- ✓ Improved image
- ✓ Turnaround time
- ✓ Strategy
- ✓ Marketing
- ✓ Sales
- ✓ Value-added services
- ✓ Accounts receivable
- ✓ Pricing
- ✓ Work in progress
- ✓ Seminars
- ✓ Webinars
- ✓ Product development
- ✓ Software creation
- ✓ Copywriting
- ✓ Team structure
- ✓ Coaching—phone and group
- ✓ Consulting

- ✓ Training
- ✓ Presenting
- ✓ Conferences
- ✓ Social media
- ✓ Branding
- ✓ Digital media
- ✓ DVD products
- ✓ Outsourcing
- ✓ Cloud technology
- ✓ Sales management
- ✓ Customer relationship management
- ✓ Benchmarking
- ✓ Group planning
- ✓ Content management
- ✓ Database creation
- ✓ Telemarketing
- ✓ Higher productivity
- ✓ Better performance
- ✓ Market share
- ✓ Revenue growth
- ✓ Wealth improvement
- ✓ Innovation
- ✓ Efficiency
- ✓ Problem solving
- ✓ Customer service
- ✓ Online business model
- ✓ How to implement
- ✓ +++

What do you currently know? Get your team involved (I did not get my team involved to create this list), and see if you can come up with a definitive list.

To create a leveraged productized business, it all starts with what you know.

What Products Can Be Created?

If you are following what I am saying here, we are moving away from the time-selling business and into the productized intellectual property purveying business. The first step is to work out what you know and the second step is work out what the package looks like.

Most accountants I meet believe that there are opportunities for additional business in their current client base. However, they don't seem that active in discovering the opportunities nor promoting the services. I think it is a BIG disservice to the client if you do not promote new ideas and new services.

We recommend that you "stay close to the numbers" with your service offerings. That way you can leverage the delivery of the services to other team members. By all means, offer high-level consulting, however typically that means that experienced (read expensive) people need to deliver them.

"Consulting is where the provider comes up with the answers; coaching is where the client is guided and the answers are coached out of the client."

One of the reasons accountants do not offer additional services is because they are unsure what the client will say and they doubt if they have the knowledge base to deliver the solution.

You have to differentiate between coaching and consulting. Consulting is when the provider comes up with the answers; coaching is when the client is guided and the answers are coached out of the client.

Financial coaching is the way to go. We recommend that your service categories fall into The Awesome 8 areas as mentioned previously. It's what your clients are interested in—over and above compliance services. As a recap, here's The Awesome 8 image.

The Awesome 8

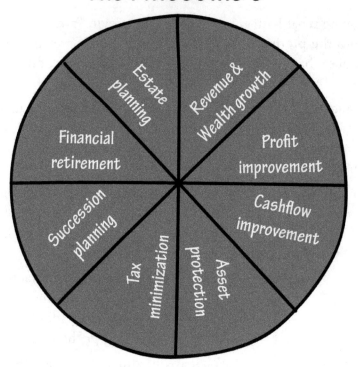

If you follow The Awesome 8, then here are 20 new services you could create.

- ✓ Revenue growth program
- ✓ Cash flow analysis, forecasting, and monitoring program
- ✓ Profit improvement program
- ✓ Debt restructuring program
- ✓ Receivables management service
- ✓ Inventory management service
- ✓ Bookkeeping (serviced from lower-cost countries)
- ✓ Virtual management accounting
- ✓ Cloud conversions
- ✓ Sort out the numbers program
- ✓ Monitoring and accountability program

> "One of the reasons accountants do not offer additional services is because they are unsure what the client will say and they doubt if they have the knowledge base to deliver the solution."

- ✓ Webinars, seminars, workshops, and events
- ✓ Planning sessions—face to face, group, or remote
- ✓ Boxed products (DVD, etc.) for a niche market
- ✓ Books, manuals, podcasts, video subscriptions
- ✓ Software or online learning—subscription based
- ✓ Challenges—100 day, six week, etc.
- ✓ Leveraged training or consulting
- ✓ Group coaching
- ✓ Cash flow in a crisis program

At the end of the day, **every client should be buying every product they need that helps them achieve their goals!** I think that's the third time I've mentioned that so far.

That should be your goal.

Follow the Digit Flow

Do you believe you're number one in numbers? If you do, then take control of the numbers. You can be a better advisor if the numbers are accurate. Your clients (in the main) do not know much about their numbers. They are making the product, buying the product, selling the product, and servicing the product. They understand their business better than anyone. You understand numbers better than anyone!

> "US General Norman Schwarzkopf Jr. . . . said one thing (that I heard at least) and that was, 'When placed in command, take charge."

I heard the late US General Norman Schwarzkopf Jr. speak once. His speech was called "Leadership: From the War Room to the Board Room." He only said one thing (that I heard at least) and that was, "When placed in command, take charge."

It's time to take charge of the numbers. I call it, **"following the digit flow."** Following the digit flow has a six-step process. They are all services that you charge for.

Step 1—Accounting software. You should be telling your clients which software (all Cloud based) they should be using. Make sure it integrates with your systems and you pay the subscription fee to the vendor—that way it's harder for the client to leave.

Step 2—Bookkeeping. Don't let the clients do it themselves, unless they have bookkeepers on the payroll. If you are following my action points in this book, then you'll be setting up a bookkeeping team offshore to do the work for you. If you have not done that, then make sure your recommended bookkeeper is updating the client numbers frequently.

Step 3—Compliance and tax. Hopefully you've already got that one nailed. If not, do it for them.

Step 4—Business advisory. Help them to manage the digits and grow the digits with cash flow, forecasting, profit improvement, and planning services.

> "Take control of the bookkeeping. Don't let them do it themselves unless they have bookkeepers on the payroll."

Step 5—Wealth development. What do they do with the money once they are making it? Either set up a division in your firm to manage and grow wealth or have a strong joint venture partner who can work with you.

Step 6—Estate planning. This involves everything from insurances, wills, structures, and succession planning. Either do it in-house or have a strong joint venture partner who can work with you.

Following the digit flow is about taking a cradle-to-grave (or womb-to-tomb) approach to the business and life of your clients.

When you take control of the numbers, you really are number one in numbers!

The Eight Nonnegotiables

If you want to run an outstanding accounting firm (a perfect firm even) that produces a fabulous profit, then you need to get the fundamentals right.

The obvious fundamentals are the right business model, the right clients, the right services, and, of course, the right team members.

"You must have the right team, clients, and model, and you MUST implement these eight critical strategies to drive profit, capacity, and growth."

The less obvious fundamentals are key strategies that I call the eight nonnegotiables. These are strategies that will hold back your performance if they are not in place or not implemented properly.

After more than 20 years working with firms to help them get to peak performance (and seeing many of them increase profits by 93 percent in the first year—see the table below for the results from 800 firms I've coached), I've seen many strategies that work and some that don't work.

Results of 800 Firms Coached

Averages – of the full financial year prior to implementation	Starting average	End of year 1	Year 1 increase	End of year 2	Year 2 % increase on year 1	Year 2 increase on the starting numbers
Revenue	$947,418	$1,556,258	64%	1,936,512	24%	104%
Profit – before partner salaries	$304,915	$587,290	93%	$801,620	36%	163%

You must have the right team, clients, and model, and you MUST implement these eight critical strategies to drive profit, capacity, and growth.

1. **Pricing upfront.** It's really simple. When you price a client project upfront, you are now directly motivated to do it as efficiently as possible. You get more margin and more time. Oh, and the clients also love it.

2. **Value pricing on special projects.** Value pricing is different from pricing upfront. Value pricing is determining your value contribution to the project and pricing it accordingly. Without you, the result is X; with you, the result is Z. Your value add is Y. Price accordingly.

3. **Client communication program.** For those clients who you want to keep, have a structured program of communication, including visits, phone calls, emails, and other touch points. You have to be disciplined with this, but the payoff is happy clients and lots of new projects.

4. **Workflow efficiency model.** Workflow is like manufacturing. Raw materials come in, they pass through a series of hands/technologies, and a finished product comes out the end. To get efficient, you need to take the bottlenecks out of the process.

5. **All clients on Cloud accounting.** When you migrate your clients to Cloud accounting and help them get more accurate numbers, you have more visibility on their financial performance. You are also more efficient at your end because the data is more accurate. Our research indicates up to a 80 percent efficiency gain at your end.

> "Workflow is like manufacturing. Raw materials come in, they pass through a series of hands/technologies and a finished product comes out the end."

6. **Marketing that works.** If you're going to create capacity with workflow management and Cloud computing, then the capacity is not going to refill itself. You'll need to get on the front foot with direct response marketing that assists in finding new projects and new clients.

7. **Sales skills.** It's a duty of care that every firm should be focused on making sure that every client they want to keep is buying every service that they need that helps achieve their goals. That is sales. Sales is a skill that can be learned. To sell is to serve, and new skills will be needed to serve properly.

8. **Business advisory services.** If you live by the following client mantra, "provide every service to every client that helps them achieve their goals," then you'll find that the additional services provided are in the advisory space. We think that accountants should stay close to the numbers with their advice. So that would be growth, profit, cash flow, assets, and structuring type advice. Financial coaching and consulting is where it's at.

By having a structured approach to properly implementing these eight nonnegotiables, you'll be able to create more profit, more capacity, and even more revenue.

Structuring for Success

The new equation means you need different skill sets. You will need a different structure to create, market, sell, and deliver the new services to new and existing services. And you will definitely need different people involved.

The traditional partnership model is a silo model. Often it has been described as "accountants sharing rent." The silo model is where each partner or division has the following:

> "The traditional partnership model is a silo model. Often it has been described as "accountants sharing rent."

- ☒ My marketing style and ability
- ☒ My sales style and ability
- ☒ My clients and client management
- ☒ My team
- ☒ My services

See the following silo diagram.

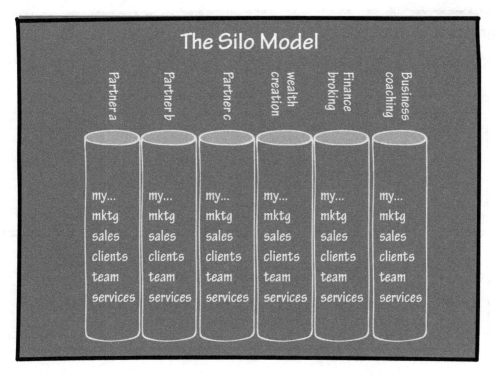

I have a cynical view as to why the silo model exists . . . so it can be pulled apart quickly if the partnership doesn't work out.

The issue is that even if there is one logo and one brand on the business card, there are separate practices operating behind it. The separation means that unless the partners (or team member in the partners' silos) can perform the project themselves, they will not internally refer to others. There are different services being delivered, multiple bosses, multiple and erratic marketing methods, different ways of doing the type of work, different pricing mechanisms, and overall inefficiencies everywhere.

> "The issue is that even if there is one logo and one brand on the business card there are separate practices operating behind it."

Enter the new corporate model, with one CEO who is given the authority to run the business as he/she sees fit. This is done with people who are creating products and services, people who are marketing specialists, salespeople who sell and manage client relationships, logistical management people who keep the office environment moving and working, and, of course, delivery people (fee delivering professionals) to do the work.

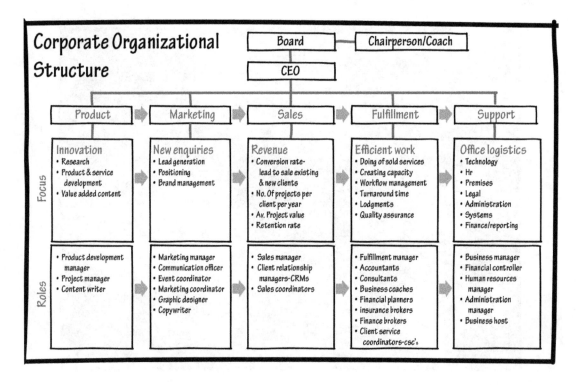

Corporate Organizational Structure

Board — Chairperson/Coach
CEO

	Product	Marketing	Sales	Fulfillment	Support
Focus	Innovation • Research • Product & service development • Value added content	New enquiries • Lead generation • Positioning • Brand management	Revenue • Conversion rate-lead to sale existing & new clients • No. Of projects per client per year • Av. Project value • Retention rate	Efficient work • Doing of sold services • Creating capacity • Workflow management • Turnaround time • Lodgments • Quality assurance	Office logistics • Technology • Hr • Premises • Legal • Administration • Systems • Finance/reporting
Roles	• Product development manager • Project manager • Content writer	• Marketing manager • Communication officer • Event coordinator • Marketing coordinator • Graphic designer • Copywriter	• Sales manager • Client relationship managers-CRMs • Sales coordinators	• Fulfillment manager • Accountants • Consultants • Business coaches • Financial planners • insurance brokers • Finance brokers • Client service coordinators-csc's	• Business manager • Financial controller • Human resources manager • Administration manager • Business host

There are five key areas that need differing skill sets and disciplines.

> **Product development people** are typically creative but with a disciplined and detailed approach to product quality and systemization.

> **Marketing people** are also often creative, and the marketing coordination team members are often introverted with a detailed focus. Start with a marketing coordinator and then grow into the other roles.

> "Salespeople must first have an inclination for sales. The skills can be taught if the inclination is there."

> **Salespeople** must first have an inclination for sales. The skills can be taught if the inclination is there. The partners and some client-facing team members of firms make excellent salespeople, because they have the client experience and natural trust. They might also be doing some client work—they might be full-time revenue generation.

> **Fulfillment people** are most of the people you currently hire. Let's not confuse what this team is doing—they are delivering on revenue that has already been sold. They are not creating new revenue. They might be creating new opportunities so someone can speak with the client. The challenge with the traditional model is that the fulfillment people also the product development, marketing, and salespeople. It just does not work. Some people just want to be an accountant—and that's OK.

> **Support team members** need to be just that—support for the rest of the business. Many firms have internal accountants (who are still doing client work) be the practice manager or the financial controller. If you want to grow, you MUST employ a full-time business manager (not a practice manager) who runs the day-to-day operations of the office—information technologies, telecommunications, receivables, accounts payable, human resources, office logistics, etc.

Now before you say, "We are not big enough to justify hiring all these people," you need to realize that all the positions in the organizational chart need to be done by someone. There might be some "multi-hat wearing" going on, and that's OK as you grow into the structure. You might also need to outsource some of the roles until you can justify a full-time (or part-time) person to fulfill the position. Your goals, courage, and resources will determine how quickly you can grow into the new structure.

THE RIGHT NUMBERS MATTER

Knowing Your Numbers

During the past 10 years, I have coached hundreds and hundreds of accounting firms to success. Every month we track their results and the average profit increase in year one is 93 percent and a further 36 percent in year two. Most firms we have coached range from $400K to $20M in revenue for a single office.

The first thing I do with a new firm is to get the people to understand their key numbers and then work on projects that positively affect the key numbers. Not revenue and profit—everyone knows those numbers. They are results-based numbers.

> "The first thing I do with a new firm is to get the people to understand their key numbers and then work on projects that positively affect the key numbers."

Our top performing firms track the activity-based numbers—the inputs. Then they implement projects that directly improve the results.

If you know the activity-based numbers, then implement projects around those numbers and your results will soar. Specifically, include activities that drive profit, capacity, and revenue growth.

Here's an example of some key activities that drive results.

Activity	Result
Number of client projects priced upfront	Profit
Frequency of invoicing/billing of work	Profit
Number of value-based fee projects per client per year	Profit
Average price increase per client per year	Profit
Number of clients on Cloud accounting platform	Capacity
Workflow turnaround time of work	Capacity
Number of administrative team members serving accounting team	Capacity
Number of chargeable hours per accountant (down, not up)	Capacity
Number of sales meetings per month—existing or new clients	Revenue
Number of projects purchased per client per year	Revenue
Number of seminars/events held per year	Revenue
Prospect database size	Revenue

How to Plan the Revenue and Profit of an Accounting Firm

Most accounting firms plan their revenue and profit in one (or a mix) of the following ways.

Our revenue (or profit) was $X last year. Let's add X percent for our target. Our costs are mostly fixed, so now we'll work out how many people we need, what the charge rates need to be, and the chargeable hours per person. It's a work-back scenario.

Or, we have X people right now who can generate work. Let's put their charge rates up by X percent and their chargeable time up by X percent and reduce the write-downs by X percent. Then we'll multiply it all out and get a revenue figure. Then we'll work out the salaries and the overheads and that will build the profit model. It's a work-back scenario.

I am going to suggest that these methods are fundamentally flawed for driving profit. I think you should do what I like to call "inside-out planning"—not work-back planning.

Let me give you a real example of a firm I worked with recently.

> "I am going to suggest that these methods are fundamentally flawed for driving profit. I think you should do what I like to call 'inside-out planning'—not work-back planning."

Michael K. has a small accounting firm in the suburbs. He has been in business for a number of years and has a fairly solid, predictable business. Here are his vital statistics for the past 12 months.

➤ He has four people (three accountants and one administrative team member) plus himself—total five.

➤ He has revenue of approximately $650,000.

➤ He was writing down $50,000 before billings.

➤ He has $125,000 work in progress at any time—70 days of revenue.

➤ He has $150,000 in receivables at any time—84 days of revenue.

➤ He has an average hourly rate (client hours) of $141.45.

➤ He has an average hourly rate (all team hours) of $77.04.

➤ He has 60 business client groups representing 85 percent of revenue.

➤ He has 120 other clients representing 15 percent of revenue.

➤ He has a profit before partner salaries of $210,000.

➤ After a notional $150,000 salary for himself, he has a business valuation of approximately $300,000.

In front of 110 people and during a 20-minute period, I did a makeover on his firm. The results were staggering. At the end of the 20-minute planning session, he was targeting a $664,709 profit (up $454,709), revenue of $1,187,709 (up $537,709), and a valuation of $2,573,545 (up $2.2M)!

Once he understood the resources, training, and methods available to him from us, he committed to implementing the following 14–step plan.

> "At the end of the 20-minute planning session, he was targeting a $664,709 profit (up $454,709), revenue of $1,187,709 (up $537,709), and a valuation of $2,573,545 (up $2.2M)!"

1. A 7.5 percent price increase for existing client work. He will add value by doing a business performance review with each client.

2. Meeting 100 percent of existing business clients following a specific meeting agenda and having 50 percent of them buy a new service from him. Normally we get up to an 80 percent conversion; however, we allowed a 50 percent conversion this time.

3. Of the 50 percent who needed something new, the average new service was priced at $4,000. This priced was based on value-based fees rather than time-based billing.

4. Finding just 24 new clients (12 from referrals and 12 from marketing methods that we suggested) at an average fee of $12,000.

   The first four implementation projects rounded out the revenue model of $1,187,709. Now he needed to deliver the $500K of new revenue. He did that by committing to the following:

5. Being 25 percent more efficient in all the work the firm did. We showed him a way to get 50 percent more efficient, however he elected for 25 percent.

6. Targeting an average hourly rate of $275 for new services to existing clients. The new services would be based on value-based fees and normally much more than $275, however they needed to be his numbers.

7. Targeting an average hourly rate of $215 for new clients. He felt comfortable with this result.

8. Having his accounting team be 75 percent productive (1,265 hours) for the year.

9. He would be 40 percent productive (675 hours) for the year.

10. He needed to employ "half" an accountant, so he elected to hire one, five-year qualified certified public accountant (CPA) offshore (in the Philippines) at a total cost of $25,000.

These six projects enabled him to create capacity and deliver the work.

Next we looked at his cost structure and cash flow:

11. He decided to give his team a 10 percent pay increase.

12. He would focus on "writing up" work rather than "writing down" work and by following our eliminating write-downs program, he would get to +5 percent write-ups.

> "These six projects enabled him to create capacity and deliver the work. Next we looked at his cost structure and cash flow."

13. He would implement our work-in-progress (WIP) training program and reduce WIP to 15 days.

14. He would implement our receivables management program and reduce receivables to 30 days.

The full details of Michael's makeover are in the following graphic.

Targets For Next 12 Months

	Past 12 Months	Benchmarks	Next 12 Months
Average hourly rate for the standard hours worked - entire team (incl. admin.)	$77.04		$153.34
Revenue Billed	$650,000.00		$1,187,709.15
Gross profit	$370,000.00		$854,709.15
Gross profit percentage	56.92%	>70	71.96%
EBIT before notional equity directors	$210,000.00		$664,709.15
EBIT percentage before equity directors salary	32.31%	>55	55.97%
EBIT after notional equity directors salaries	$60,000.00		$514,709.15
EBIT percentage after equity directors salaries	9.23%		43.34%
EBIT per equity director before directors salaries	$210,000.00	>1,000,000	$664,709.15
EBIT per equity director after directors salaries	$60,000.00		$514,709.15
Business Valuation based 5 x EBIT after directors salaries- excl WIP & Receivables	$300,000.00		$2,573,545.75

The Ultimate Accountants Metrics Guide

If you are going to improve the profit, capacity, and revenue of an accounting firm, there are certain fundamentals that you must measure, understand, and improve. The following table highlights the key metrics, formulae, and strategies.

"If you are going to improve the profit, capacity, and revenue of an accounting firm, there are certain fundamentals that you must measure, understand, and improve."

Terminology	Definition and Comments	Equation
Revenue model— internally focused	Most firms operate under the old traditional model of generating revenue. This model is internally focused and causes write-downs and low profitability. Most firms do not even realize they are using this model, which suggests that if they get more employees, make them more productive, charge higher rates per hour or record less of their time, then they will increase revenue. If a firm is operating with this model, it is typically pricing the work after the work is completed. This method invariably involves write-downs, because the partner who is doing the billing thinks there was too much time on the clock and marks some of it down.	Number of chargeable people x average chargeable time x average charge rates - write-downs = revenue billed For example, 8 x 1,181 x \$176 X -10 percent = \$1,496,436
Revenue model— externally focused	The best revenue model is one that is externally focused, namely on clients. It is about the number of clients, how they are serviced, and what they buy on an annual basis. Progressive firms track these indicators and look to increase client count, retention rate, average project value, and the number of projects per client per year. They look for value-based fees projects that attract a higher margin per hour. If you are focused on this model, then you would be planning the client project in advance, advising the client of the price and scope, and getting written (or electronic) sign-off from the client before proceeding to do the work. The client knows how much the project will cost and the firm is directly incentivized to do the job in the least amount of time possible.	Starting client count x retention rate x number of projects per client x average project value = revenue For example, 335 x 95 percent x 2.7 x \$1,750 = \$1,503,731

Terminology	Definition and Comments	Equation
Gross profit—GP	The way to measure gross profit is to take revenue minus cost of goods sold (COGS). The question is what should be included in COGS. For simplicity's sake, let's use direct labor. Most firms have a GP of 55–65 percent. The high-performing firms achieve GP of more than 70 percent.	Revenue minus direct labor costs (chargeable team members) For example, $1,500,000 revenue $400,000 direct labor GP = $1.1M = 73 percent
Net profit or EBIT (earnings before interest & tax)	There are two ways to measure basic profit in a firm—before partner compensation and after partner compensation. Both are legitimate approaches. Most firms use a partnership model, so for the sake of consistency it is easier to measure profit before compensation of partners. There was a standard model operating in the last century of one-third for labor, one-third for overhead, and one-third for profit. We're not sure who came up with this, but we know it to be obsolete and wrong. Most firms have a profit margin (before partner compensation) of 25–35 percent. The high-performing firms achieve a net profit margin of more than 50 percent. The trick is to drive up profit without the partners having to do significant amounts of chargeable work. Partner chargeable time can be below 30 percent and net profit above 50 percent.	Revenue minus all costs (labor and overhead) before partner compensation For example, $1,500,000 revenue $500,000 direct labor $250,000 office overhead $750,000 net profit = 50 percent

Terminology	Definition and Comments	Equation
Revenue per full-time equivalent—FTE	This is a measure that incorporates many components, including efficiency, pricing, margins, team mix, value-based fees, and workflow management. Most firms are either side of $150,000 per FTE (all team members) in revenue. The top performers achieve more than $300,000 per FTE.	Revenue divided by number of FTEs For example, $1,500,000 / 10 = $150,000
Work in progress—WIP	Your WIP balance is the amount of inventory you have that has not been billed or completed. WIP sits on the balance sheet, and it should be minimal at all times. It's an indicator of your billing processes, your efficiency model, and your client service levels. Many firms have negative WIP because they bill in advance. The objective should be to have a WIP balance of below 10 days of revenue at any time of the year.	WIP / revenue for year x 365 = WIP days For example, $300,000 / $1,500,000 = 20 percent x 365 = 70 days
Accounts receivable—A/R	Your accounts receivable balance is a direct indicator of your cash management processes. Most firms send invoices and then wait. And they wonder why their receivables are high. The progressive firms notify their clients as to the prices in advance, have direct debit (or credit card) arrangements and have specific, documented systems to collect any outstanding balances. The objective should be to have the A/R balance below 20 days. Many firms have A/R days in the single digits, and many have negative A/R.	Balance of AR / revenue for year x 365 = A/R days For example, $200,000 / $1,500,000 = 13.3 percent x 365 = 48 days

Terminology	Definition and Comments	Equation
Lock-up	This is the sum of WIP and A/R combined. By reducing lock-up, a firm can free up an enormous amount of cash. Best practice would be to have less than 30 days on average in lock-up. Reducing lock-up is the fastest and simplest way to accelerate cash flow in an accounting firm.	Dollar value (or days) of WIP + AR = lock-up. For example, $300,000 + $200,000 = $500,000 or 70 + 48 = 118 days
Average hourly rate—AHR	This is a measure of how much a firm earns for every hour spent on client work. There are two ways to monitor AHR. Based on total time taken to do the client work—best practice would be more than $350 per hour. Based on the entire team (including partners and administrative staff) employed and how many hours they work to produce the work. Best practice would be more than $150 per hour. Method two is a better way to monitor the performance of a firm, as it takes into consideration team mix, productivity, efficiency, and pricing. Driving AHR is an excellent means to increase profit in an accounting firm. The way to do this is to price higher upfront and then be efficient in doing the work—less time on the job. Your AHR should be increasing every month.	Total revenue / team member hours to produce the revenue For example, **1. Client hours** $1.5M / 9,500 hours taken = $158 AHR **2. Team hours** $1.5M / 14,000 team hours worked = $107 AHR

Terminology	Definition and Comments	Equation
Write-downs	Taking write-downs is discounting before billing. A firm will charge all chargeable time to the WIP account. Then before billing, they think they cannot bill it all, so a portion is written down. This is a complete waste of profit and is easy to eliminate. It's amazing that some firms actually budget for write-downs—they expect to fail before they've even started!	The difference between what was WIP versus the amount billed is the write-down. For example, $1,650,000 charge to WIP -9 percent write-down = $1,500,000 billed—$150,000 written down
Write-ups	Write-ups occur when a firm prices the project upfront and then because of efficiency completes the project in less time than expected. Standard hourly rates multiplied by the number of expected chargeable hours will give you the normal price. If the original sold price is higher than the actual chargeable time, you have a write-up. The only ethical way to earn write-ups is to price the project upfront, have your client sign off on the engagement, and if you are more efficient than anticipated, you will have a write-up. The price remains the same but the margin increases.	Price the client project upfront, beat the budget, and create a write-up. For example, old system—25 hours x $200 AHR = $5,000 new system—$5,000 = 15 hours x $333 AHR If regular charge rates are used, a $2,000 write-up has occurred.

Terminology	Definition and Comments	Equation
Productivity/ utilization	This is a measure of "charged time as a percentage of available time." Typically, firms work on a 40-hour per week basis x 52 weeks or 2,080 hours (which is known as standard hours). So the productivity is the measure of how much of that time was charged to clients. Most firms run at an average of 1,300 chargeable hours per accountant. If a firm prices its services after the fact, and it is "driving productivity," then it encourages people to go slower (more time), pad their time sheets (more time), or make mistakes (more time). This results in a higher fee for the client. If you're resourcing your team correctly, and setting all prices in advance, then team members will likely hit their revenue targets. Partners should limit their personal productivity and spend most of their time on sales and leadership.	Worked hours = 40 Client time charged to WIP = 32 32 / 40 = 80 percent
Average fee per client	Most firms do not know exactly how many client family groups they have and the average fee per group. This is important information. What you can measure, you can manage.	Revenue divided by number of client groups = average fee per client For example, \$1,500,000 / 300 = \$5,000

Terminology	Definition and Comments	Equation
Number of projects per client per year	Most firms do not know this information; yet it is critical to increasing revenue and client services. If you can work out how many times a client buys from you, you can see what other services/products/projects the client needs. A project is a singular task (product or service) that has been completed for a client. A project could be, for example, the annual tax return, audit report, review or compilation report, cash flow analysis, loan proposal, or information technology study. Most firms only sell their clients essential services, namely compliance. Some clients will be buying more projects than others, but the average is typically about two projects per year. A firm needs to get to at least four projects per client per year on average to be servicing all their clients properly. The objective is to "provide every service to every client that helps them achieve their goals." This means that some clients might buy three services, some might buy ten services.	Number of invoices divided by client groups For example, 750 invoices / 300 client groups = 2.5 projects per client
Average fee per project	With upselling, bundling, price increases, and value-based fees, this number should grow dramatically over time.	Revenue divided by number of projects For example, $1,500,000 / 750 = $2,000 per project

Terminology	Definition and Comments	Equation
Churn/ attrition rate	Most accounting firms keep clients for a long time. However, this is changing. To keep clients, firms must now offer a better level of service and a wider range of services. It takes a lot of effort to get a new client for the first time—the best return on investment comes from the energy you spend on keeping them!	Client churn rate = number of clients that left during the year / total number of clients at start of period. For example, 25 lost clients for year / 250 clients at start of year = 10 percent churn
Lifetime value—LTV	Most accountants do not truly acknowledge the lifetime value of each client. Clients stay with accountants for a long time for three main reasons—(1) relationship, (2) service, and (3) financial intimacy. They leave for exactly the same reasons. If a firm focuses on the lifetime value of a client, they will treat them better, serve them better, and build deeper relationships with them.	Churn rate percent x 100 = years x average fee per client = LTV For example, 10 percent x 100 = 10 years x $5,000 = $50,000 LTV

Terminology	Definition and Comments	Equation
Client acquisition cost—CAC	How much does it really cost to acquire a new client? And how much are you prepared to spend to acquire a new client? Based on the LTV of a client and a good return on investment, you have good reason to allocate resources to acquiring new clients.	CAC = sum of all sales and marketing expenses (including partner salary portion) / number of new clients added For example, marketing costs + partner costs (say $100,000) / 50 = $2,000 CAC
Turnaround time	Turnaround time is the elapsed time from when a project is started to the delivery of a finished product. A project can take anywhere from one day to six months or more. It's a customer service measure. Faster turnaround time equals better perceived client service. It's a matter of setting reasonable time parameters, managing expectations, and doing things on time.	First piece of information received to final product delivered to client For example, May 1, first information received, June 30, final product delivered = 61 days turnaround time

THE ENTREPRENEURIAL ACCOUNTANT—AN OXYMORON?

Entrepreneur: Definition

"One who takes the initiative to create a product or establish a business for profit. Generally, whoever undertakes on his/her own account an enterprise in which others are employed and risks are taken."

Are partners of accounting firms entrepreneurs? This is an interesting question. According to the definition, they own a business (although most did not start the business they own), they employ people, they take risks, and they provide products and services—hopefully for a healthy profit. Does this make them entrepreneurs? Would most partners of accounting firms describe themselves as an entrepreneur? Probably not.

> "Would most partners of accounting firms describe themselves as an entrepreneur? Probably not."

What do they call themselves? Normally they say, "I am a partner in an accounting practice," or words to that effect. Rarely do they say, "I am an entrepreneur who owns an accounting business."

In this chapter I will challenge every aspect of your partnership model and hopefully convince you to operate under a different—more commercial—model.

Why Are Partners, Partners?

Although most accounting firms are operated by sole practitioners (one owner), by my educated guess there are approximately three partners for every accounting firm in the world. And according to a global research company, there are more than 1,270,000 firms in the world. So, there are somewhere in the order of 3,500,000 partners. Worldwide, it is estimated to be more than a $500B profession.

That is a lot of accounting firms and a lot of owners of accounting firms. Far too many of both in my opinion!

So how do the partners become partners? Here are some typical (and perplexing) scenarios. As accountants go through the ranks and learn their craft, at some point in time they "make partner"—as if it is their given right. Sometimes a team member puts pressure on the partners and threatens to leave if they do not become a partner— and the partners cave in. Sometimes current partners think they must elevate team members to partner status just to keep them—so they do. I even know of partners who have become partners without knowing the financial situation of the firm they are buying into. Who would want to be in business with someone who did not understand the financial situation of the business he or she were buying into?

There are too many partners who are there for retention reasons—not good business reasons.

What about the partner who starts his/her own firm? These are the real entrepreneurs in this profession. It's interesting how they come to be. The individual in question starts life as a junior accountant or graduate, learns how to do that part of the job, stays in the current firm for a few years, gets more experience, and then shifts firms. They stay at the next firm for a few years and then maybe shift firms again. All the way observing how each of the partners conduct business.

> "Who would want to be in business with someone who did not understand the financial situation of the business they were buying into?"

One day (usually in their thirties), they wake up and say to themselves, "I am sick of being an employee of an accounting firm. I'm a good accountant. I want to go out on my own. I want to start my own firm." They have just had an entrepreneurial seizure!

Off they (you?) go, believing that just because they are a good accountant they know how to run a successful accounting business that provides great accounting services. Nothing could be further from the truth. Being a technician (knowing how to do the work) and being a business owner (knowing how to run a business that works) are two vastly different scenarios.

Here's the issue. How did this new entrepreneur learn to run the business he/she just started? From the partners that they worked for. They learned by osmosis. And where did those partners learn their great (tongue firmly planted in cheek) business skills from? The partners before them. And so on and so forth.

If you want to run a better business, you must first become a better businessperson.

If you stick to the traditional practice model, the only real way to create wealth in this business is to have fewer partners in your firm and a higher leverage of people per partner.

> "The issue of low profitability starts when you have too many partners and the leverage (people per partner) is low."

There are plenty of sole practitioners around the world who hire more than 20 people, and as such they are typically making more than $1M profit per annum. The issue of low profitability starts when you have too many partners and the leverage (people per partner) is low. It's easy to prop up profits in an accounting firm—just have the partners charge more time. They have the highest (apparently) charge rates, so all time charged by partners is, theoretically, all profit.

Recently I asked a simple question at one of our coachingclub meetings. "If you could wave a magic wand, then the ideal business partner is someone who . . ." And then I got them to answer the question. This is what the group came up with.

The "ideal" partner in an accounting firm is someone who . . .

1. Brings something to the table—complements existing partners.
2. Is a good cultural fit in the firm.
3. Is a good communicator at the partner level.
4. Is a good communicator with team members.
5. Is a good communicator with clients.
6. Is stable—emotionally and financially.
7. Is profit and growth motivated.

8. Has a good work ethic.

9. Is reasonably fit and healthy.

10. Is at the same stage in life mentally.

11. Shares similar values and ethics.

12. Has an ability to respect other partners.

13. Knows what they want—goal oriented.

14. Is supportive of new ideas.

15. Is flexible in their thoughts and actions.

16. Is a good business builder.

17. Is fun to be with.

18. Shares the vision.

19. Walks the talk, not just talks the talk.

20. Acts in the best interests of clients and the firm at all times.

21. Can bring in new business.

How many of these 21 ideals can your current partners answer favorably? Maybe some partners you have are not a fit. Do you need fewer, more, or different partners?

Maybe some change needs to happen in your firm at the partner level.

Partner Remuneration

How much should a partner of a multi-partner accounting firm be paid? Should it be equal pay because you have equal shareholding? If it is going to be equal pay, then each person must pass the checklist of the ideal partner. It's my opinion that most partners should not be paid equally.

I have a view that a lot of partners in this profession are overpaid senior accountants. They are doing the work of a senior accountant but being paid substantially more.

As I mentioned, there are many partners who are partners because of retention reasons rather than good business reasons. In today's

> "In today's money, you can employ a senior accountant for $150K (or thereabouts) to do the work of most partners."

money, you can employ a senior accountant for $150K (or thereabouts) to do the work of most partners.

If I am paying someone $300K–$500K (with dividends), then I would expect them to operate differently from a senior accountant who does the "delivery" side of the work. As a minimum, I would be expecting partners to bring in new business from existing and future clients. Partners need to have the skills, motivation, and abilities to bring in at least $1M of new business per year.

I think high-contribution partners should be following my 30:60:10 rule and only do three things.

1. **High-end work for a low percentage of time.** Advisory work at value-based fees with high margins for no more than 30 percent of time. That means no compliance work and time allocated to not more than 500 hours per year.

2. **Sales activity.** Increasing the average fee per client with additional services sold and finding new clients. Spending about 60 percent of time in a sales function.

3. **Leadership.** Driving performance of the firm and leading the team. For about 10 percent of time.

So how much should you pay them?

To start the discussion, you need to separate employee and owner. There is no right or wrong answer (to how much), however I think a rule of thumb needs to be, "What would it cost me to replace this person with another employee?"

By nature of the answer, it means that there needs to be differing salary levels among partners.

I am talking about rewarding people with a package based on their contributions to the business. It is farcical to think that all employees of a business (partner group) should be paid the same amount, if they are contributing in different ways.

> "I think a rule of thumb needs to be, "What would it cost me to replace this person with another employee?"

As an example, if one partner is bringing in $300K worth of new clients per year and doing $200K of personal chargeable work, then he is far more valuable than someone doing $500K of personal chargeable work and not bringing in any new business.

To get it close to right (and the number will never be right), there are three considerations to the total salary package of an employee or partner.

1. **Salary** earnings—an amount that it would cost to replace you as an employee.
2. **Bonus** earnings—an amount based on "above salary" contribution—it must promote overachievement.
3. **Equity** earnings—an amount based on your equity percentage and your dividend policy.

Excluding equity, as an overall employee package, you should be thinking about "on target earnings"—OTE.

Here are some examples of differing pay scales based on differing contributions.

NOTE: The salary levels are a guideline only. You'll need to check the various salary surveys to get accurate numbers for your location, types of work performed, and the various skill levels of people.

Partner 1. If you have a partner who wants to be the business manager of the firm with no clients, then he should be paid accordingly. Maybe the OTE is $100K–$150K.

Partner 2. If you have a partner who wants to be a workflow, delivery person (say 65 percent productive or $350K personal chargeable time), manage $1M of team revenue, and do zero client nurturing, then she should be rewarded accordingly—like a senior accountant. Maybe the OTE is $125K–$200K.

Partner 3. If you have a partner who does 50 percent chargeable time (say $300K of personal revenue), manages $1M of team revenue, and allocates 10 percent of his time to sales (and he actually does it), then that would be approximately 100 sales meetings at an average of 50 percent conversion at an average $5K extra work for each sale—or an additional $250K of work that has been brought into the firm. Maybe the OTE is $150K–$250K.

"If one partner is bringing in $300K worth of new clients per year and doing $200K of personal chargeable work, then he is far more valuable than someone doing $500K of personal chargeable work and not bringing in any new business."

Partner 4. If you have a partner who does 30 percent chargeable time (say $200K of personal revenue), manages $1M of team revenue, and allocates 30 percent of his time to sales, then that would be approximately 300 client sales meetings at 50 percent at $5K = $750K of new business. Maybe the OTE is $200K–$300K.

Partner 5. If you have a partner who does 20 percent chargeable time ($150K of personal revenue), manages $500K of team revenue, and allocates 50 percent of her time to sales (approximately 500 sales meetings at 50 percent at $5K = $1.25M of new business. Maybe the OTE is $250K–$350K.

Partner 6. The most valuable partner in the firm is the one who has zero chargeable time and spends say 20 percent of the time with potential new clients (say 100 leads generated by the marketing team), and say 50 percent of the time with existing clients, then the numbers are vastly different. This is 100 prospect meetings x 75 percent conversion x $10K each = $750K (recurring) business plus 500 meetings at 50 percent at $5K = $1.25M of new business from existing clients. Total new revenue of $2M. Maybe the OTE is $300K–$500K.

> "Are your partners best at the "revenue delivery" role or the "revenue production" (sales) role?"

This is part art and part science. Which partner are you? Which partners are your partners?

Are your partners best at the "revenue delivery" role or the "revenue production" (sales) role?

This is going to hurt, but delivery people are a dime a dozen. People who can generate revenue from existing clients or convert a prospective client with full services are not.

The Last Trusted Advisor

I believe accountants are the last, natural, trusted advisor.

Think about it . . .

➢ In the 1970s, the insurance people lost their position of trust when they started selling "whole of life" policies and other "products"—trusted advisor status revoked.

➤ In the 1980s, the banks started closing down the branches and subsequently the bank managers had their status revoked.

➤ In the 1990s, we had the rise of investment bankers and then they destroyed their position of trust with the global financial crisis.

➤ The financial planners started off OK but got their trusted advisor status well and truly revoked with "less than above board" commissions and failed investment (typically property or agricultural related) scheme after failed investment scheme.

Sure, there are some less-than-scrupulous accountants who put their fingers into the trust accounts (always with the view of paying it back) or blatantly stealing from clients.

I remember one memorable meeting at a "soon to go into liquidation" accounting firm for well below the line (illegal) activities. I casually asked one of the long-standing employees, "So how much of clients' money did you put into these failed investment schemes?" Answer, "I dunno, somewhere in the order of $200M–$300M during a 10-year period."

I was utterly gobsmacked. Even though the track record was failure over the years, they still had enough trust to extract $20M—$30M per year from the client base. The firm was getting 10–15 percent commission on the money, regardless of the success of the program. Incentives like that drive the absolute wrong behavior. No wonder most of the financial planners who have been selling "commission based products" get themselves into so much trouble!

Even with big accounting scandals, such as Enron Corporation and Arthur Andersen LLP, the trusted advisor status of the accounting profession remains.

It's almost like when you become qualified you get your fancy certificate that you proudly hang on the wall, and it comes with a permanent tattoo for your forehead, which says, **"Trust me—I'm an accountant."**

So why do we trust accountants? Is it the ethical standards that they are bound by? Is it that there have not been that many scandals (in the scheme of things)? Is it that we are told to trust them? Is it that the professional bodies (that

> "So why do we trust accountants? Is it the ethical standards that they are bound by? Is it that there have not been that many scandals (in the scheme of things)? Is it that we are told to trust them?"

all real accountants are members of) actually mean something? Is it the piece of paper on the wall? Is it that clients are typically referred to an accountant and we trust the referee?

All of these certainly help, however, I think the main reason we trust accountants is that they know more about our financial affairs than anyone else does. And financial affairs are a personal and confidential matter. Accountants know the intimate details of our profit, debt, wealth, revenue, and cash flow. Accountants can influence positively (by offering additional help) and negatively (by doing nothing) our profit, debt, wealth, revenue, and cash flow.

They have financial intimacy over the client.

To give you an idea of the size of your level of trust, consider the following equations.

Profit TRUST Equation. With the annual compliance results, add all the profit that your business clients achieved during the past 12 months. If your average client did $250K in profit, and you had 200 clients, then that would be $50M profit that you could positively or negatively influence.

Revenue TRUST Equation. Using the annual compliance results, add all the revenue that your business clients achieved for the past 12 months. You might have 200 business clients, and they had average revenue of $1M each, then that would equate to $200M revenue that you could positively or negatively influence.

Debt TRUST Equation. With this equation, add all the business and personal debt of all of your clients—business and personal. You might have 200 business clients with an average business debt of $350K, and 300 personal clients with an average household debt of $250K, so that would be $190M of debt that you could positively or negatively influence.

Cash TRUST Equation. If your business clients have an average free cash flow balance of $100K per year and you had 200 clients, then that would be $20M of free cash flow that you could positively or negatively influence.

Wealth TRUST Equation. Take the net balance sheet position of your business and personal clients. If you had 200 business clients with a net balance sheet average of $1M, and 300 personal clients with a balance sheet position of $500K, then that would be a whopping wealth under your custodianship of $350M that you could positively or negatively influence.

"Having trusted advisor status is a privileged position to be in. It's a big responsibility."

Having trusted advisor status is a privileged position to be in. It's a big responsibility.

I think it is the accountants' duty of care to leverage the trusted advisor status and positively help clients by offering additional services that really make a difference to the clients' financial conditions.

I think that if the accountant is the trusted advisor, then they need to make sure to "provide every service to every client that helps them achieve their goals."

It's How You Think

If you want to run a thriving accounting business, you need to need to change the way you think. How you think and what you think about is crucial to your success. I meet many accountants who have low self-esteem.

It's my belief that the "order taker" and "clock watcher" mentality drives a level of thinking that is not conducive to business success. Self-esteem plummets when you don't have to work that hard for new business (the government changes the rules and you get some more), when 90 percent of the revenue comes in every year regardless of what you do, and when you are not required to market, sell, or build client relationships—they keep coming back!

With low self-esteem, accountants tend to talk a lot *at* clients—telling all the time rather than asking and listening. It's like you have been taught to bamboozle clients at accounting school with fancy terms so that you look good in front of the client.

> "Low self-esteem also drives accountants into the most arrogant activity of all—prejudging what clients will or will not do."

Low self-esteem also drives accountants into the most arrogant activity of all—prejudging what clients will or will not do. I have heard partners say, "Don't send them the newsletter— they'll never read it." And, "They will never turn up to the seminar." Or, "They will never buy that service."

How dare you prejudge a clients' future!

I also hear, "We can't find any good people." Are you sure? There are hundreds of thousands out there; they just don't work for you! Or this one, "We don't have any clients who will buy that." How do you know that you don't have the right clients? Have you asked them all? And when a good idea is presented, which has worked in countless other firms before you, I get this response, "We could never do that." Hmmm.

This level of "stinkin' thinkin'" is driving down business performance and eroding self-esteem.

You must change your attitude and mindset to one of abundance, confidence, and self-belief that you can do it. Believe that you are worth more and believe that if you get out of your comfort zone, learn from others, and be proactive you will get different results. Once you change your thinking, you will start to run a better business.

Here are two great quotes that I live by and teach my clients to live by.

"Whatever the mind of man can conceive and believe, he can achieve."

—Napoleon Hill, author of the bestselling book *Think and Grow Rich,* 1936

"If you think you can do a thing or think you can't do a thing, you're right."

—Henry Ford

A couple of years back, my wife, Nat, and I had the privilege of spending four days with my favorite entrepreneur and business hero, founder of the hugely successful Virgin Group—Sir Richard Branson. The reason I got to spend time with Sir Richard at his private retreat in Morocco was because the previous year, for my fortieth birthday, Nat bought me a ticket into space on Virgin Galactic. There were 12 "future astronauts" (as I shall be called from now on) and their respective partners at the gathering, and we all had a blast (pardon the pun) trekking, cycling, eating, partying, and generally hanging out together.

> "Once you change your thinking, you will start to run a better business."

After reading about his entrepreneurial and adventure exploits for years, I was excited to spend some quality time with Richard. So much so that I compiled a list of questions to ask him! I wanted to know how he worked and how he thought. On the first morning, I changed my mind and decided to toss the questions in the trash.

It felt too contrived. Once I relaxed and got into the groove, I was quite surprised to learn how he ticked. During breakfast one morning, I even witnessed a fellow entrepreneur "pitch" his idea to Richard. After four days, my synopsis as to what makes this man different from mere mortal entrepreneurs is fivefold.

1. He thinks much BIGGER than anyone I have ever met.
2. He has bucketloads of courage and self-belief.
3. He surrounds himself with the best people—and lets them get on with it.
4. He chooses high-volume business vehicles.
5. He always takes calculated risks and, as he frequently says, he "protects the downside."

How big is your thinking? Are you limited by negative self-talk and limiting beliefs? Is your potential stymied by the people you associate with and the information you are putting into your mind?

When I ask accountants to change one of the most basic of business tactics—price upfront versus price in arrears—I am typically met with fear and trepidation. "What will the clients think" and "How will they react" are the typical thoughts. When the accountants finally implement the change, it is never as scary as they thought and the client acceptance rate is close to 100 percent.

You can reprogram your thinking and your self-belief system. You must first want to. There are thousands upon thousands of books, articles, stories, learning programs, seminars, and courses that you can attend and absorb. Become a student of business and personal development. I was fortunate that at the tender age of 17, I "got into" self-help material, and throughout the years I have amassed an impressive library of knowledge in many formats.

Remember this. You will become the person you want to be by the people you associate with and the material you absorb. Someone in the world has done what you want to do—seek them out and learn from them.

> "I was fortunate that at the tender age of 17, I "got into" self-help material, and throughout the years I have amassed an impressive library of knowledge in many formats."

Let me leave you with a little saying that I heard recently.

"Watch your **thoughts;** they become words.

Watch your **words;** they become actions.

Watch your **actions;** they become habits.

Watch your **habits;** they become character.

Watch your **character;** it becomes your **destiny.**"

MONEY, MONEY, MONEY

Improving the Profit of Your Accounting Business

The purpose of any business is to find and keep customers. So, you have a marketing and sales function to find them, and then you have great service and services that WOW them into staying with you.

That's all well and good for your clients. What about you? You've taken a risk to start/buy your business (it's not a practice and you need to stop practicing—you've been practicing long enough), and you need to be rewarded. In my opinion, you need to be rewarded well for your intellect, your contribution, and your risk. I think the benchmark is more than $1M profit per partner with partners doing minimal client work. Unfortunately, the average partner makes about one-third (or less) of that number.

> "The problem with comfort is that you stop seeking, striving, developing and then apathy tends to kick in"

Now you might be comfortable with your current number and that's OK for now. The problem with comfort is that you stop seeking, striving, and developing, then apathy tends to kick in. You need a healthy discontent for the present to change. The output of change is profit and cash.

Here's a dialogue between my son, Hugh (when he was six), and me.

Me: Hugh, it's time to teach you about profit.

Hugh: Dad, what's profit?

Me: It's the selling price minus the buying price. (equation on the whiteboard)

Hugh: Oh, sell take off buy.

Me: Yes, mate, the profit is the result of sales minus costs.

Hugh: Oh.

Me: Hugh, what's profit?

Hugh: Profit is GOOD!

Me: Hugh, how much profit should we make?

Hugh: Hmmm—as much as possible.

You've gotta love young capitalism. Instill it into them young, I say. We still talk about that conversation all these years later (at the time of writing this book, he's 21) and in business it's an important part of life.

The six-year-old kid got it. Do you?

Sadly, the accounting professionals seem scared to talk about their own profit and money. "Why?" I ask. It's not a dirty word—it's a healthy word. A healthy vibrant business makes lots of it. A driven business owner makes decisions to get more of it.

And here's the kicker. If you are supposed to be a leader of business, then why are you not making more money than your clients? I think you should be making more than ALL OF THEM WHO YOU ADVISE ON BUSINESS MATTERS.

OK, rant over. You get my message. I think you deserve more profit and you have the business vehicle to do it. But to maximize the profit, you have to change your business model.

> "If you are supposed to be a leader of business, then why are you not making more money than your clients?"

Here's how you increase the profit of an accounting firm. There are eight primary ways.

1. Your mindset and culture
2. Your pricing structure
3. Your cost structure
4. Your efficiency model
5. Your number (and type) of clients
6. Your services
7. Your clients buying more services
8. Your leverage

Your Mindset and Culture

I have heard it time and time again, "We're not motivated by more money" or similar trite answers. It's a rubbish answer. There is not a business owner on the planet who if they were handed an extra $1M in income wouldn't take it. I don't care if you give it away to charity or your kids or waste it at the casino. Either way, it'll make you feel better. I understand that you don't promote the fact to your clients that you

> "Here is the best pricing advice I can give you. STOP PRICING BY THE HOUR!"

want to make more profit, but I do think you need a profit-driven mindset within you and your team. That means you are always looking for cost-saving ideas, new revenue, and better pricing methods. You are always looking for ways to sell something new to clients (only if they need it) and always looking for new clients.

According to the six year old, profit is good, and you should make as much as possible!

Your Pricing Structure

Here is the best pricing advice I can give you.

STOP PRICING BY THE HOUR!

Seriously, it'll keep you in the poorhouse and the overworked house. It's a really dumb way to price anything. It assumes the hourly rate was correct, and the time to do it was correct. Neither are ever close to being correct. The worst model is when you price based on time taken multiplied by the hourly rate AFTER the work has been done. This model causes inefficiencies, waste, padding of time sheets, go-slow mentality, and other nasty behaviors. What if you priced every job upfront with a 15 percent increase from last year? And please don't write it off. What if you assessed your value contribution to the project and priced (in advance) on your value, and then worked as hard as you can to deliver the project in the least amount of time possible while maintaining quality control?

According to the six year old, profit is good, and you should make as much as possible!

Your Cost Structure

Many firms we work with are seriously looking at (or have already implemented) offshoring with their businesses. The biggest cost structure in any accounting firm is how much you pay for labor. There are not many savings to be made in an accounting firm other than labor. When you can hire five-year qualified CPAs in the Philippines for $5 per hour, it does make it tempting to at least explore the opportunity. If you have accountants in your office who spend most of their time processing work and doing administrative chores (which means they are not really adding value to the client), then you can get that done elsewhere for four times less cost. The accounting firm of the future is one that has a local, client-facing team and everything else is done somewhere else in a more cost-effective location.

According to the six year old, profit is good, and you should make as much as possible!

Your Efficiency Model

There is so much waste and inefficiency in an accounting firm it's not funny. Think of the volume of hours it takes to "check" client data or the enormous amount of time it takes to get all "the missing information" from a client. The human brain can go so much faster if it is under pressure. People can type faster than they currently can if they are trained properly. Accountants spend much of their day doing "administrative tasks associated with the accounting job" instead of doing accounting work. Why not overhaul your systems and the way you interact with clients, so you are more efficient? Why not move all your clients to a Cloud accounting system, so you can be more efficient? Why not hire professional administrators to do the administrative work, so you can be more efficient? A word of caution: Unless you price jobs upfront, your price will go down with your efficiencies, or you'll end up doing more work for the same amount of money.

> "The accounting firm of the future is one that has a local client-facing team and everything else is done somewhere else in a more cost-effective location."

According to the six year old, profit is good, and you should make as much as possible!

Your Number (and Type) of Clients

So, you want to improve profit. To do that someone has to pay for your services. Enter your clients. Every accounting firm I have ever trained, coached, or even spoken to has clients who are costing the firm money. They won't change, they are disruptive, they are disorganized, and they waste accountants' time. If you are on a fixed fee with these clients, then that is profit gone. Not to mention the distraction factor and opportunity cost. Start by asking them to leave. Get rid of the bottom 20 percent of clients. Find clients who appreciate your work and you can make a profit on. Every firm has excess capacity (especially when they implement our workflow procedures), and that excess capacity should be used on attaining more clients. If you got rid of the 20 percent of clients who are "bottom feeders" and replaced them with new clients who are A-class, then your profit would sharply increase.

> "Time and time again I ask accountants if their clients need additional services that they have the skills to deliver. I get the same answer every time. YES."

According to the six year old, profit is good, and you should make as much as possible!

Your Services

Some services you offer are just not profitable. They are low-value services that attract a low-value price. Just like you measure average hourly rate or net firm billing rate on the business (at least I hope you are) why not start by doing that on every invoice and every service. It's a simple equation—invoice value divided by hours taken. You'll soon start to see which services have a low margin compared to others. Once you know the margin, you can make a decision—keep or go. If you keep the service or product, then can it be done more efficiently by someone else, somewhere else? Remember, you are not a community service. You do not have to do everything for everybody. Focus on services that have a ridiculously high margin, and you'll improve your profit.

According to the six year old, profit is good, and you should make as much as possible!

Your Clients Buying More Services

I have yet to meet an accounting firm that has "tapped out" every client with every service it has to offer. The objective is to "provide every service to every client that helps them achieve their goals." That means you know the goals of the clients, and you are matching services to those goals. Time and time again, I ask accountants if their clients need additional services that they have the skills to deliver. I get the same answer every time. YES. The cool thing about additional services to existing clients is that it is not more compliance work. It's more useful business advisory and value-added services work. And the other cool thing is that these new services can be priced differently because the client has not bought it before and it has more value to the client. More value to the client equals more margin for you and more profit.

According to the six year old, profit is good and you should make as much as possible!

Your Leverage

> "Yes. Fewer partners and greater leverage equals more profit per partner."

Most firms are "over partnered" and "under leveraged." This means that the ratio of people to partner is typically low. Many firms operate under the old practice model that they need about $1M in fees per partner and that means about four to five people on that team. What if there were 15–20 people on the partner team? Or more. You'll get more leverage and your profit per partner will sharply increase. If you have low leverage, then consider restructuring your firm so the next two levels under the partner have must more client contact, thus enabling the firm to have more clients per partner and more revenue per partner. There are too many overpaid accountants who because of tenure and cash are currently partners. They are not bringing in new business—merely looking after existing business. It's crazy to pay (with dividends) a partner who adds a minimal growth value of $350K when you can hire a senior accountant for a third of that and still get the same effect. Yes. Fewer partners and greater leverage equals more profit per partner.

According to the six year old, profit is good, and you should make as much as possible!

How to Be Superefficient and Still Make Money

When a partner of an accounting firm says to a colleague or team member—

"I want more billable hours out of you," or

"I need you to get more time on the clock," or

"Your utilization/productivity is low—fix it."

What is he or she saying?

They are basically saying that the individual is not performing. When in actual fact they might be. The individuals that you are "performance managing" might actually be superefficient; however, the traditional business model says they are not.

> "Accountants fill the available time with what work they have to do."

The traditional business model of an accounting practice (not a business) is to "put time on the clock" for a client, and then the hourly rate of the individual(s) doing the work will determine the price. When you say you want more time on the clock from the person, typically bad behavior starts to enter the equation. Team members work slower, they "pad" time sheets, they make mistakes, they go "hunting" for issues, they double/triple check everything, and basically spend more time than they need to.

Don't you think it's amazing that when you say to an accountant, "You've got $5,000 worth of billable time on this job," just like magic, the job comes in at about $5,000? You see, it's human nature—people fill the available time with what work they have to do.

Let me make it clear: If you are pricing in arrears and driving more billable hours, then this is a bad thing. You are not promoting efficiencies. You are promoting inefficiencies.

If you continue to price in arrears and you do decide to get efficient, then what happens is the price either goes down with the new efficiencies or you end up doing more work for the same amount of money. Not a good look!

Being more efficient is the way to go; however, you MUST price the project upfront if you want to capitalize on the investment you have made in being more efficient.

The following diagram shows the new profit model for a modern and progressive accounting firm.

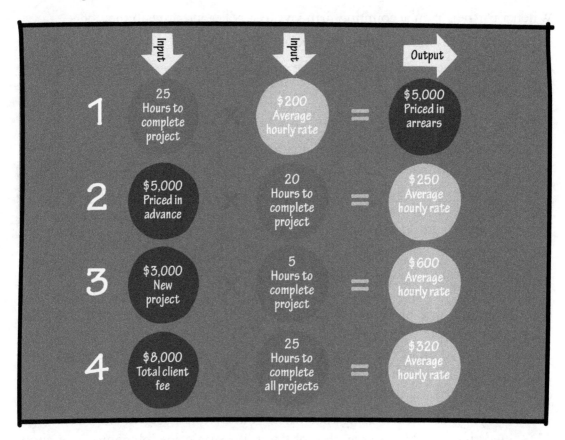

Here's how it works.

Step one is the old model. You put time on the job (input), you have charge rates (input), and the price pops out the end as an output. You are promoting inefficiencies and write-downs. Stop doing this immediately.

Step two is part one of the new model. You price upfront (sometimes for the same amount), you get as efficient as you can and take time out of the job (in this case five hours taken out) and the average hourly rate (in this case $250) pops out at the end.

Step three is part two of the new model. You value price a new project (in this case $3,000) to the same client, you use the "saved" hours (in this case five) to deliver the new project, and the average hourly rate (in this case $600) pops out at the end.

Step four is the outcome of steps two and three. Your new fee to this client is $8,000, the time taken is still 25 hours, and the average hourly rate is now $320.

Imagine if you did this across your entire firm. Imagine taking your average hourly rate (or net firm billing rate) from $200 to $320. What if your firm did 10,000 client hours? Your previous revenue was $2,000,000 and your new revenue for the same 10,000 client hours is $3,200,000. The difference ($1,200,000) is mostly profit. Are you excited yet?

> "I have observed that there are eight key ways to get superefficient with any accounting or advisory project."

But how do you do this? How do you get efficient (I'll deal with pricing upfront and value pricing later) and take time out of every single client job?

After many years helping accounting firms to be more efficient, I have observed that there are eight key ways to get superefficient with any accounting or advisory project. The premise on this list is that you have a good team of people, so I am not covering that here. Here is the list of eight key ways.

> "Imagine taking your average hourly rate (or net firm billing rate) from $200 to $320."

1. Client service coordinators
2. Self-imposed deadlines
3. Policies and rules
4. Visual management
5. Technology
6. All information in from clients
7. Getting rid of bottlenecks
8. Scheduling work

Let's look at each one.

Client Service Coordinators

It's a known fact that accountants spend a big chunk of their day doing administrative work as part of every accounting job. Depending on the skill level of the team member, the number of hours per person per day varies. Often the more skilled and senior they are, the more administrative work they do. Typically, the average is one-and-a-half hours of administrative work (associated with the accounting task) per accountant per day. If you have 10 accountants, that's 75 hours per week. If they work for 48 weeks of the year, that's a whopping 3,600 hours spent per year doing administrative work. If you have an average hourly rate (net firm billing rate) of $200, then that's equivalent to $720,000 of administrative time (also known as opportunity cost) per year. If you hired two new people (called client service coordinators or CSCs) to look after the 10 accountants and take the administrative tasks from them, then you'd free $720,000 of capacity. Even if you filled 50 percent of the new capacity, you'd still be a mile in front on what you pay the CSCs.

> "If you hired two new people . . . to look after the 10 accountants and take the administrative tasks from them, then you'd free $720,000 of capacity."

Self-Imposed Deadlines

It always makes me laugh when I observe people who are about to go on vacation for a few weeks. Have you noticed that they are superefficient in the final weeks leading up to the vacation? Their meetings are shorter, they talk faster, they type faster, and emails are much shorter and to the point. Previously, they used to give a long-winded answer and now they simply say "NO" and hit send. Why? Because they had a self-imposed deadline, and they didn't want to go away and still be thinking about work. The efficiencies are real when you have self-imposed deadlines on accounting work. Here are some examples of self-imposed deadlines.

- You could tell the client when you'll be getting the work back to them—you could even book the presentation meeting.
- You could have a maximum hours budget on every job.
- You could impose a 10-day turnaround time on every job.
- You could create an internal competition on time taken and accuracy.

When you get a culture of self-imposed deadlines, you build a culture of efficiency seeking.

Policies and Rules

What rules or policies have you got regarding your workflow management process? You can have client policies and team policies. For example, every project has a "maximum hours budget" (not a dollar budget as the price has already been set) and that budget is always challenged down. You should always be asking the question, "How can we do this job in half the time?" You could collect some money from clients before proceeding. A rule could be that you don't start the job before all the client information/data has been collected. A policy

> "A nonnegotiable rule is that every job is priced upfront and the client is notified of the scope of works and the price of the project."

should be not to go outside of the scope of works—only do what you're supposed to do and everything else is priced separately. A nonnegotiable rule is that every job is priced upfront and the client is notified of the scope of works and the price of the project. If you're going to have rules, then make sure you stick to them.

Visual Management

Some accountants like to hide behind screens and spreadsheets all day. Have you ever wondered what they actually do all day as they sit there quietly? It's easy to hide behind two or three computer screens. It's not so easy to hide behind a big screen or whiteboard that shows their real-time performance. A visual management system is great for motivation, accountability, and transparency. The following template is a good one. The thing I like about this "whiteboard" is that it has three self-imposed deadlines built in. The due date, the maximum hours, and the 10-day turnaround commitment. Every day the job is in the shop, a day is added. Every day the board is updated with "hours to go," based on the maximum hours budget. You can see which clients/jobs are on schedule and off schedule. The objective of this board is to get the work in and out in 10 days with a credit balance on the hours at the end. Once the job is finished, a file note is created of how many hours it took and the margin on the job. That way you can beat it next year!

Workflow Whiteboard

Accountant	Client/Job	Due date	Max Hrs	1	2	3	4	5	6	7	8	9	10	Hrs. to go
Mary	Coleman	3/2	24	24/1	25/1	26/1	27/1							12
	Dunn	4/2	16	26/1	27/1	28/1	29/1	30/1	31/1					5
	Pillans	5/2	28	26/1	27/1	28/1	29/1	30/1						28
John	Henson	31/1	9	28/1	29/1									0
	Vanjicki	15/2	15	3/2	4/2	5/2	6/2							1
	Fitzalan	12/2	21	6/2	7/2	8/2	9/2							12
Hamish	Ware	1/2	8	5/2	6/2	7/2	8/2	9/2	10/2	11/2	12/2			2
	Hillig	22/2	44	3/2	4/2	5/2	6/2	7/2	8/2	9/2	10/2	11/2	12/2	-6
	Mansel	16/2	22	26/1										18
Jane	Wilson	5/2	12	28/1	29/1	30/1	31/1	1/2	2/2					7
	Kelly	9/2	8	26/1	27/1	28/1	29/1	30/1	31/1	1/2	2/2			-4
	Challenger	11/2	9	26/1	27/1									9

Note: 24/1 means January 24. It's a convenient way to express a date. Make sure everyone in your firm follows the same style.

Once you have the screen or whiteboard in place, it's the perfect place to hold the daily stand up workflow meeting.

> "Find out what the bottlenecks are and fix them. They are causing you to be inefficient."

Technology

Many accounting firms I visit and initially work with are operating with technology from more than 10 years ago. They still have servers, paper management systems, single screens, and their clients are on multiple versions of accounting software. Time to get with the program, folks. **The advent of Cloud technology is THE most significant efficiency gaining tool ever created for accounting firms.** No more version control issues, all documents are on the Internet, real-time data from clients, and supercomputers are doing the processing work. You need to actively and assertively get all your clients on a Cloud accounting system. You need to convert your practice management system to a Cloud system, and you need to get rid of the filing cabinets. When you get your clients on a Cloud accounting system, you can consolidate their data into software and offer valuable business advisory services to them. **Your clients' data can be accessed anytime, on any device, and from any location with Internet service.** What's not to like about that?

All Information in from Clients

I find accountants have a nasty habit of not being clear about what they want their clients to send in. I also find that clients have a nasty habit of not sending in everything when they are asked. I also find that accountants are not that quick to follow up on the missing information. All this missing information leads to "job pick up, put down" and massive inefficiencies. So, fix it. All you need to do is get your new client service coordinator to send a (plain English) questionnaire to the client with enough detail so he can locate what you need. Then have the CSC call the client to check that he got it, that he understands it, and then make him accountable to a date to have it all sent in. Give the client the deadline plus a day, and then call to see where the information is. If he misses the new deadline, then have the CSC physically go to the place of work and collect it. Do not let accountants send an email to the client asking for the information and then wait. Waiting and waiting and waiting. Have the CSC manage the process.

> "All this missing information leads to 'job pick up, put down' and massive inefficiencies. So fix it."

Getting Rid of Bottlenecks

When you apply "the theory of constraints" to a manufacturing line, it'll be the slowest part/section/process/person that holds up the speed of throughput. A manufacturing line exists in an accounting firm and every accounting project. There is a process to follow, there is information to collect, and a product needs to be created from the process and the information. Along the way, there are bottlenecks that are slowing progress. There could be a bottleneck with clients, technology, certain team members, and even the partners. Find out what the bottlenecks are and fix them. They are causing you to be inefficient.

Scheduling Work

I visit accounting firms and I see piles and piles of folders and paper. It's like a visual filing system is going on. There are low-rise piles and high-rise piles. Sometimes the piles fall over, because they are so high and unstable. Sound familiar? There can only be one logical reason that there are so many jobs in the shop at any one time. There is no scheduling of when it is supposed to come in. Clients are just sending in their "stuff" when it suits them. When I go to a dentist, I have to book an appointment, as the dentist can only see one person at a time. Schedule the known work (when you're doing it and when you need it) at least six months in advance, and make sure each accountant has no more than three open jobs at any one time.

The pursuit of efficiency is what you must do to thrive in this profession. You'll need to stop driving billable hours and, if you price every job upfront, refill the newfound capacity with business advisory services so you'll make a lot of money and you'll have happy clients.

$1M Profit Per Partner

Most accountants make nothing close to $1M profit per partner. Most are in the $200K–$400K range. I personally think that is waaayyyy too low.

For the risks you take, for how smart you are, and the value you add, I think you're worth $1M or more profit per partner. But you must believe it first.

Now you might not want to make $1M profit per partner. However, you might want to double your current profit.

The old way is to follow the labor hire business model. Get more accountants to do the work; get them to charge more time and that will increase your revenue. Yes, that is true—your revenue will increase. And so will your cost structure. Unless you have a high leverage of people to partner ratio and decent charge rates, you'll rarely get there.

Chasing "the billable hour" or "more chargeable time" is chasing the WRONG thing. After two decades of coaching accounting firms, I've found that if you chase the following strategies you'll have more of a fighting chance to crack the $1M profit per partner mark.

> "For the risks you take, for how smart you are, and the value you add, I think you're worth $1M or more profit per partner. But you must believe it first."

1. **Better leverage and fewer partners.** There are too many overpaid partners who are really glorified managers. Don't accept new partners unless they are "rainmakers." All non-rainmaking partners should not be partners. You need at least an 8:1 ratio for team members to partner and at least $2M revenue per partner.

2. **More administrative/marketing team members.** Get the admin team to do the admin work associated with the accounting jobs and have a marketing person generate leads.

3. **Better quality clients.** Only have A-class and B-class clients who have some "upside." Get rid of the "bottom feeders" who are not ambitious and do not want to grow. Find new clients who are ambitious and want to grow.

4. **Value-based fees.** For special projects, price based on value created not a "time and charge rate" system.

5. **More projects per client.** Work out how many projects each client buys from you, and then see what else they can buy from you. Make sure the new projects are priced on value, not time based.

6. **Offshore labor.** Look at your delivery costs. You can often hire cheaper labor elsewhere with the same quality.

7. **Efficiency methods.** Look at every process/tool and see if it can be done faster another way. Often technology can play a major part in this.

> "Work out how many projects each client buys from you, and then see what else they can buy from you."

8. **Better utilization of partner time.** You can certainly prop up profits by having the partners charge more time. They have the highest charge rates. If you get partners focused on high end work (30 percent of time), sales (60 percent), and leadership (10 percent), then you'll achieve a much better result.

9. **Less time for accountants.** Stop beating them to a pulp. The objective should be less time on a client job, not more. When you price upfront, you should reward efficiency (less time) not inefficiency (more time). A solid accountant should work for no more than 1,800 hours and be effective for no more than 1,300.

10. **Average hourly rate increase.** When you price a project upfront, your average hourly rate should be increasing every month. It indicates you are pricing better, adding value, and getting more efficient every month. If it's not increasing every month, then it's either your pricing, your efficiency, or your value.

The following table is an example of a sole practitioner model of $1M profit. It's just an example (that does add up), and you'll need to amend it for your business for the number of partners you have.

$1M Profit per partner

Key Area	Now
Partners	1
Accountants	4
Administration & Marketing	3
Client numbers - groups	200
Average project value	$2,200
Number of projects per year per client	4
Average fee per client group per year (projects x fee / project)	$8,800
Revenue	$1,760,000
Salaries - Excluding partners	$450,000 (74% GP)
Office overheads	$310,000
Total costs	$760,000
Profit before partner salary	$1,000,000 (57%)
Productivity / Utilization - Partners	30% - 506 hours
Productivity / Utilization - Accountants	75% - 1265 hours
Average Hourly Rate (AHR) - client hours	$316
Average Hourly Rate (AHR) - All team All hours worked	$130

If you want to make $1M profit, then you can. However, your mindset and business model need to change. It'll take discipline, alignment, and desire before you take action.

Time Is Not Money

Someone coined the phrase—time is money. What a load of nonsense. Time is not money; money is money. A good use of time can turn opportunities into money—but time itself is not money.

Accountants have turned this "time is money" mantra into a sophisticated art form.

An elaborate system has been created of recording time and then charging the time with a charge rate per hour, rather than charging for the value of the work. Seeing how smart accountants are, I find that strange. You might say that the time and rate model does create the true value of the work. I beg to differ. You see, how do you know what your work is really worth? The true determiner of the value of your work is what your client is prepared to pay for it. If clients have a problem that you solve, and the impact of solving it is huge for the clients, then they should pay based on the value of the outcome—not by the time taken.

Think of this analogy.

> "You might say that the time and rate model does create the true value of the work. I beg to differ."

"A washing machine repair person comes to your fix washing machine. She takes one look at the machine, pulls out her trusty mallet, and hits it in precisely the right spot. The washing machine now works. She prepares an invoice for $200. You ask her to itemize the invoice. She writes, "Parts and materials, $1. Knowing where to hit it, $199." BAM!

You know where to hit it, yet you charge by parts and materials!

Using the above analogy, your parts and materials are accountants' time and disbursements. Most accountants have allocated their time to be six-minute units—so there are 10 units per hour with each unit having a set price. If the accountants' charge rate is $250 per hour, then each unit is theoretically "worth" $25.

As the accountant is doing the work for a client, these "units" are ticking away in the background. That means that when a new job is started (typically without the client knowing the final price until after the job is complete), or an existing job is worked on, an electronic clock is keeping score. Theoretically, if the accountant has to do something else not related to the client (like go to the rest room or reply to an internal email), then the clock should be stopped and restarted. I know for a fact that this is not the case. Often, the clients' clock remains active in a lot of cases when personal and company activities are going on.

Let's say you take a phone call from the client (and, of course, you have stopped the clock on another client) and it takes 15 minutes. Your employer has instructed you to start the clock with every "matter" on every client. How much time do you put down? Is it two-and-one-half units? I highly doubt it. My guess is you round it up to three units. You just ripped the client off!

Can your worth really be determined by a six-minute unit? Does the unit price really set the correct price? What a burden to segment your life into small compartmentalized amounts.

> "Can your worth really be determined by a six-minute unit? Does the unit price really set the correct price? What a burden to segment your life into small compartmentalized amounts."

No wonder accountants are looking for the "quick fix" on everything. You are so time driven that you miss the big picture. This method of determining your worth must surely drive low self-esteem, and it must drive you crazy at billing time—I know it promotes the wrong behavior.

The wrong behavior with this business model is threefold.

1. Not charging for everything that you do for a client.
2. Being rewarded for taking more time and being inefficient.
3. Not focusing on client needs because you are scared the bill will be too high.

Let's look at each one.

Not Charging for Everything That You Do for a Client

Whenever I have a group of accountants in a seminar, I ask important questions, such as, "Put your hand on your heart and honestly tell me, when you do the work for a client, how much time actually hits the clock?"

I have asked more than 5,000 fee-earning accountants (employees) this question. The answer is always predictable. If there are 100 in the group, there will be two or three who say 100 percent (they're lying). There will be five or so who say 95 percent. There will be 10 or so who say 90 percent, and the overwhelming response is about 85 percent (they tell the truth)—many say 80 percent or less. The first time I asked this question, one of the partners of the firm I was working with (Judy) pulled

> "Put your hand on your heart and honestly tell me, when you do the work for a client, how much time actually hits the clock?"

me aside at lunchtime and said "They're stealing from me."

I don't get this. Your business model says charge by time, yet your employees are making judgment calls at the time of doing the work about how much the work is worth. Last time I looked it was not your employee's business!

I was on the way to golf one day and I called Susan who was the client manager with my previous accountant. My inquiry was in relation to a new car I was buying for my wife. Susan asked me some questions, gave me the answer, and then said "and if you do it that way you'll have a tax break between $5K and $20K." She then hung up the phone. It was an eight-minute car ride and the call took seven minutes of it. Did she give me good customer service? You might say so, because she answered my question. I have to tell you I had no idea what she said—yet she gave me (potentially) $5K–$20K worth of value. I inquired of Peter (partner at the firm) how much I was charged for this call. You guessed it. Zero. It didn't even make the time recording system.

To value her expertise and give me better service, here is how the call should have been handled.

Rob: I am going to buy a new BMW for my wife—what is the best way to finance it?

Susan: It sounds like you are driving, so I was wondering if this is an urgent matter.

Rob: No—not urgent. I am on the way to golf.

Susan: OK then. The best way to handle this is I need to ask you a whole series of questions, and then I will write you a detailed letter of advice that you can take to the finance person. The letter will spell out exactly the best way to finance the vehicle and exactly what you need to do. Depending on your answers, you will get anywhere between $5K and $20K tax break on the purchase. So that you can be completely focused, I would like to set up a telephone meeting with you (for about 10 minutes) later today when you get back from golf. As I said, you will be able to get between $5K and $20K tax benefit when you do it the way I tell you to do it. My fee for doing this will be $495—is that OK with you?

Rob: Sounds great. I'll speak with you at [time].

Susan: I will send you a quick confirmation email now, and I will call you at [time].

After the call, Susan can use a standard template (which was used before with another client) with an embedded spreadsheet, send me the letter, and now I have something tangible to take to the finance manager at the dealership.

Being Rewarded for Taking More Time and Being Inefficient

You promote a "productivity" target to your accountants. The way you typically define productivity is "client charged time as a percentage of available time." Some accountants work on a 37.5-hour week for 45 weeks during the year—available time of 1,687.5 hours. Normally this productivity figure is about 80 percent of the 1,687.5 hours—or 1,350 of client charged hours per year per accountant.

> "I don't get this. Your business model says charge by time, yet your employees are making judgment calls at the time of doing the work about how much the work is worth."

This focus on productivity causes accountants to go slower, make mistakes, inflate the time taken on time sheets, work longer hours (so your team can get their targets), hoard work, and not care too much about the client. You are actually rewarded for doing the wrong things.

The right thing to do is to get the job done quickly and accurately for the client. Under this productivity-driving model why would you do that? You'll get less revenue.

With a focus on productivity (selling time) you have inadvertently set up a labor for hire business. The more labor you get, the more revenue you will get. However, this does not drive profitability. What happens with the productivity-driving model is you end up with far too many people to do what work you have to do.

You are not in a labor for hire business—you are in the knowledge selling business. You turn your intellectual capital (what you know) into intellectual property, which is tangible. Your intellectual property comes in the form of letters, reports, spreadsheets, emails, diagrams, manuals, and plans.

If you adopt a **pricing upfront** model and a **focus on driving time down,** then you will run out of standard work. This is a good thing. You can downsize your team, increase your client base, and sell additional services to existing clients without adding to your cost structure. When we work with our coachingclub clients and have them adopt this model, 100 percent of them run out of work in the first year. Typically, what took the firms 12 months to do last year, they do in 9–10 months the first year they adopt the new model. In year two, they typically do the same work in 6–8 months.

Not Focusing on Client Needs Because You Are Scared the Bill Will Be Too High

A seminar attendee (client manager) said to me, "I want to get out and find out what clients need. I want to sell. I am unable to, because the partners want me to have 80 percent productivity."

I think that sums up the entire issue. It's a conflict.

If you are focused on charging the clients for everything, then you will miss out on really helping the clients with what they need. This behavior does not encourage relationship building. I think it is a self-esteem issue. You seem to be more comfortable just "charging time" for the reactive work, rather than really finding out what the clients need—and proactively helping them. I find that most accountants think that the price will be too high (self-esteem again), and the client will not pay the higher fee.

You have to get to the point where you do not have to charge for everything. Your projects should have enough margins in them that you do not have to worry. You should not be charging for quick phone calls or emails. If the clients know that you charge for everything, then they will only do the bare necessities with you. They will limit the number of calls they make and the meetings will be efficient but little time will be allocated to relationship building. The client is constantly thinking, "I hope I am not getting charged for the time he is asking about my family and the dog—I wish he would just get on with it." How can you build a relationship with a client when the client is thinking this?

> "David Maister once said, 'What you do with your billable time determines your current income, but what you do with your non-billable time determines your future.'"

All interactions with a client are opportunities to discover additional needs. Many phone calls are "intellectual property selling opportunities" in disguise. You need to train yourself and your team to look for them—and not charge for the time used in finding out what the client needs.

As the world-renowned author (now retired) on professional services firms David Maister once said, "What you do with your billable time determines your current income, but what you do with your non-billable time determines your future."

With this focus on time, another waste phenomenon occurs—**write-downs!**

What typically happens is the project is worked on by the accountant and when it comes time to draft the bill the **gutless partner** "writes down" (discounting before billing) the value of the work. What a self-esteem destroyer. Your accounting team does the best job they can and by way of your actions you tell them they are not worthy. The partners think the client will not pay the full price—how do they know that? Sure, from time to time an accountant "stuffs up" or there was more work in the project than first thought. If there was more work in the project, then you should have communicated this to the client during the work in progress and invoked a "change order" on the original engagement letter. Oh, I forgot. You did not price the job upfront. You'll have to wear the write-down in that case.

Write-downs are one of the easiest things to fix. It's a decision. You decided to write-down. You can decide to write-up. Here's how you eliminate write-downs once and for all. This piece of advice is worth millions of dollars.

> "If you are going **to be completely ethical** and true to your time-based business model, then you should be charging by the hundred-millionth of a second, not a six-minute unit."

1. Make a decision to stop writing-down.
2. Price every job upfront with client sign-off.
3. Drive time down and take the write-up.

It's that simple. Be warned, though. If your business model is charging in arrears and you write-up a client's work, then you have been unethical. I do not care if you were superefficient, your business model said charge for the time that was taken. There have been many cases of accountants going to court for overbilling. Take a look at the 1993 movie *The Firm,* starring Tom Cruise. In the last scene, the law firm was brought unstuck for overbilling. These are write-ups using a time-based, price in arrears model.

I have said it before, and I'll say it again. You are doing your clients a complete disservice by focusing on charging them for everything and not building relationships with them.

To sum it up. How can this time and rate model ever work? When . . .

- The price per hour is based on an accountants' salary level.
- The time to do the job is never properly recorded.
- The time taken varies from person to person.
- You are rewarded for taking longer and being inefficient.

If you are going **to be completely ethical** and true to your time-based business model, then you should be charging by the hundred-millionth of a second, not a six-minute unit.

I think this entire method of pricing by time is not only bad for you; it is bad for your client. It is highly unethical. There is no winner. There has to be a better way. The good news is that there is a better, more ethical way.

It's called value pricing.

It's all about working with the client to scope and then price each project based on what value the client gets out of the project. You price the project so there is fair and equitable remuneration for you and a dramatic return on investment for the client. You do this before you commence work on the project. You communicate in writing the scope, price, and value to the client and then get the client to approve the project.

HOW TO DETERMINE THE PRICE

The M Zone

I am sure you have had that feeling when everything you do just seems to work. It is working so well that you feel like you are in the "zone." It is a good feeling.

There is a new zone I want to take you to. It's called the margin Zone—the M Zone. This is the place where you get the greatest return for your intellectual capabilities. It's the place where profit margins skyrocket and where happiness (shareholders, team, and clients) is at its highest.

When you are in the zone, you have three things working for you in sync.

> "It's the place where profit margins skyrocket and where happiness (shareholders, team, and clients) is at its highest."

1. You have **courage** to charge what your intellectual property is really worth.
2. You **price every job in advance**—and communicate the price to the clients.
3. You are as **efficient** as possible in performing the work.

The diagram below highlights the links among the three.

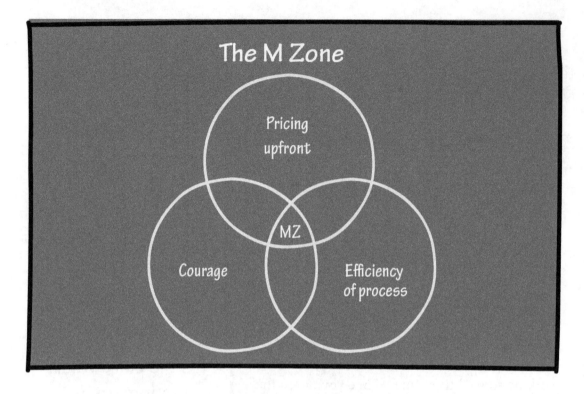

You might be courageous in your pricing approach, but you do not tell the clients the price and you are not that efficient. Lots of bravado—thus profit margins not maximized.

You might price every job in advance and you might tell your clients the price, but you have limited courage and the firm is not that efficient. It takes months to get work out and when it does get out, the client gets a great price—thus profit margins not maximized.

> "You may have all the best systems and be superefficient, but you lack courage and you do not price upfront."

You might have all the best systems and be superefficient), but you lack courage and you do not price upfront. High quality control is present, however, profit margins not maximized.

You might have lots of courage and price every job in advance; however, the systems are not working as well as they could. Messy business and profits are not maximized.

You might price every job in advance and you are fairly efficient, but you have limited courage. Smooth operation and profit margins are not maximized.

You have lots of courage and you are efficient, but you price in arrears. You might get a reasonable write-up and you will probably end up justifying your fee, because the client was unaware how much it was in the first place. Profit margins are not maximized.

The optimum of course is the middle, the margin zone (MZ). This is where you are as efficient as possible, you price and communicate every job in advance, and you are courageous in your pricing approach.

Here's an exercise to do. Have your entire team rate the firm (one to ten) in each of these three areas. Take an average of the team scores, and this will give you an indication of where you need to focus your energy. Preface the team that you want to double your average hourly rate in six months with write-ups. You might get a different score!

There are many ways, ideas, and strategies to get more courage, to price upfront, and to be more efficient. Here are a number of suggestions contributed by my coachingclub firms who are in the MZ and achieving fantastic margins.

Courage—How to Get More of It

- ✓ Look at the volume of work and realize you do not need to say yes to everything.
- ✓ Have an abundance mentality—not scarcity.
- ✓ Use a buddy system—do not price anything until someone else looks at it (partner, colleague).
- ✓ Be accountable to an external source.
- ✓ Take the emotion out of pricing.
- ✓ Discipline yourself and focus on higher margins.
- ✓ Believe in yourself—you truly are worth more.
- ✓ Value articulation—learn how to find the value to the client in every job.

> "The optimum of course is the middle, the margin zone (MZ). This is where you are as efficient as possible, you price and communicate every job in advance, and you are courageous in your pricing approach."

- ✓ Educate the team on the firms' value of each job.
- ✓ Leverage past successes—if you've done it before, it should be more next time!
- ✓ Unbundle what you do and realize the value of each component.
- ✓ Brainstorm, before pricing, the client value in the job with others.
- ✓ Strengthen relationships with your clients.
- ✓ Practice role plays—as corny as it is, practice in the mirror, not on your clients.
- ✓ Say "No"—be prepared to walk away from clients or work.
- ✓ Put yourself out on a limb—take a guess ... you'll probably be wrong.
- ✓ Have confidence in knowing it will be done well in the office.
- ✓ Look at worst-case scenarios by putting your prices up.
- ✓ Toughen up—maybe you are just too nice!
- ✓ Look at how you are different from your competitors.
- ✓ Shout it from the rooftop—talk it up how good you are.
- ✓ Learn/train in new skills—self-development.
- ✓ Acknowledge feedback, testimonials, case studies, recognition, awards.
- ✓ Look at your infrastructure, intellectual property, risk.
- ✓ Associate with positive, forward-thinking people.
- ✓ Look successful.
- ✓ Select clients—have criteria and say no or goodbye if the criteria are not met.
- ✓ Examine your motivations—goals, dreams, legacy, incentives, pain solved, or pleasure gained.

And the BIG one ... **Take some courage pills!**

Efficiency—How to Be More Efficient

- ✓ Get your team to buy-in to your plan.
- ✓ Use information technology (IT) systems—electronic work papers, three screens every desk, intranet, etc.
- ✓ Police IT usage—No Internet goof-off time.
- ✓ Utilize electronic systems and procedures—everything "e."

> "There are many ways, ideas, and strategies to get more courage, price upfront, and to be more efficient."

✓ Create budgets on every job—in hours only.

✓ Monitor non-chargeable time.

✓ Adjust the right mix of jobs/projects.

✓ Assign the right people to do the tasks at hand.

✓ Communicate with clients—what promises have been made?

✓ Have administrative people do the administrative tasks associated with the accounting job.

✓ Get rid of bad clients.

✓ Create an organizational structure.

✓ Redesign an efficient office layout.

✓ Focus on picking the job up once.

✓ Develop an information-gathering system with clients.

✓ Prioritize workflow systems.

✓ Monitor and share intellectual property and systems throughout the office.

✓ Have an efficiency competition—small prizes to motivate the team.

✓ Provide skills training.

✓ Hire a business manager to run the operation.

✓ Hire a professional development training manager to train the team.

✓ Have self-imposed deadlines on every job.

✓ Ensure that all clients are on Cloud accounting.

✓ Work on one job at a time.

✓ Make certain there are no interruptions while working on client work.

✓ Create productization and systemization of everything.

And the BIG one . . . **Gather all the client information before starting!**

Pricing Upfront

> "And the BIG one . . . Gather all the client information before starting!"

✓ Ensure 100 percent policy—every job must be priced and scoped upfront and communicated with clients.

- ✓ Presentation of all services to clients.
- ✓ Practice scripts/role plays.
- ✓ Look for the value-pricing opportunities, don't give answer right away.
- ✓ Involve the team—this comes up all the time.
- ✓ Create templates—if you think you will do it again, turn it into a system or template.
- ✓ Write statements/letters of advice.
- ✓ Acknowledge the engagement process.
- ✓ Communicate during WIP—if there is scope creep or scope seep.
- ✓ File notes on previous projects for future reference.
- ✓ Capture sold price in system for future reference.
- ✓ Create a menu of services.
- ✓ Have two prices—external price to clients and internal hours to team.

And the BIG one ... **Write to your clients and tell them that you will be pricing upfront—accountability!**

Getting into the MZ is easy. Get some courage, price everything upfront, become more efficient, and you will get there. Simple really!

Charge Rates and Value Pricing

It's like the saying, "blue and green should never be seen together." The same goes with charge rates and value pricing—they do not go together.

> "How can you really value price a project if in the back of your mind there is a charge rate hanging over your head?"

How can you really value price a project if in the back of your mind there is a charge rate hanging over your head? You will constantly struggle with the charge rate and not focus on the value of the work.

So get rid of the charge rates—all of them! Once you start pricing all jobs upfront, the charge rates are surplus to requirements.

Be warned, though. Do not get rid of charge rates until you are pricing every project upfront. I would advise that you initially keep time sheets (and put the charge rate at $1 per hour per person) for measurement purposes. However, as soon as you are comfortable with the strategy and highly profitable, also eliminate time sheets.

Once you get rid of charge rates, you can have this wonderful conversation with a client or prospect when they ask you, **"What are your charge rates?"**

"Just about every accounting firm in the country uses charge rates. Those firms that use them are directly rewarded for how inefficient they are. The longer they take, the more money they get. In our view, that is unethical behavior. We don't think that is fair to you, so, here at XYZ, we don't use charge rates. Instead, we will give you a fixed price for the work that we undertake. You will receive that price in writing and in advance of us starting. When we get into the work if we are inefficient, then that's our problem—the price remains the same. If the scope of the work changes as we get into the project, then we will inform you of any price changes. Normally the price does not change because we spend quality time with you at the outset to determine the exact scope of the work. Overall we think this is a fairer way to do business."

You just promoted how your firm is different and more client focused and, at the same time, you gave every one of your potential competitors a "back hander."

When my son, Hugh, was 12, he asked if there were some jobs he could do at the office. I told him I needed 1,000 stickers adhered to 1,000 paper bags. He said, "How much will you pay me?" I said 10 cents a unit. "Is that 10 cents for the bag and the sticker?" he asked. Smart kid. "No—10 cents per completed item." On the first morning, he did 200 bags in three hours and I gave him $20. He was thrilled. I told him he made about $7 per hour and then I said, "When you come back next week to finish the remaining 800, do you want to be paid 10 cents per unit or $7 per hour?" As quick as a flash he said, "10 cents a unit—I'll probably do it faster next week."

> "Never charge by the hour. It'll send you to the poorhouse."

If a 12 year old gets it, then what is your problem! Never charge by the hour. It'll send you to the poorhouse.

Moving to Value Pricing

The idea of value pricing is that your clients know how much the price will be before the work commences and you get a healthy margin in return for your intellectual capital/property.

With the implementation of value pricing, your average hourly rate (AHR) should increase dramatically. There are two ways to measure AHR.

> "Once you get rid of charge rates, you gain a new value-priced focus but lose some of your measurement metrics."

The first is if you have time sheets then it is **revenue divided by client hours charged.** So, if your revenue was $3M and your fee-earning team (including partners) did 10,000 client charged hours for the year, then your AHR would be $300.

Once you get rid of charge rates, you gain a new value-priced focus but lose some of your measurement metrics. You can however measure AHR based on your total employee base. The equation becomes **revenue divided by total working time.** So, if your revenue was $3M and you had 10 people (total team including partners) who were paid for 1,687 hours for the year then your total working time is 16,870 hours. That would mean your AHR without time sheets is $178.

The objective is to increase your AHR every month—or as a minimum every quarter. Most firms start their journey with time sheets and an AHR about the $150 mark.

There are six logical steps to increase your margins, as illustrated in the following model. As you move through the steps, your AHR should be going through the roof.

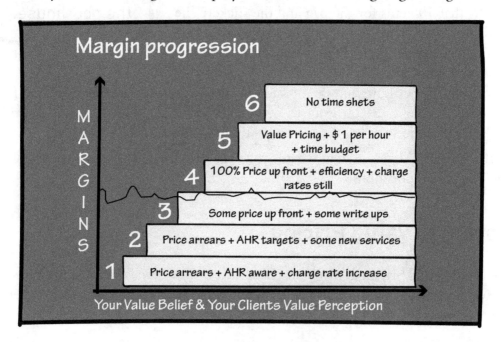

Your margins will increase based on three key factors.

1. Your value belief in yourself and the project—courage and self-esteem.
2. Your clients' value perception—how much value they perceive they get.
3. The tactics and strategies you adopt—the six steps implemented.

> "If you are operating below the waterline, you will be drowning in margin poverty. If you are above the waterline, you will be surviving in margin abundance."

I am going to deal with numbers one and two in the next section on "How to Price Based on Value." For now, I want to focus on the tactics and strategies as you quickly move up the margin ladder.

You will notice that there is a "waterline" halfway through the strategies in previous the margin progression image. If you are operating below the waterline, you will be drowning in margin poverty. If you are above the waterline, you will be surviving in margin abundance.

As you understand each step, do not be concerned that you have to take one step after another. You can jump steps and go right to level five or six. You need to get above the drowning point as quickly as possible. The faster you get to the top, the higher your margins will be.

Step 1. Price arrears + AHR aware + charge rate increase

Most firms start here. They price in arrears with time sheets and they are aware of their AHR. They might not be happy with where the AHR is, but it is where it is. To increase your margin, simply put your charge rates up. Put them all up by 15 percent. Do that today. No one will notice and make sure you do not adjust salaries at the same time. If you do 10,000 client hours and your AHR was $150, with a price rise of 15 percent it is now $172.50. You just made an additional $225,000 profit. I knew I should have value priced this book!

Step 2. Price arrears + AHR targets + some new services

You are still pricing in arrears (with an increased charge rate) and now you have an AHR target. The price rise got you to $172.50 AHR, and now you might set an initial target of $200. To get to a higher target you might need to introduce some more valuable services that are worth more to your clients and more to you—such as business advisory or management accounting services. As you move through the levels and keep having a higher and higher AHR target, however, be warned. Once you get into value pricing, the focus cannot be on the AHR target because you will start to price services based on the target—rather than the value of the project. You are still drowning in margin poverty.

Step3. Some price upfront + some write-ups

You have gone through the first two steps and now you have "put your toe in the water" and tested some upfront pricing on a few clients. The clients are always happy and as a result of this you inadvertently become more efficient and you get some write-ups. You are just starting to put your head above the drowning line and heading toward margin abundance. However, it's a bit like being pregnant with this price upfront strategy. You can't be half pregnant and you can't be half doing this strategy—you either are or you are not.

Step 4. 100 percent price upfront + efficiency + charge rates still

Now you're starting to move into margin abundance. You have committed to price every project upfront and now you are really driving time down by being more efficient. Your margins are climbing, your write-downs are eliminated for good, and you are getting through the work much faster. You'll be running out of work soon—be prepared. You are still holding onto charge rates. While you still have charge rates, your internal budget will be based on a dollar figure, which the team will achieve ("you have \$X worth of time to do the job"), and you will set the price based on your AHR target or based on charge rates—albeit they are higher than before.

Step 5. Value pricing + \$1 per hour + time budget

It's now time to get rid of the charge rates and the AHR targets. If you get rid of the charge rates and move to \$1 per hour per person, you will be less inclined to price based on time but more inclined to price based on the value of

> "If you get rid of the charge rates and move to \$1 per hour per person, you will be less inclined to price based on time but more inclined to price based on the value of the project."

the project. You can still measure and monitor what is going on because you have not eliminated the time sheet recording system. When you do an internal team budget (for the project), you should do it in hours not dollars, and the team cannot associate the time taken with the price the client has agreed to pay. You should always challenge the time and drive it down by being more efficient. Your team is even more inclined to record all the time and you'll get an accurate AHR. Your write-downs were eliminated in step four—you will only achieve write-downs in step five if you are REALLY inefficient. Every firm that has gotten to step five will never go back to having charge rates. They are redundant and surplus to requirements.

Step 6. No time sheets

This is the step every accountant wants to take but is scared to take! Getting rid of the time sheets. The tyranny of time will finally be lifted when you do. However, be warned. Many firms have eliminated time sheets too early. I think it is a sensible option, and one that you will not regret. You should do it when the time is right. I know some firms that have eliminated time sheets too early and they have nearly gone broke in the process. I know some firms that have eliminated time sheets and not priced jobs upfront—they literally made up the price after the fact. What a mess. I know firms that have eliminated time sheets and have had a blowout of people costs. I think the time to eliminate time sheets is when your AHR with time sheets is already high (say more than $400), your turnaround time on jobs is fast (say less than two weeks), and your profit margin is already high (around the 55 percent mark before partner salaries). Once you get rid of time sheets, some of your measurement systems also go. This is not a bad thing. Your main KPIs now become profit, turnaround time (not WIP), receivables, and AHR (based on revenue/total working time). It certainly simplifies things and saves a huge amount of time filling the darn things in.

> "I know firms that have eliminated time sheets and have had a blowout of people costs."

These steps are there to be jumped. Get to level five as quickly as you can and you'll never look back.

Let me tell you about a large firm that nailed this. I'm going to use a large firm example because the larger the firm, the harder it can be to implement. If you're a one-to-five partner firm, it's easy to implement. Make a decision and just do it.

This large firm had 14 partners. They were super successful and writing down work and pricing in arrears. They had 5,000 clients and for years, they were pricing in arrears. They were also writing down $1.6M per year. They were champions at write-downs. They budgeted for 10 percent write-downs each year, and they expected to fail before they started. They nearly hit their goal as they were achieving 8 percent write-downs each year. Their average hourly rate charged was $120, and their profit before partner salaries was 25 percent.

They were a big example of a typical small firm.

So, this is what I did to fix it. I realized that if we wanted to change the behavior, then we must first change the system. The first thing I did (after the partners bought into the program) was get the team members onboard. We ran a seminar to educate the team about all the new changes. I then drafted a one-page letter (following this example) to send to their clients to announce the change in the system. They sent the letter to 3,500 of their 5,000 clients.

The team and the partners were now accountable to the change. We drafted a series of standard "price upfront" engagement letters and as the client work came in they sent a letter with the scope and had the client sign off on it. Now they were directly incentivized to be as efficient as possible.

Within six weeks, they eliminated $1.6M of write-downs and started writing up work. Within 12 months, they had $500,000 in write-ups ($2.1M profit improvement) and an average hourly rate of $176—a 46 percent increase in margin.

When you price upfront, you are now incentivized to drive the time down not drive the time up! Fewer billable hours, not more billable hours. You get more capacity and you get more margin. Your clients love it (you have to trust me on that one), because they have certainty on price before the project starts.

It's not that hard when you have the structure, the systems, and the tools to do it.

This is the exact letter I had the large 14-partner firm send to their clients.

> "When you price upfront, you are now incentivized to drive the time down not drive the time up! Fewer billable hours, not more billable hours."

Dear [client],

Since our firm was started in [year] we have been using a "time multiplied by rate per hour" method to determine the price of the work. Nearly every accounting firm worldwide uses this method.

We have come to the realization that this method is an archaic method of pricing. It is also a conflict of interest because what it means is (as a profession) we are directly rewarded for how inefficient we are. The longer we take to do the job, the more we get. It is not promoting good customer service of faster completion time. This also means you have no idea how much the job will be until the bill is received. We don't think that is fair to you. As a courtesy to you, we think you deserve to know in advance how much the job will cost and what it entails. As a modern and progressive firm, we have decided to change this "old" business practice as of [date]. This means that before every job starts, we will advise how much it will cost. There will be a written communication that you will need to sign. If you are uncertain about the project, the price, or the benefits, you will have the opportunity to discuss these with us at the outset. To get the new system up and running, we are clearing out all the time that we have accumulated to date on your behalf under the old system. Accordingly, please find enclosed an invoice, which brings you up to date. Other than for minor incidentals that we attend to from time to time, this is the last time you will receive such an invoice from us. We are indeed bringing in a bold new era for accountants. We appreciate your business and are confident that this new method of pricing will enable us to give you far better service. We look forward to working with you under the new arrangement.

Yours sincerely,

[partner name]

By sending this letter, the firm cleaned out its work in progress in one go and made themselves accountable to the strategy. To change behavior, we changed the system.

How to Price Based on Value

The most popular question I get is, "How do you determine the price?" Unfortunately, there is no easy answer to that. If you were in the commodity business (selling the same things that others sell), then it would be relatively easy—see what your competitors are selling their comparable products for and price yours higher or lower based on the quality of your products and services.

You are not in the commodity business—unless, of course, your business is personal income tax returns and you are competing against the "sandwich board" style tax agents on the sidewalk. They market personal income tax returns as a commodity with a low price and as such they have "commoditized" the service.

With a commodity, you can have a major differential in price depending on the circumstances. Take a 600ml bottle of water, for example. In the supermarket, in a pack of 24, the water retails for about 30c each. The same water at the convenience store retails for about $2. The same water at the airport retails for $4, and in the five-star hotel minibar it retails for $5 or more. Scarcity and circumstances can drive price. **Circumstance pricing!**

> "You are not in the commodity business—unless, of course, your business is personal income tax returns and you are competing against the 'sandwich board' style tax agents on the sidewalk."

Your products are unique. Your products are based on what you know. You turn your (and your firm's) intellectual capital into intellectual property. You do not sell a commodity service and you have no true competitors—because no one is you. Yes, there are many other accounting firms who sell compliance, business advisory, and consulting services. Yet you are unique with your special blend of relationship and customer service.

So, if that is the case, then the only determiner of your product price is what the market is prepared to pay for it.

This means you need to test different packages and approaches to see what your market is prepared to pay for your product. It means you need to listen to what the market is saying (Do they have fee questions or fee objections?) and reprice or

> "If you adopt a new model of listening to your market, then that means you need to adopt a new model of testing."

repackage accordingly. It means you cannot dictate to the clients what they are prepared to pay. That would be extremely arrogant. Yet under the "hours times rate" model, that's exactly what you do. You tell (rather than listen) the clients what they will pay.

If you adopt a new model of listening to your market, then that means you need to adopt a new model of testing. Here's an example.

I received an email from one of our coachingclub members (Sean,) which was titled "Win for the Day." Sean is the business manager of an extremely successful accounting firm—it has won our coveted "Accounting Firm of the Year" award twice in the past four years. The story was about one of the partners (Marc) who was about to go into a client meeting. Before he went into the meeting, Sean asked Marc to role play what he was going to say, how he was going to say it, and what he was thinking of charging the client. Marc explained his case to Sean and said, "I am thinking of $25K for the project." Sean said, "I would be prepared to pay $45K for it. And when you get to telling them the price do not say "umm" in front of the price—say it with confidence."

By simply speaking with someone else before getting to the price, Marc now had a different perspective on what the job was worth.

So Marc gets into the meeting, explains the opportunity to the client, and, of course, the client says, "How much will it cost?" Marc says (with great tonality and confidence), "The fee will be $50K." The client said, "Yes" without hesitation! Sean's email continued—"Four years ago before we joined coachingclub, we would have charged about $5K."

I saw Marc a few weeks after receiving the email and I asked him specifically (when the price was mentioned) what the client said and how the client said it. Marc said at the time he mentioned the price, the client put both thumbs up and said, "That's an excellent use of money."

> "There is no right or wrong price. However, if your clients are continually saying 'yes' to your price, then the price is wrong. The right price is just before 'no.'"

The client said yes, without hesitation. The price was probably wrong! Could Marc have gotten $60K or $70K for the project? Probably. Was Marc ecstatic with what he got? You bet.

There is no right or wrong price. However, if your clients are continually saying "yes" to your price, then the price is wrong. The right price is just before "no."

One of our most successful firms looks at client jobs and says (based on volume/weight), "There's about $2,000 worth of value in this job—no more than four hours to do it." Next job comes along and he says, "There's about $5,000 worth of value in this one—no more than 10 hours to do it." His current goal is $500 per hour in client work. Based on weight/volume/value the price is set. Then the time is set based on target average hourly rate. **Weight-based pricing!**

The same accounting firm will go to a meeting with four prewritten implementation plans with four different prices. Each implementation plan has a color-coded sticky note on it. As the meeting progresses and depending on the mood of the meeting, he decides which color he pulls out. He's been known to pull the wrong color. **Mood-based pricing!**

Put the price up and **let the marketplace tell you** when you've gone far enough. If you push the boundaries and you get lots of "no" answers, then back it off a bit and settle on a price that has a great margin for you and a good return for the client. There are two bright sides to getting a NO.

1. You don't have to do the work.

2. Every NO you get means you're closer to a YES.

As you have probably gathered by now, the problem with pricing by the hour is the assumption that the price per hour is correct (often calculated by a salary multiple) and the time to do the task is correct. The assumption is that hours multiplied by the rate equals the correct price. In my view, nothing could be further from the truth.

When selling intellectual property, to price in arrears based on hours and rate is a bizarre pricing model. You are valuing what you know and the outcome the client gets based on a salary multiple (to get to the charge rate) and the time taken to do the task. Strange! I understand it's an easy way to calculate a price. The issue is this model does not value how smart you are and the impact you make.

There has to be a better way. And there is. It's all about value pricing. Value pricing is where you price the job upfront based on the value you create for your client. You cannot value price after the fact. That means you must "scope out" the project first (by talking with the client and doing some research), find the value you are adding, and then present an implementation plan to the client based on how you are going to help them.

Now for historical work, you have a challenge with pricing. And that's price parity. You might think it is worth more, but if the client has been paying $X for the past few years then they might pay $X plus a bit more—but not the price you think it is worth. For a new project that the client has not bought before, then that's a different story.

If you know the numbers in advance (Cloud accounting helps enormously), then you can scope out projects that make a difference with your clients. If you can articulate your value in advance and present it in such a way that makes sense financially and emotionally, then you'll win the business.

Most people get the concept of value pricing as price based on your value.

The biggest question I get about this topic is, "How do I work out the price?" Here is the definitive way to price knowledge-based services. If you follow this simple guide, you'll never need to ask the question again.

There are only three areas you need to focus on to get to the right price.

> "If you can articulate your value in advance and present it in such a way that makes sense financially and emotionally, then you'll win the business."

1. Your value belief in the project, your team, and yourself.

2. You value contribution to the client's condition.

3. Your client's value perception of what you are doing for them.

The following diagram will help you determine the right price.

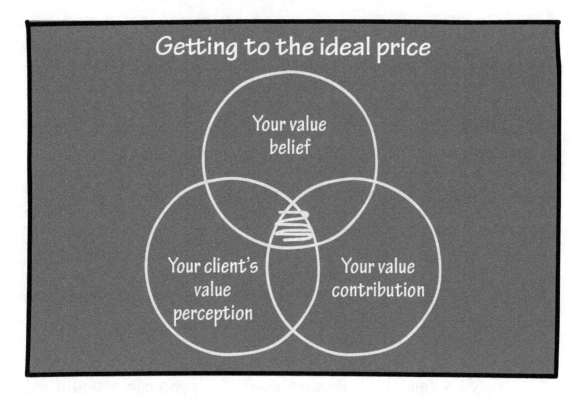

Here are some pricing scenarios about these three critical pricing areas.

Let's say you have a high-value belief and your contribution is high, yet you have not articulated your value to your client, then you will not maximize your price. Let's say your client value contribution is high and your client's perception of your value is high, yet your self-belief is low, then you will not maximize your price. The worst one is when your client's value perception is high and your value belief is high, yet your contribution is low, then you will not maximize your price—you're basically lying!

If you want to maximize your price and get a great return on your intellectual property, then all three areas must be working together.

Let's look at each one in detail and see if I can help you with the dark art of pricing.

"Unless you believe in yourself and what you and your firm know is worthy of a high price, then you will always price low."

Your Value Belief

It all starts here. Unless you believe in yourself and what you and your firm know is worthy of a high price, then you will always price low. I find self-esteem in the accounting profession to be a major issue when it comes to pricing. You might be different, but most of those who I meet lack the confidence and courage to price appropriately.

As you look at the scope of work to do, and as you work out the value, you'll scratch your head (like the accountant in the following image), and you'll have a lot of "chatter" going on in your head. You'll be thinking of charge rates, value, competitors, and the one you most think of is "What will my client think?"

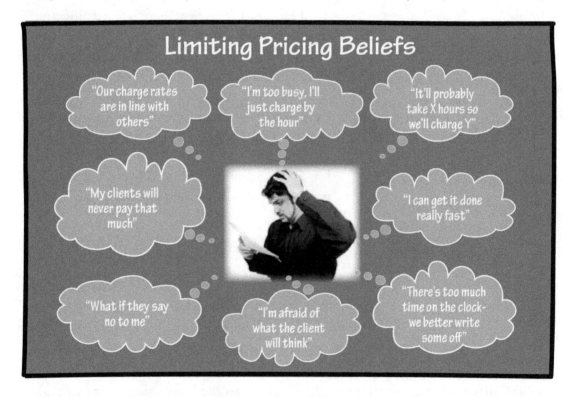

Who cares what others think?

Get over yourself. They are not really thinking about you. They are too busy worrying what you think of them! What people think of you is none of your business anyway, that's their business.

Get some courage and believe in your self-worth as an awesome, smart accountant. It's taken years to get to where you are today. You used to do the same project in five days; now because of your experience you can do the same project in two hours.

You should be rewarded for your years of experience, not how long it took to do the project.

Here's your new value belief system.

"I really value what I know. I articulate my value eloquently.

I sell my intellect and information based on my value contribution rather than my time."

Here is a great example of value belief. In my live seminars, I will often have the accountants tell me how much they have charged for certain projects. This one is a standard project that most accountants have done and one that invokes some interesting prices.

> "I have come to the conclusion I know nothing about how much to charge—I keep putting my prices up and they keep saying yes."

The scenario is you have an existing (retail shop) client who does $1M in revenue with a $250K profit. The clients' bank has requested that a budget and a cash flow projection be prepared for the next three years. The bank has requested the forecast because it wants to be confident that the client can support the existing $50K overdraft and the new $300K working capital loan. Your job as the accountant is to do some analysis and prepare the report so the client can take it to the bank.

How much have you charged in the past for this service?

I have everyone write what they have charged in the past for this service. The results are staggering. The current low price is $500 and the current high price is $30K—and everywhere in between. A 60-times variable for the same instructions!

There have been two accountants at $30K, three at $25K, and hundreds near the $10K mark. I asked one of the accountants (Chris) who had charged $30K, why so much? Chris' response, "Without us, they cannot get the loan—that's our value add!"

WOW—now there is an accountant who understands his value. Who am I to tell you how much to charge when there is a 60-times variable. I have come to the conclusion I know nothing about how much to charge—I keep putting my prices up and they keep saying yes.

Recently I was in a hotel, and I was having a massage. I was paying $150 for the hour-long service. As I lay on the massage table, I started thinking about accountants—

yes, sad, I know. The reason I was thinking about you is because here I was happily paying $150 for a service where the effects would not last more than a day. I started thinking about all the accounting firms where their average hourly rate is well below $150, yet the effects of the services they provide often last a lifetime.

> "Without high-value contribution, you will not maximize your price."

The more you understand what your clients get out of implementing your services and the value you create, the more you will believe you are worth more. Your value belief and self-esteem will improve as will your courage to charge more.

Your Value Contribution

To work out the value contribution you are adding, you need to think about the following:

Without me, they can achieve "X" result. With me, they can achieve "Z" result. The difference ("Y") is your value that you can add. The impact might be financial, emotional, or both.

Let's look at a couple of examples.

Cash-flow improvement. If clients are constantly juggling cash, never have any surplus money, and are always stretching creditors and arranging payment plans, then that is their current situation. Educate them, put systems in place, show them how to improve profit, then monitor their behavior, and let's say the outcome during the year is that they are $200,000 better off. Your cash "value add" is $200,000. They are also sleeping better at night, are less stressed, have more working capital to expand, and are generally happier. Your emotional value add is massive. How much would you charge? Well a 10:1 return is a really good deal. So maybe $20K–$30K.

Tax minimization. If your client has a tax exposure of say $550,000, because of her current structure and trading environment, then that is the current reality. You come along and restructure the affairs and negotiate with the tax department and you get the exposure down to $150,000. Then your cash value add is $400,000. What can she do with $400,000? Maybe expand the business, pay the family home off sooner, retire early, and get some of her life back. Your emotional value add is huge. What's that worth to the client? Pick a number—maybe $30K–$60K.

Without high-value contribution, you will not maximize your price. You need to work it (value contribution) out in advance and show the clients with confidence that you can help them.

I play a great game with my coaching clients and seminar attendees called "Where's the Value?" It's all about you articulating the value of what you do. I always start with basic annual compliance, and typically the accountants draw a blank on the real value of compliance. After some prodding I get frustrated and I say, **"As a result of understanding and using your compliance product, tell me what it will enable the client to do and tell me how your client can use it."**

Now the real value of the compliance product comes out. They say as a result of understanding and using the product the clients can . . .

- ✓ Make better and more informed management decisions.
- ✓ Increase their credit lines with suppliers.
- ✓ Appease financiers.
- ✓ Get more capital.
- ✓ Value their business.
- ✓ Mitigate risk by increasing insurance levels.
- ✓ Sell their business.
- ✓ Improve the profit in their business.
- ✓ Use it as a basis for cash flow management.
- ✓ Sleep better at night.
- ✓ Have peace of mind that their affairs are looked after.
- ✓ Increase their wealth.
- ✓ Improve their lifestyle.

Amazing amounts of value in a seemingly "valueless" product.

Once you understand how the client can use your product or what result the client can realize by implementing it, you will have a much easier job of articulating the value of your product.

At a recent coachingclub meeting, I asked the accountants to play the "Where's the Value?" game and to articulate the value that they had created for a client. Each accountant had to bring a current project to the meeting and tell everyone what value the client got out of the project. Sheryl turned up with her compliance project and it had 12 points of value attached to it. I told her that was awesome, and then she told me that she originally drew a blank and did not come up with any of them. She confessed that she emailed her client and told him that she wanted to anonymously talk about the client in a meeting and could the client tell her the value that she created for him. The client emailed back 12 points of value.

Sometimes you need to ask others what value you create.

One of the reasons that you do not think in a "value that you create" way is because you are constantly thinking about **activities and inputs instead of results and outputs.** What I mean is you are thinking (and subsequently articulating) about things—three of these, one of these, and two of those—rather than what the client gets out of implementing your things.

Your Clients' Value Perception

How you articulate how you are helping your clients improve their conditions will make a massive difference in whether (1) you win the business in the first place and (2) you maximize your price. It's all in the language. And if you want to master the dark art of pricing, then you need to become an eloquent user of value pricing language.

Here's the problem that must be addressed.

Most accountants talk to their clients about what they are going to do, rather than what they are currently achieving for the clients.

What I mean is most accountants talk about inputs (activities) rather than outputs (results). Most accountants relate the work they have to do, rather than what benefit the clients get when they buy the work.

I see engagement letters that look like this.

Included in this project are the following.

> "If you want to master the dark art of pricing, then you need to become an eloquent user of value pricing language."

- ➤ Analysis of your current situation
- ➤ Recommendations to improve your structure
- ➤ A cash flow forecast statement
- ➤ Tax planning for entities X, Y, and Z
- ➤ Annual financial returns for entities X, Y, and Z
- ➤ Personal financial returns

Throw in an audit and you have the entire shopping list at the grocery store!

Selling Outputs Not Inputs

[X]	Analysis	✓	Profit
[X]	Advice	✓	Growth
[X]	Budgets	✓	Cashflow
[X]	Tax planning	✓	Security
[X]	EOY statements	✓	Wealth
[X]	Meetings	✓	Retirement
[X]	Valuations	✓	Success
[X]	Consulting	✓	Peace of Mind
[X]	Structuring	✓	Lifestyle
[X]	Time	✓	Hope

You must change your language and articulate the BENEFITS of the project. It's the oldest radio station in the world W.I.I.F.M—what's in it for me!

Talk to me about profit improvement, wealth creation, asset security, lifestyle improvement, etc. Just tell me how much better off I'll be by buying your ideas.

At the end of the day, the only right price is what the market is prepared to pay for it. That means the right price is just before NO. In other words, if they keep saying YES without hesitation, then the price is too low.

Value pricing is a wonderful tool to use. It gives certainty to the client about the price and the scope, and you maximize the years and years of experience you have.

> "Most accountants talk to their clients about what they are going to do, rather than what they are currently doing for the clients."

Now you can get creative with this and give your clients an enhanced version.

You could package several services (known ones) and give your client an annual accounting service, which is an annual fee divided by 12 to get a monthly fee. Then have direct debit authority for the monthly fee.

You could promote known services into packages on your website. It's the old small, medium, and large idea.

Basic	Intermediate	Advanced
Cloud accounting software	Cloud accounting software	Cloud accounting software
Filing of Quarterly BAS/Tax/GST	Filing of Quarterly Tax	Filing of Quarterly Tax
Filing of annual return	Filing of annual return	Filing of annual return
Year end Review meeting	Year end Review meeting	Year end Review meeting
Unlimited phone and email support	Unlimited phone and email support	Unlimited phone and email support
Regular tax updates	Regular tax updates	Regular tax updates
	Interim financial statements	Interim financial statements
	Year end tax planning	Year end tax planning
		Annual cashflow forecast
		Monthly cashflow report
$250 per month	$450 per month	$750 per month

Note: This is a guideline only and not designed to be the prices to charge or the packages to promote. Also, I am sure you could come up with more creative titles than I have here.

"If the clients buy it too easily, then play with the pricing until you get some saying no. If they consistently ask for this but not that, then play with your packaging. Let the marketplace tell you what it will buy and how much it will pay by testing."

Or you could simply scope out every project and offer a written price to your clients before you start.

I am reminded of an old marketing saying, "It is arrogant in the extreme to dictate to the marketplace how much it will pay and what it will buy."

What that means is you come up with an idea/price/package and you "put it out there" and see how the marketplace responds. If the clients buy it too easily, then play with the pricing until you get some saying no. If they consistently ask for this but not that, then play with your packaging. Let the marketplace tell you what it will buy and how much it will pay by testing.

If there was a magic formula, this might be it.

To settle on a price, work out what tangible results a client gets from using your service, work out (by asking them) what other intangible benefits they will receive, then settle on a price that is a good return for you (based on your value contribution and the intellectual capital you bring to the table) and a dramatic return on investment for your client.

When you adopt these methods, your profits (and enjoyment levels) will improve out of sight.

Below is an actual letter and invoice I received from a sole practitioner ($980K in fees). Read the letter and see the invoice! Now that's value pricing!

Accountants for Free Enterprise

- Management & Financial Accountants
- Forensic Accountants
- Registered Tax Agents
- Certified Practising Accountants

Director

Graeme Gillard

Dip. Comm. Grad. Cert.
Forensic Studies (Acctg)
CPA FTIA

Associate Director

Vivienne Gillard

B. Comm. (Acctg)

Postal Address:

PO Box 2530

Southport

Q 4215

Office Address:

Level 1, Suite 3

101 Ashmore Road

Bundall Q 4217

Telephone:

(07) 5561 1909

Facsimile:

(07) 5504 6752

Email:

info@affe.com.au

Liability limited by
a scheme approved
under Professional
Standards Legislation

ACN 066 780 612 Pty Ltd
ABN 43 392 191 260
Trading as Accountants
for Free Enterprise

8 July 2013

Attention Rob Nixon

Proactive Accountants
PO Box 1339
Fortitude Valley
Brisbane Qld 4006

Dear Rob

We forward herewith a copy of the invoice we issued for our biggest fee ever.

By way of background I thought I should tell you about the journey that has taken place with our business for us to be able to issue such an invoice.

I remembered years ago when I went to the Results boot camp with Paul Dunn where I came away excited about changing the accounting perception of accountants.

The one thing that stuck in my mind from that boot camp, was I purchased a bread making machine, so when clients came to the business they would smell the aromas of freshly baked bread.

This aroma would stay with the client and everytime time they went for some bread they would remember our business.

However, in those days there was no follow up or any process to make sure that what you took away with you from the conference was being implemented and hence the excitement slowly died as you immerse yourself back into to old habits.

So when we were approached to join Proactive I was fairly reticent as I thought I had heard it all before and this was just another marketing organization.

Thankfully to my CFO (Viv) who has not been damaged over the years with sarcasm, she finally convinced me to join the network as what we were doing was taking us nowhere.

Once we joined the network I was still resistant to change (just because of whom I am and possibly my age) but since joining Proactive it has truly changed my process.

The changing point for me was Queenstown when Taggarts were pricing their account and the various prices that came from the floor.

I said to myself they are no different to us (except a little bit younger than me) so what is holding us back.

Accountants for Free Enterprise is a CPA practice.

Accountants for Free Enterprise

- Management & Financial Accountants
- Forensic Accountants
- Registered Tax Agents
- Certified Practising Accountants

As you know I spoke to you about this client as I was on the back foot as this job started just before we joined your organization and we had not priced it up front.

I had worked out a fee that I thought was really outrageous, but after Queenstown I decided that there was no real price except the one I thought was reasonable.

I came home from Queenstown and re assessed my pricing (copy of my calculations enclosed).

As you have often stated it's selling the value and what it's worth to the client.

On the day I meet with the client I took my rough calculations with me so I could re assure myself that the price I chose could be explained in value terms.

After asking the client what this tax ruling meant to him and the tax savings I had achieved for him, I decided that the 11% option was fair.

When this was put to the client (I was nervous as all hell) he looks at me and asked me to repeat what I had just said.

At this point I thought I'm down in straight sets.

I repeated the value to him and what this meant to him which he had just told me and waited for an answer.

He looked me straight in the eyes and said "I think that is fair as we all need to win".

The relief was unbelievable as I tried to contain my excitement.

I walked out of the meeting with the amount scratched out on a piece of paper to show the team who were all spelled bound and were waiting in anticipation.

Needless to say I took him out for lunch.

This would not have happened if we had not joined Proactive, and we want to thank you and the team at Proactive for giving us the belief that anything is possible if you have belief and a system to support the belief process.

I have mentioned this to some of my contemporises who don't believe what we have done as they are still in the time warp of trading dollars for hours.

As one expert who I consulted too said how "did you justify the hourly rate?"

We are truly indebted to Proactive as we purchased a ticket to go on a journey and have won Tattslotto.

Director

Graeme Gillard

Dip. Comm. Grad. Govt.
Forensic Studies (Acctg)
CPA FTIA

Associate Director

Vivienne Gillard

B. Comm. (Acctg)

Postal Address:

PO Box 2530

Southport

Q 4215

Office Address:

Level 1, Suite 3

101 Ashmore Road

Bundall Q 4217

Telephone:

(07) 5561 1909

Facsimile:

(07) 5504 6752

Email:

info@affe.com.au

ACN 046 780 612 Pty Ltd
ABN 45 392 191 260
Trading as Accountants
for Free Enterprise

Accountants for Free Enterprise is a CPA practice.

Accountants for Free Enterprise

- Management & Financial Accountants
- Forensic Accountants
- Registered Tax Agents
- Certified Practising Accountants

Tax Invoice

OUR BEST ACHIVEMENT TO DATE **Date:** 16 May, 2013

Director

Graeme Gillard

Dip. Comm. Grad. Cert.
Forensic Studies (Acctg)
CPA FTIA

Associate Director

Vivienne Gillard

B. Comm. (Acctg)

Description

Agreed success fee in relation to income tax ruling, in relation to carry forward losses.

Postal Address:

PO Box 2530

Southport

Q 4215

Office Address:

Level 1, Suite 3

101 Ashmore Road

Bundall Q 4217

Telephone:

(07) 5561 1909

Facsimile:

(07) 5504 6752

Email:

info@affe.com.au

Liability limited by
a scheme approved
under Professional
Standards Legislation

ACN 066 780 612 Pty Ltd
ABN 45 392 193 260
Trading as Accountants
for Free Enterprise

Amount Due: 930,692.40

The Amount Due Includes GST of $84608.40

Please detach the portion below and forward with your payment

BPAY | Biller Code: 117382 | **Remittance Advice**
Ref: 1255926

Telephone & Internet Banking - BPAY®
Call your bank, credit union or
building society to make this payment
from cheque, savings or credit
card account. www.bpay.com.au

® Registered to BPAY Pty Ltd
ABN 69 079 137 518

Cheque ☐ Mastercard ☐ Visa ☐

Card Number

16 May, 2013

Amount Due: $ 930,692.40

Cardholder .... Signature   Expiry Date ....

BSB 034-215 Account# 197-045 Visa & Mastercard will incur 1.5% surcharge

Accountants for Free Enterprise is a CPA practice.

CPA

Delivering AWESOME Service

Communicating until It Hurts

If a client pays you a high fee, do you communicate with them more? Absolutely, you say. Should you wait for them to pay you more before you communicate with them? Or should you communicate with them more before they pay you more? I think the latter should apply.

- If you increase the level of communication, then you'll increase the level of trust.
- If you increase the level of trust, you'll increase the level of relationship.
- If you increase the level of relationship, you'll increase the level of fee per client.
- If you increase the level of fee per client, you'll increase the referral rate.
- If you increase the referral rate, you'll increase the happiness level.
- If you increase the happiness level, then everything is sorted!

> "If you increase the level of relationship you'll increase the level of fee per client."

It all starts with increasing the level of communication. How much communication and in what format is the key. After years of working with accounting firms and their clients, I have worked out that the following diagram is the ultimate communication schedule. It should be applied to all clients you want to keep.

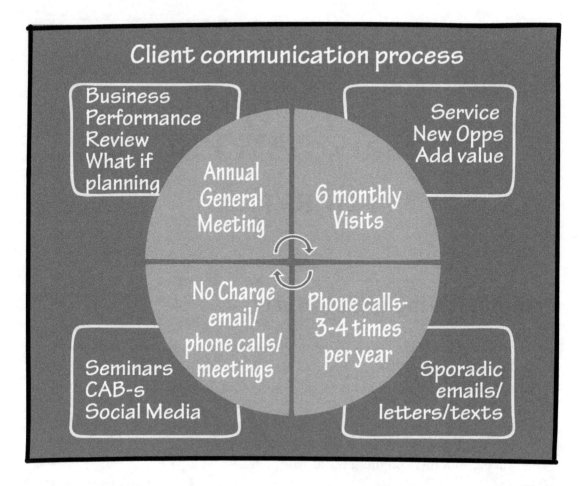

There are four parts to this schedule.

1. An annual general meeting
2. Visits to see how the client is doing
3. Phone calls and sporadic communication
4. No charge for "attendance" communication

"Is it all those inane 'sign here' stickers with little or no explanation? Do you email/courier/ mail the draft accounts for signing? I hope not."

The Annual General Meeting

Every year you finalize the annual accounts for your client. What is your process at this point? Is it all those inane "sign here" stickers with little or no explanation? Do you email/courier/mail the draft accounts for signing? I hope not.

My guess is that the majority of your clients get a substandard explanation of the previous year's financial performance. As a business client, I have two main questions at year end: (1) How much tax do I have to pay and why, and (2) Where did the cash go?

If you are glossing over this, then you are missing out on loads of opportunities. You are missing out on great customer service and potential revenue opportunities. I recommend that you have an annual general meeting (AGM) process. This happens once per year. Of course, all the signing needs to take place but, more important, an explanation also needs to take place.

When it comes to clients understanding what you have done, typically the reports that come out of your tax preparation software are not that great. If you just send it to your clients, then they don't understand it. It's full of numbers and words that confuse them.

The accountants that we work with are using a different process. They are adding a business performance review, which is a three-year historical review of the clients' financial affairs in one easy-to-view screen. The business performance review is a conversation starter. It shows trends, issues, and opportunities in critical areas of a business. It is designed to be simple, so the clients can see what is going on. It is presented on a screen (the bigger, the better) and, of course, you can print it. You can do some financial modeling and "what if" based analysis. It typically results in the clients asking, "How do we fix it?"—or words to that effect.

> "This AGM meeting should be conducted with every business client you want to keep. Never charge for this meeting."

The objective of this meeting is for clients to understand their current situation fully (by knowing the numbers and asking questions), understand their objectives going forward (by asking questions), and having a discussion about how you can help them get there.

This AGM meeting should be conducted with every business client you want to keep. Never charge for this meeting. It's on you and it's a value-adding opportunity, and, who knows, you might win some more business from it. At a minimum, you'll give some great customer service. Typically, clients will ask, "How do we improve the numbers?"

Client Visits

> "You want to build a better relationship with clients and building a relationship with a client takes communication."

All clients love it when you visit them at their place of business. Most accountants don't do it enough and some accountants don't do it at all. If you don't do it, you are missing out on massive opportunities to add value and create new business from existing clients. I used to call this meeting a "nurturing" visit. A few years back, I changed the terminology to a sales visit.

The purpose of the meeting is to understand your clients' current situation more, to understand their short- and long-term objectives, and to see if you can help them achieve their objectives. It's a sales meeting. As a sales meeting, you do not want to leave anything to chance. You need a systematic approach to the meeting, so you can get a predictable outcome. Follow my 12-step meeting approach in the sales chapter in this book and you can't go wrong.

Client meetings need to happen at least every six months. If you are a typical partner of an accounting firm, then you'll have about 120 business clients. That averages out to 20 per partner per month on average.

Proactive Phone Calls

Throughout a two-year period, I interviewed 1,077 business clients on behalf of 126 accounting firms. There were approximately eight clients per meeting in a client advisory board format. The questions to the clients were primarily about what they like, what they don't like, and what they would like to see improved or added if they were running the firm. The partners were not in the room, and I would give a report after the meeting. One of these meetings stood out. I got to the improvement of service question when a paint retailer, Barry, said the following.

"I would love it if the partner who looks after me, Greg, would phone me up from time to time and ask one simple question—how's business? I would tell him what is going on, and, who knows, there could be an opportunity for Greg to help me and win some more business from me."

This happened in a recorded meeting from a client! They want you to call them and send emails, letters, or useful information pieces. How often are you proactively calling them with no agenda? I think for the clients you want to keep, you should call three to four times per year. You don't even have to speak with them. You could leave a message and say you're just checking in.

Ever since that client advisory board meeting, I have been promoting proactive phone calls with a "how is it going" agenda. The accountants who do it are creating better relationships with their clients.

> "As a sales meeting, you do not want to leave anything to chance. You need a systematic approach to the meeting so you can get a predictable outcome."

Not Charging for Communication

I still find it bizarre that accountants want to charge for phone calls and meetings. I know firms that have wanted to charge clients for receiving newsletters and travel time. I don't think there are too many (unlike your legal colleagues) who still charge for letter writing, courier fees, faxing, and other meaningless disbursements.

Think about it. You want to build a better relationship with clients, and building a relationship with a client takes communication. And you want to charge for communicating with them. What the . . . ?

Imagine if you were a client who knows your accountant charges for phone calls and meetings. Guess what? He will only call you when he absolutely has to. And he will want to keep the conversation short and not get involved in "small talk" for fear of being charged for the chitchat. What a wasted opportunity to find out what the client really needs. What a wasted opportunity to find out the client's deep problems and hidden opportunities.

The successful firms who are smashing it with growth are not charging for phone calls, emails, and quick meetings. In fact, they are telling the clients that they do not charge for these communications. They are using this as a differentiator against other firms.

Imagine if you get a call from a prospective client, and she asks, "What are your charge rates, and how do you charge?" There are two ways you could answer that question.

Option 1

"We charge by the hour for everything we do, and the price per hour is dependent on who does your work. If you use the graduates, they are $120 per hour. The seniors are $160 per hour. The client manager is $220 per hour, and as the partner, I charge $350 per hour."

Option 2

"Thanks for asking. Here at XYZ, we don't have charge rates and as such we don't charge by the hour. The vast majority of accounting firms charge a graduated fee based on the skill levels of the people they use. They also typically charge for every phone call, email, and meeting. We don't charge you for any of that. We charge you a set fee on each project that we agree on together before the project starts. Included in every project are unlimited phone calls, emails, and meetings for anyone who is working on the project. That way there are no surprises with the fee and no barriers to doing business with us. We want you to call or email us as many times as you need throughout our time together. We think that is a fairer way to do business with you."

> "Even if you do not currently charge for phone calls, emails, and meetings, you must tell the clients."

As a client of an accounting firm, give me option two any day. I have certainty of price and there are no barriers to picking up the phone or shooting off an email. Most partners of accounting firms think that clients will abuse the privilege. Let me assure you, they will not. Even if you do not currently charge for phone calls, emails, and meetings, you must tell the clients. They think you are like every other accounting firm.

The same goes for low-value seminars, client advisory board invitations, and social media. I know some firms that want to (and sometimes do) charge their clients to attend the firm's annual Christmas party. If the seminar has value, then by all means charge. If it is a sales pitch, then don't charge. Client advisory boards are an awesome way to communicate with clients. Social media is a tool to communicate with clients.

Stop thinking like a labor hire business where you have to charge for every interaction on the clock. It'll keep you in the poorhouse.

For you to thrive, you'll need to dramatically increase the communication levels with all your clients. Communicate a lot first. Increase the fee levels later!

Retaining Clients

Most firms have a high retention rate per client. That means their clients stay clients of the firm for a long period of time. Somehow the accounting profession has got most of their clients bluffed that it is hard to change accountants. It's actually not.

> "I do not think retention rate is high because of great service, relationships, value for money, or services offered. I think retention rate is high because of **financial intimacy**."

Partners will argue that clients remain with the firm because of the great relationship they have with their clients. I beg to differ. How can you have a great relationship with someone when you see them once or twice per year?

Imagine what your relationship would be like at home if you only saw your life partner once or twice per year? For some of you reading this, it might be better!

I do not think retention rate is high because of great service, relationships, value for money, or services offered. I think retention rate is high because of **financial intimacy.**

I think retention rate is high because you know things about the client's financial affairs that no one else does. **It's financial intimacy.** Period. Most people do not speak openly about their financial affairs—it's a private matter. And if they only speak to a couple of people about a private matter, a lot of trust is built up. Not relationship—trust.

Your clients trust you to not tell others. So, they don't leave.

However, the real measure is how happy they are to be a client of your firm. I think that metric is based on the number of referrals you receive each year per client and how many projects they buy from you each year.

For starters, work out the average referrals per client. If you divide the number of referrals (inquiries) you get annually into your total client base, this will give you a startling reality of how happy your clients actually are.

Now the flip side to that is they might want you all for themselves and they do not want to refer! Possibly. The easiest way to increase the number of referrals is to systematically ask for them. If you deserve a referral (great service, etc.), then you'll get referrals. Most clients do not refer for three reasons.

1. You've never asked—we didn't know you wanted any.
2. You seem to be too busy—we don't want our service levels to drop.
3. We're not happy—something has happened in the past.

If you focus on those three, then you'll get more referrals. This chapter is not about marketing and referrals; it's about clients and WOWing them into staying with you.

> "The more projects a client buys from you, the better they are served and the more you put a fence around the client."

Focusing on retaining clients is not about increasing the retention rate, it's about making memorable experiences with existing clients so they buy more from you and refer more to you.

As a measure of great retention, you should be aiming for an actual retention rate of 95 percent, at least one referral per client per year, and at least four projects per client purchased each year.

Let's explore the **number of projects per year** that clients buy from you.

The more projects a client buys from you, the better they are served and the more you put a fence around the client. It makes it harder for them to leave your firm if they are buying (on average) four or more services from you.

This KPI however should not be about retaining clients (although that will happen); it should be about servicing them properly. The internal mantra should be "provide every service to every client that helps them achieve their goals."

If you are doing your job currently by building close relationships with your clients, meeting them frequently at no cost, you will get to know them and you will find many projects and opportunities.

To work out the number of projects per client, take your invoices sent number and divide the number of clients into it. Typically, it will be about two projects per client per year.

Here's a simple test. In a table, list all your services across the top and all your clients on the left-hand side. Apply a "tick" or a "cross" to each client and each product and see how many ticks you come up with. This is a measure of your product penetration. It's called a client product matrix. It looks like this.

> "If you are doing your job currently by building close relationships with your clients, meeting them frequently at no cost, you will get to know them and you will find many projects and opportunities."

Client/product matrix

	Corp Secretarial	Annual Accounts	FBT/other tax	SMSF/401K audit	Budget	Cashflow	Planning Session	Monitoring-mthly/quarterly	Tax planning	Health Check	Asset protection	Coaching	Systems development
Client name	✓	✓	✓	✗	✗	✗	✗	✗	✗	✗	✗	✗	✗
Client name	✓	✓	✗	✗	✓	✓	✗	✓	✗	✗	✗	✗	✗
Client name	✓	✓	✓	✓	✗	✗	✗	✗	✗	✗	✗	✗	✓
Client name	✓	✓	✗	✗	✗	✗	✗	✓	✗	✓	✗	✗	✗
Client name	✓	✓	✓	✗	✗	✗	✗	✗	✓	✗	✗	✗	✗
Client name	✓	✓	✗	✓	✗	✗	✗	✗	✗	✗	✗	✗	✗
Client name	✓	✓	✗	✗	✗	✗	✗	✓	✗	✗	✗	✗	✗
Client name	✓	✓	✓	✓	✗	✗	✗	✗	✗	✗	✗	✓	✗

My guess is that less than 15 percent (or less) of your clients buy every service you offer! Yet many clients need your additional services—they just don't know the services exist because you have never offered them. What an opportunity!

If you have a focus on "all clients you want to keep," then you will make sure they are buying what they need to succeed. A systematic approach is needed with a consistent questioning and interview process.

Another measure of your retention rate is how much the **average project value** is per client. The higher it is, the happier they are.

A project is defined as a singular piece of work. So, annual bookkeeping is a single project, annual accounts—one project. A budget, audit, cash flow forecast—all one project. How many projects (on average) do your clients buy from you?

What is your average project value? It's simple to work out. All you need to do is divide the number of invoices sent into your revenue for the year. If you have multiple invoices for one project, then that should be classed as one invoice.

> "Another measure of your retention rate is how much the average project value is per client. The higher it is, the happier they are."

Your average project value multiplied by the number of projects per client per year will equal your revenue per client.

It's a great way to look at your client base. If you have a small average project value (but lots of clients) you will have a large administrative function just for invoicing. With a small average project value, you will also have a higher than normal attrition rate—it's no big deal if the clients leave.

The objective should be to increase the average project value while increasing the number of projects that each client buys from you each year. If your business clients are not spending at least $10,000 with you annually and buying at least four projects from you (therefore the average project value is about $2,500), then I think you are massively under-servicing your client base.

As you work out your numbers for your firm, it might look something like this.

Revenue	$2,000,000.00
Invoices sent	639
Average project value	$3,129.89
Number of clients	192
Number of projects per client	3.3
Average fee per client	$10,416.67

You have low attrition because of high financial intimacy. You get higher financial intimacy by delivering amazing service and making sure to "provide every service to every client that helps them achieve their goals."

Keep a Watchful Eye on Clients Every Day

I love the way Cloud technology is shaping the future of the accounting profession. I love it because for the first time in history you can "see" what is happening in your client base as it is happening. If the client is on a Cloud accounting system, as they are transacting every day, their software is automatically being updated with those transactions.

"One of the challenges you'll have when a lot of your clients migrate their old systems to the new Cloud system is the volume of data that you can now potentially see."

As they make a sale, buy inventory, pay an invoice, or receive money from a customer, it is all getting updated. Since you are the trusted advisor, you have access to their accounting system. That means you can go and look into their finances every day, if you choose. If you wanted to look, you could spot trends, issues, and opportunities. With your analytical accounting hat on, you could even predict major issues before they happened. It is hard to do that if your client is on an old-fashioned, hard-drive-based accounting system.

This is a good reason to promote Cloud accounting to your clients. One of the challenges you'll have when a lot of your clients migrate their old systems to the new Cloud system is the volume of data that you can now potentially see.

You can overcome this by consolidating all your clients' Cloud data (from multiple accounting packages) into one easy-to-read dashboard.

When you see what is going on (good and bad) you could send them a quick email or text or call them in for a meeting if something "untoward" is happening. You might have noticed that sales have dropped, inventory has risen, receivables have increased, and cash has gone down. It looks like they are in for a cash flow grind if they are not already in one.

This sort of intelligence is cool, and it will help you deliver the ultimate in client service.

For more than 20 years, I have been advocating that you need to be proactive. It's actually quite hard and frustrating to get accountants to do that. With cool new dashboarding tools that alert you to what is going on, you no longer need to be proactive. All you need to do is react (tongue firmly in cheek) to what you see in front of you. Just do it every day!

Delivering WOW Every Day

As you've already read, I have been telling accountants to be proactive and add value ever since I started working with them in 1994.

You need to, and your clients want you to be **proactive and add value**. That means the level of WOW needs to improve.

As mentioned previously, the main reason clients stay with you is because of financial intimacy. They leave you for another firm because of the following reasons.

1. **Service**—the client service experience was poor.
2. **Services**—the value for money was poor, or they thought they needed more but were not getting it.

> "If an accountant sees an issue or opportunity in the client details, then they are obliged to tell the client."

The services must be complete ("provide every service to every client that helps them achieve their goals") and the customer service must be WOW.

Here's the thing. If accountants see an issue or opportunity in the client details, then they are obliged to tell the client. The problem is most accountants are "store blind" and are not focused on seeing ways to really help clients.

Here are some quick thoughts on how you can add value to what you are doing.

1. Offer free phone calls, emails, and meetings all year.
2. Conduct a business performance review every year with every client.
3. Conduct a finding opportunities, brainstorming exercise on every client every year.
4. Create a closed networking group on one of the social media platforms and connect your clients.
5. Visit every client two times per year (free) to see how you can help.
6. Call every client four times per year (free) to touch base and see how they are doing.
7. Run client advisory boards to get feedback from clients on how you can improve.
8. Run seminars and workshops and teach the clients something new.

I came up with that list in five minutes! Ask your team what else you can do and create your adding value list. Your team might focus on customer service ideas like the following.

✓ Offer beverages and food with a menu upon arrival.

✓ Follow up on every interaction with a quick call.

✓ Write a thank-you note when the clients pay their bills on time.

> "Call every client four times per year (free) to touch base and see how they are doing."

✓ Remember their names when they come in.

✓ Put their name on the "welcome board" for every visit.

✓ Have a "candy salad" on the front counter.

✓ Call them on their birthday.

✓ Send cards/gifts at appropriate times throughout the year.

✓ Have fresh flowers in the office.

✓ Send snippets from newspapers/magazines that might interest them.

✓ Let your clients know when you'll be finishing their projects and exceeding the deadlines.

✓ Return phone calls and other communication the same day.

I am sure your team can come up with many more. The service levels in the profession are fairly poor, so it's not hard to deliver WOW service every day.

When you get a lead for a new client, you are so excited. It's almost like a potential new love has entered your life. To seal the deal you really "woo" the potential client in the dating period, and you dance for a few weeks while you make all sorts of promises. Finally, he commits to being engaged to you and agrees to your promises and charm. You are even more excited. The moment of truth is about to happen—marriage. The client signs your engagement letter and you send the mandatory ethical clearance letter to the previous accountant. Although you might not show it at the time, you are probably having a party on the inside, as your excitement levels hit an all-time high. You are ecstatic—you have just signed a new $20,000 per year client, and you proudly tell your other partners of your lovemaking and courting prowess. They are equally impressed, and they secretly wish they had your skills because they did not bring in any new clients this week.

And then it turns horribly wrong.

The client thought you would be doing the work (you didn't tell him otherwise), however he is handed to an "underling," who he has not met—sometimes the work is outsourced overseas without the client even knowing. The client finds that dealing with the front office customer service is less than cordial—he never met that person either. The initial work takes an inordinate amount of time to get done (again you didn't tell him otherwise), with constant back and forth of information needed (why can't you do it in one go, your client wonders). Finally, the draft work arrives for signing, and then a finished copy arrives some weeks later.

During the course of the year, the client calls you from time to time; however, he hesitates to do so because every time he does, he gets a bill. When the client comes to see you, he does not spend much time on chitchat, he gets right down to business because he knows you charge by the hour. You told the client you would be

> "You are ecstatic—you have just signed a new $20,000 per year client and you proudly tell your other partners of your lovemaking and courting prowess."

"proactive" in your advice, yet all the client ever receives is a useless newsletter and letters from time to time when the government changes the compliance rules. You never randomly call the client to see how he is doing and heaven forbid, you never visit the client—you would have to charge for that!

You say you have good relationships with your clients, yet how can you when you deal with them in this way?

Building enduring client relationships is all about how you deal with your clients and how you communicate with them.

So how do you define a great client relationship? I think a definition of a great client relationship is when . . .

"Clients call you before they do things where you are the expert."

From the outset, you need client service performance standards. Your performance standards will define the way you work with your clients. Once you have developed your performance standards (remember, it is your business, so you design them anyway you want), you should promote them at every opportunity. In particular, as part of your client induction process, each client should be stepped through each performance standard.

> "In particular, as part of your client induction process, each client should be stepped through each performance standard."

Here is an example of 12 critical performance standards that you can duplicate and use!

Performance standards

1. We lead the business community by example by running exceptionally well rub business
2. You will always know the price and scope of every project before we start
3. You will be totally delighted with what we do and how we do it – if you are not then there will be no change for that project
4. You will be greeted and farewelled by name with eye contact and with a smile
5. If at fault, we will apologize and make restitution the same day
6. You will never receive a 'financial surprise' from the tax department or other financial institutions
7. We will proactively communicate to you for free whilst we follow our 10 step client communication process
8. Once all your information is received you will receive your complete project within 10 working days
9. You will always fully understand what we say because we do not use technical jargon when communicating with you
10. We will always tell you the 'candid truth' so you can make the right decisions
11. Any queries or complaints are owned by the team member who receives them and are addressed within the same business day that they are received
12. We always reply to all communication by the end of the same business day that it was received

---

It's a "sea of sameness" out there when it comes to accounting firms. Each one looks and acts the same. If you want to differentiate, then it will not be via the quality of your work. Each firm says its work is of the highest quality, yet how would the client know if it is or is not when you have a disclaimer on everything—you don't even think the work is correct!

> "The only way that you can differentiate is by building an enduring relationship with the client while giving them outstanding client service."

Your Clients on Your Terms

It's interesting how accounting firms evolve with their clients. It seems that throughout the years, the clients have just "turned up" (via referral mainly), and you have accepted all who walk through your door. It's almost as if your firm is a community service or a charity. As time passes, the clients stay with you and many of them are not that enjoyable to deal with. Many of your current clients do not fit your direction, and they supply information in a format and time frame that suits them. It's not your clients' business, it's your business!

It's time to take control of your clients and redesign the clients (and their behavior) you want to work with.

Taking Control

Why is it that accountants' work in progress (WIP) management is well above 10 days and receivables are more than 10 days of revenue? There is only one person to blame—you.

Typically, the client controls the cash flow of the firm. It has everything to do with the way the firm sets the client up, explains the rules (or lack thereof), and then works with the client. Remember, it's your business, not your clients' business. The relationship needs to be on your terms.

Consider this. Clients are accepted into the firm by referral (normally because they are unhappy with the current accountant), and the new accountant sends an engagement letter (in most cases only because he has to, according to professional body rulings) explaining charge rates (not a fixed price for the project) and broadly how the firm works with new clients. The client might or might not sign this letter.

When it comes time to do the work, the accountant might send out a simple letter or checklist (most cases she does not) and generally the accountant simply "lets" the client send in the work in a format that the client chooses in a time frame that the client chooses. The new work (called work in progress—WIP) arrives and an accountant picks up the work to get started. As the accountant gets into the job, she realizes that something is missing. So she puts the job down, communicates with the client about the missing information, and then waits. A few weeks (sometimes months) pass and the missing information turns up. The accountant picks the job back up, reacquaints herself with it, starts doing some more work, and then realizes something else is missing. Damn it! She puts the job back down, communicates again with the client, and then waits some more. Finally, the other missing pieces turn up and the job is completed.

> "The most efficient firms (in turnaround time per job) are limiting each accountant to work on no more than three jobs at a time."

While all this madness is going on, an accountant can be working on 15–30 jobs at a time—called "open jobs."

I was once in an accountants' office (four partners and 20 accountants) and casually asked, "How many open jobs do you have at the moment?" "No idea," was the response. With a few keystrokes of the computer, they worked out that they had 440 open jobs! That's a whopping 22 open jobs per accountant. "Let's take a look," I requested. We went past the façade of reception and into the engine room. You could see the open jobs. There was stuff all over the place. One said, "Wait, there's more." One of the partners opened a cupboard door and there was more of it piled high on shelves. At that moment, it started to fall out onto the floor. What a mess!

A couple of days later, I was at a dinner party and I met a dentist. I was telling the dentist about the firm I had just visited and the number of open jobs they had at any one time. He said, "That would be like me having five patients on five different chairs at the same time—no wonder they're inefficient."

You can't make this stuff up.

The most efficient firms (in turnaround time per job) are limiting each accountant to work on no more than three jobs at a time and focusing on fewer than 10-days average workflow turnaround time for all jobs in the shop. I met a partner of a firm the other day, and he has his accountants work on only one job at a time—turnaround time is fewer than three days average for all jobs. Now that's customer service!

In addition to having too many open jobs per accountant, I also find that fully trained accountants are doing a lot of administrative work associated with the job—sometimes up to three hours per accountant per day. An example of administrative work (that needs to be done—just not by an accountant) is setting up work papers, collecting information from clients, chasing missing information, data entry, making appointments, monitoring and managing workflow, filing, lodging work, and generally advising clients of *mundane information—such as their tax file number!*

As I have coached firms throughout the years, I developed a list of 30 standard administrative tasks (associated with accounting work) with on average 22 of them being done on a regular basis by accountants. When we do time and motion studies in firms, we find that on average each accountant spends one-and-a half hours per day doing (our definition of) administrative tasks—sometimes up to three hours per person per day. If a working year is 225 days, then that is 337 hours per accountant per year doing things that they should not be doing. If you have 10 accountants, that's 3,337 hours per year at an average hourly rate (let's say) of $200. That's a huge $674,000 per year in opportunity cost. A small firm of 10 accountants might only have revenue of $2.5M and to have 27 percent opportunity cost is just incredible.

> "An example of administration work (that needs to be done—just not by an accountant) is setting up work papers, collecting information from clients, and chasing missing information."

What an Opportunity!

You can unleash this opportunity cost by employing specialized administrative people—what I like to call client service coordinators (CSCs). If your accountants are spending one-and-a half hours on average doing these administrative tasks, then you will need one CSC per five accountants. The CSC job is to keep the accountants busy by freeing them from the administrative tasks associated with the accounting job.

If you think of your accounting business like a manufacturing business, then you will manage your workflow management process vastly differently from the way you do now—and become more efficient in the process.

> "If you think of your accounting business like a manufacturing business, then you will manage your workflow management process vastly differently."

In a manufacturing business, the salesperson (partner or client manager) scopes and sells the product; they then give the order to the manufacturing manager (CSC) who manages the overall production. The manufacturing manager (CSC) works out what raw materials are needed, has those gathered by the warehouse person (CSC), and sets the job up on the manufacturing line. The manufacturing team (accountants) produces the product, and then it goes to the quality control manager (client manager) for final sign off. The shipping manager (CSC) sends the product to the client and the salesperson (partner or client manager) follows up to add some value and sell the next product.

Eighteen-Step Workflow Process

If workflow is like manufacturing, then you'll realize that there are four parts to efficient workflow.

1. **Selling.** Selling the value of the job, getting client sign off before beginning.
2. **Setup.** Collecting all the raw materials and getting the job ready to action.
3. **Doing.** Creating the product.
4. **Selling.** Presenting the finished product, selling the next project, and asking for a referral.

To make workflow make sense in an accounting business, here is an 18-step workflow process that when implemented drives faster turnaround time, less time on the job, exceptional cash flow, and high client satisfaction.

18 steps workflow process

Steps in process	Who manages or does
1. Schedule the work in advance-using calendar system	Client Service Coordinator (CSC)
2. Meet with client to scope and sell the value of the job	Partner or Client Manager
3. Value price the job, communicate in writing (scope & price) to client	Partner or Client Manager
4. Client signs off on scope/price and pays deposit or full amount	Client Service Coordinator
5. Send checklist and gather raw materials	Client Service Coordinator
6. Check everything has been received	Client Service Coordinator
7. Contact the client for any missing information	Client Service Coordinator
8. Log the job onto your electronic and visual workflow system	Client Service Coordinator
9. Do a draft internal team budget-in hours	Client Service Coordinator
10. Set up the electronic workpapers-basic data entry	Client Service Coordinator
11. Challenge the hours budget (drive time down), lock in max time	Client Manager/Accountant & CSC
12. Allocate & explain the job to the person doing the work	Client Manager
13. Do the job & find any Awesome 8 opportunities for the client	Accountant
14. Communicate any technical queries to client & then finish job	Client Manager and Accountant
15. Review the job and fully understand Awesome 8 opportunities	Client Manager and Accountant
16. Print/Collate/Bind/Prepare final Invoice/File	Client Service Coordinator
17. Meet Client-present job, explain new ideas and sell next job	Partner or Client Manager
18. Ask for a referral at least one per year- and follow up!	Partner or Client Manager

If we go back to our selling, setup, doing, and selling process then.

➢ Steps 1–4—Selling
➢ Steps 5–12—Setup
➢ Steps 13–16—Doing
➢ Steps 17–18—Selling

Follow all 18 steps in sequence. You can blend them together, but don't miss any!

A sole practitioner (Brian) with $500K in fees joined our coachingclub program and at that time his total lock-up (WIP and receivables combined) was more than 200 days. It was his first meeting and I told him he needed to reduce this dramatically in the next 90 days. By the time the next meeting rolled around, he had reduced it to about 50 days—combined. Amazed at the result, I asked how he did it and how much time he spent

"I have $100,000 extra in the bank." I responded with, "WOW, $100,000 for 40 hours of work. At $2,500 per hour, a good use of your time, Brian."

reducing it—I was hoping he had not written it all off! He told me he went line by line through his WIP ledger, billed everything he could, and then put in place a diligent collection process. Total time of 40 hours worked during a three-month period. I then asked what the material benefit was to the firm. Brian answered with, "I have $100,000 extra in the bank." I responded with, "WOW, $100,000 for 40 hours of work. At $2,500 per hour, a good use of your time, Brian."

Here's an update on this story.

I checked Brian's figures (now a two-partner, $1.5M firm) on our online monitoring and benchmarking system and his lock-up is typically 39 days—14 days in WIP and 25 in receivables. He cleaned it up once and kept it there.

Take control of your workflow and re-educate your clients on the way that you want to work with them. Change the system to suit your terms and be strong. It's your business, not your clients!

Finding Opportunities

There is a massive amount of value in compliance accounting! It's the perfect lead generator.

Oh, I have wanted to say that for a long time!

> "There is a massive amount of value in compliance accounting! It's the perfect lead generator."

You see, there is a massive amount of value in compliance—however, rarely does the accountant understand the value in compliance and as such neither does the client. So, while the client does not understand the value, then they will always see it as a grudge purchase.

If you make the invisible visible (meaning explain what is in the bound-up paperwork), then you and your client will understand the value. It's a simple process of thinking about the value the clients get out of their annual compliance accounts—and then explaining it to them.

If you really think about it, here is the value of compliance to the client. My (client speaking here) annual "have to" compliance records help me to . . .

✓ Understand my business better.

✓ Have comparisons from one year to the next.

- ✓ See trends.
- ✓ Make management decisions going forward.
- ✓ Plan for the future by analyzing the past.
- ✓ Use as a basis to improve my cash flow.
- ✓ See where the money went.
- ✓ Improve my profitability.
- ✓ Value my business.
- ✓ Bring on a successor or sell my business.
- ✓ Increase my wealth.
- ✓ Improve my lifestyle—as a result of all the above.

> "Now, few clients realize that what is seen as a grudge purchase is actually a hidden treasure trove of ideas, strategies, plans, and a MASSIVE AMOUNT OF VALUE."

Now, few clients realize that what is seen as a grudge purchase is actually a hidden treasure trove of ideas, strategies, plans, and a MASSIVE AMOUNT OF VALUE.

As a client, I will always think it is a grudge purchase if you have never explained it to me. Message to self—please explain it to me. Your clients are not accountants—they do not understand this stuff.

What other opportunities are there in compliance?

Here's a short story from a few years ago. True story of what my business looked like then.

I am a typical client of yours. I am a small to midsize business (SMB) that employs 15 people. With my previous accountant, I was paying about $4,000 per year for compliance-only services. I switched accountants three years ago, and in the past three years I have gladly paid the new firm $219,650—about $73K per year—or an 18-times increase in fees. Before you say, "We'll do it for less"—I am not interested. I am deliriously happy with what I have bought from the new firm . . . and it wasn't all compliance.

Recently I was running a workshop (about 60 people or so) with one firm, and I asked the partners and accountants (after I told them my story), "How many clients do you think you have that you could increase their fees by 10 times?"

Many of them looked at me strangely, but after some pressing I got their answers—and as you can imagine the answers were 1, 2 ,4, 5, or maybe 10 clients at a push—low numbers.

I then told them that they just prejudged their entire client base. The real answer is that you have no idea who needs what, and what they will pay for it.

I then educated the group on potential other services (and how you take them to clients) that can eventuate from compliance if . . .

> "I then told them that they just prejudged their entire client base. The real answer is you have no idea who needs what, and what they will pay for it."

1. You spend some time thinking about what additional services the client needs.

2. You go to the client with some conversation starters (ideas) and then ask leading questions that identify THEIR opportunities and THEIR issues that need to be acted on.

3. You then design a service offering to match their needs.

4. You articulate the value of those additional services to the client.

5. You price the new services based on value—not time charged.

6. You write an implementation plan (with options that the client can take) and present it to the client.

7. Client picks an option—your team does the work. Everyone happy!

The workshop exercise was with real client files. We worked on 12 typical clients and between us we had solutions (initially conversation starters) that the partners could take to them. I called the exercise finding opportunities in compliance.

The idea of the exercise is that you brainstorm potential conversation starters with the client. As an example, you might find opportunities in . . .

➤ Sales or breakeven analysis.
➤ Benchmarking on expenses, revenues, margins.
➤ Gross profit analysis.
➤ Any trends—year to year.
➤ Marketing analysis and expenses.
➤ Number of clients.
➤ Frequency of purchase per client.
➤ Average spend per client.

- Insurance spend.
- Cash flow—tax interest payments, bank interest, overdraft (OD).
- Receivable or payable days.
- Tax structuring.
- Debt or equity structuring.

With these ideas, they brainstormed each client. Then I asked the question again—now, if you follow my process, how many clients could you increase the fee by 10 times?

This time the minimum score was 20 percent of clients they could increase the fee by 10 times. WOW. A re-education process, the clients are better serviced, and you get a higher fee with a much higher margin.

Within the process, there were also role plays, scripting, proposal templates, questions to ask, and interview techniques.

I think the thinking has gone out of accounting. Years ago, when it was ink/lead and paper, the accountant had to think about the client situation. Now the software does the thinking. It's time to bring the thinking back into accounting.

> "If you spent just 20 minutes on each client at the end of the compliance project and brainstormed what else you could do for the client, you are sure to find additional ideas to deliver."

If you spent just 20 minutes on each client at the end of the compliance project and brainstormed what else you could do for the client, you are sure to find additional ideas to deliver. Gather a small team of four and the person who knows the client the best shows the set of accounts to the others in their team. They explain the client situation and then the four of them brainstorm what else you could do. Under the guise of The Awesome 8, new ideas and services will flow that you can take to clients.

We have done this exercise with more than 2,000 accountants in the past 10 years. So far there is a 100 percent success rate. With a group of 12 accountants in Sweden, we had three teams and three different clients. The first team found one idea, the second team found four ideas, and the third team found eight ideas. In 20 minutes, we found 13 potential projects in three clients.

The new mindset is that **there is another project in the current project.**

It's a duty of care that the profession has to make sure all clients are properly serviced. They need to be buying all projects from you that help them achieve their goals.

They Should All Be A-Class Clients

Every client you have should be an A-class client.

You have all sorts of clients. Some have great potential—they are open to new ideas, pay their bills on time, are pleasant to your team, and are generally great to deal with—they might be your A-class clients. Others have no potential, are close-minded, moan and groan about everything, and a general pain in the rear—they might be classed as a D-class clients.

There is no right or wrong criteria—each firm is different with the types of clients they want to deal with.

If I was running an accounting firm, here are my criteria for an ideal client.

1. It is an existing trading business with employees—not a startup.
2. The business has potential.
3. The business makes an existing profit (pick a number!).
4. The business type is in line with my niche market(s) that I want to serve.
5. The owners are ambitious.
6. The owners are open to new ideas.
7. The owners are nice people to deal with.
8. They understand and play by my rules—pay me on time, adhere to my workflow requests, etc.
9. I can make more than 80 percent gross profit (client fee less direct labor costs) on the client.
10. They are not "price shoppers" looking for the cheapest accounting firm.

> "Every client you have should be an A-class client."

That would be my list—you make up your own criteria. Whatever your ideal list, my guess is that only 20 percent (or less) of your current client base fit your new criteria. My guess is also that your current 20 percent represent about 80 percent of your fee base—or at least a substantial part. So, the question is begging to be asked—**Why do you keep the rest?**

Normally you keep the rest because of cash flow reasons. If you just had one criteria of profit per client (your profit, that is), then you would be staggered by how unprofitable most of your clients are. Do this exercise. Put all your clients into a spreadsheet with the following four columns.

Client Name	Annual Fee	Total Hours to Deliver Annual Fee	Average Hourly Rate

Divide the annual fee by the total hours and you can work out the average hourly rate per client.

If you had a firm-wide average hourly rate (revenue divided by client hours charged—so if your revenue was $2M and you had 10,000 client hours charged, then your firm-wide average hourly rate would be $200) of say $200, then you will find that your client range would be from about $100 to $300. Many of your clients would be well below your average—some of your largest clients (by fee) will be under the average.

Maybe you need to have a discussion that goes something like this with clients that you are undercharging.

"Mr. and Mrs. Smith, we are thrilled that you have been a client of the firm for the past 10 years. You are great to deal with and we appreciate your business. What we have found, after some careful analysis, is that we have actually been undercharging you for the past 10 years—by about 30 percent per year. What we are not going to do is send you a whopping great big bill to rectify the problem. That's our mistake and your gain. Going forward, however, your work needs to be charged at X, otherwise I am sorry we cannot do your work anymore."

Give your C-class and D-class clients a shot at being A-class and B-class clients. If you communicate your new direction and criteria, they might want to play ball—at least give them

> "Give your C-class and D-class clients a shot at being A-class and B-class clients. If you communicate your new direction and criteria, they might want to play ball—at least give them a chance."

a chance. If they do not want to be on the new team, then get rid of them—quickly. They are sapping business oxygen from you and your team. They are making you miserable, and they are sending you to the poorhouse.

Your decisions of the past got you where you are today. So be it. You can always change. It does take some courage to change, however, if you remember that you are only on this planet once (OK, some would say otherwise) and it is your business, then why not change? Why not take some courage pills and let them go? It is a cathartic experience to ask a client to leave. The angst, energy, and frustration caused by clients you do not want to deal with can be an enormous drain on team morale and sanity.

While I'm at it, most of your new business clients come from referrals. Make sure you never accept a referral from a D-class client—their friends are also idiots!

One of our coachingclub members started his journey years ago with 256 clients—all types of clients accepted by the firm throughout many years. The firm made a conscious decision to set a criterion for the type of work it wanted to do for clients—which was a minimum of quarterly reporting. The partners communicated with all their clients to see who wanted the new level of service. Most did not, so they were referred to other accounting firms. They also educated their referral sources (bankers, brokers, lawyers, etc.) of their new direction and asked them to only refer prospects who fit their criteria. After a lot of culling, they ended up with 109 clients and an average fee of $32,000. Profit at this stage was running at about 40 percent. Eighteen months later (after joining coachingclub), they did another cull and now they have 70 clients with an average fee of $45,000. Their profit now runs about 50 percent.

> "Make sure you never accept a referral from a D-class client—their friends are also idiots."

Take charge. Make some decisions and design your client base with who you want to deal with in the manner you want to deal with them. I'll say it again—**it's your business, not your clients' business.**

Clients Wants or Needs

If you have gotten this far, you would realize that clients want **service** and **services** from you. They want a better client service, with a few extra services at good value for money. The client **wants** these things. Is that what they **need?**

I am suggesting that clients need more than they get from you. However, generally the client dictates the terms—what they want from you. You are the expert in what you do, so how would the client know what they need?

To give clients what they need, you have to find out what they need. If you find out what they need (over and above the mandatory compliance), then you will build a stronger relationship with them. If you build a stronger relationship, you will have more loyalty. If you have more loyalty, you will get more referrals. More referrals come with a choice of who you work with and a larger more profitable business.

> "If you find out what they need (over and above the mandatory compliance), then you will build a stronger relationship with them."

If all you deliver to a client is the bare necessity of compliance, then that is equivalent to a grudge purchase. A client does not want compliance—they have to buy it. Compliance-based services are part of the cost structure of doing business.

Remember this.

"If you are part of costs, they can easily get rid of you.

If you are part of profit, then they can't get enough of you."

What does that mean?

If you are focusing on what clients think they want (costs), then they can get rid of you. If you are really helping them to improve their condition (profit), then they can't get enough of you.

So how do you find what clients need?

Simple—ask them! However, you are not about to say, "What do you need?" You see, this is the tricky bit—they do not know what they need. You have to be investigative and ask lots of leading questions before you determine what they need.

You can be investigative when you are doing other work for them. As you do the compliance work, think about the clients' situations and come up with some new ideas that you can take to them.

One of our coachingclub members (Craig) came up with a simple but powerful idea. What he did was incorporate The Awesome 8 into his end-of-job process. So as the accountants are finalizing the work and filling in the checklist, the accountants have to fill in some extra answers to questions.

> "You have to be investigative and ask lots of leading questions before you determine what they need."

The accountants are trained to look for opportunities as they do the work and then it goes into the review process. The client manager adds their ideas and a meeting is called with the client to present the potential opportunities.

Graphically Craig's process would look like this.

Finding Opportunities in Compliance

1. • Train accountants to look for opportunities while they are doing the work

2. • Add it to your review process – what other opportunities can you identify for the client?

3. • Get the Client Manager or Partner to add their ideas

4. • Have a meeting with your clients and present the opportunities you've identified with ideas on what they can do

To make this happen what you have to do is have your accountants ask questions on every single client project that they work on. You need to make this part of the review process. That means you will not review the job until the questions are answered.

Here are the nine key questions to ask on every single client you work with.

1. What ideas do you have to help this client **grow** revenue or wealth?
2. What ideas do you have to help this client increase **profit?**
3. What ideas do you have to help this client understand and improve **cash flow?**
4. What ideas do you have to help this client **protect** assets?
5. What ides do you have to help this client with **succession** planning or selling the business?
6. What ideas do you have to minimize **tax** for this client in the future?
7. What ideas do you have to help this client to financially **retire?**
8. What ideas do you have to help this client with **estate planning?**
9. What other opportunities are there to provide extra services to this client that he or she is not already using?

> "You have to be investigative and ask lots of leading questions before you determine what they need."

Changing Accountants—Part 1

I was running a teleseminar with more than 500 firms listening. I was interviewing an accountant (Shane) who specialized in medical businesses. He said that he dedicated every Wednesday to visiting his clients at no cost. The purpose of the meeting was to find out what the clients needed and if appropriate, to sell additional services to satisfy their needs. My existing accountant at the time (Peter) was listening in, and he called me immediately after the meeting and said that it was a great idea to visit clients and he should start with me. I had been Peter's client for 11 years and never once had he visited me—even though for nine of those years my office was no more than 1 mile from his office. I guess it was too far to walk. I was paying Peter for compliance-based services only. That night I went home to my wife and said, "You're not going to believe this, but Peter is coming to visit me next Tuesday—I think he is getting better!"

So Peter turns up and I did what clients do. I explained my business, showed off my premises, and indicated I had a few problems. I told him I had some overseas income coming in and didn't know what to do with it. I told him I wanted a referral to a lawyer, as I felt I needed to do some intellectual property protection and I questioned if my structure was right for tax effectiveness. Peter said, "I'll get right on it." That was in October, and by April the following year I had had enough of waiting for Peter to get right on it, so I left and found a more proactive accountant.

Changing Accountants—Part 2

I know thousands of accountants, and I finally chose a three-partner firm I liked. I called the first meeting and told my new accountant (Matt, the partner) that the first project he needed to work on was tax planning—I am a proactive client. Matt dismissed my request and said, "Before we get into tax planning, let me understand everything about the Nixon Group—what you have now and what your objectives are." He was in control of the meeting at this point. Matt drew a line two-thirds of the way across on my whiteboard. On the left side, he wrote "now" and started asking my wife and me a whole series of questions about our structures, profit, cash flow, kids, wills, assets, liabilities, insurances, and so on. He drew diagrams and pictures and when it all unfolded I turned to Nat and said, "What a bloody mess that is." Nothing seemed to link together or resemble any sort of order. Matt ignored my comment.

> "If you ask the right questions in the right order you will find out what your clients really need—not what they want?"

He then went to the final third of the whiteboard and drew a large "T." On the left, he wrote "Rob," and on the right, he wrote "Nat." He then asked a whole series of questions about our goals and ambitions. He started with my wife, then me. The whiteboard was eventually filled. He then said the following, which I will always remember, ***"You have great goals and ambitions and to achieve them you need to be financially well organized. You are not financially well organized; you are financially disorganized. Your structures are not right, you have debt in the wrong places, your wills are out of date, you do not have the right share structure, and your trusts are not set up for maximum tax*** *effectiveness. With every new client (and every three years thereafter) we make sure you are financially well organized from the outset. We will work with you to get this right so your estates are looked after and you are set up for maximum tax effectiveness. Our fee to do this is $10K (I was thinking $15K) plus legal fees to get this right—when do you want to get started?"*

I said yes, and that's how we started a great relationship.

If you ask the right questions in the right order, you will find out what your clients really need—not what they want. Not doing so is doing your clients a complete disservice.

Let's Make Some Targeted Noise

Your Marketing Objectives

The strategy of growing a business is relatively simple. If you know who your target market is, if you have an active **database** of them, if you have a healthy **brand,** and you do loads of **activity,** then you'll win business and grow. The database needs to be of your target market, clean and complete. You brand needs to stand for something and the activity must invoke a response.

What's the point of having a great service offering, fantastic client results, great people, and an inspiring vision if only you and your team know about it? Your business might be a finely tuned instrument, but if it is not played in the orchestra then no one will hear it.

> "The purpose of marketing is to sell your message in a leveraged way so that people respond to it."

It's time to make some noise, make some music, and tell the world (including your existing clients) how good you are and what you can do for them. It's time to do some marketing!

Before I get into my definition of marketing, I need to clear up a misconception in the marketplace as to what marketing is and what the purpose is. Many people think marketing is all about "getting the word out there," or "building awareness," or "branding." Yes, they are all important and they need to be done. However, unless you understand the core purpose of marketing and what it is all about, you will waste a lot of time and a lot of money on activities that do not work.

My definition of marketing is this: **"Marketing is salesmanship multiplied."** The purpose of marketing is to sell your message in a leveraged way so that people respond to it. The purpose of marketing is to invoke a response—hopefully a positive one.

If you think a billboard/ad/flyer with your firm's name, a catchy phrase, and a picture of your partners sells what your firm can do for me, then good luck to you. It's not going to work. The only people who get excited by that are the partners—provided the photo is good. It'll be a waste of time and a BIG waste of money. But the partners will feel good.

> "If you think a six-page, full-color brochure of your people, the brand values, your premises, your services offered, and how many years you have been in business is going to work, then think again."

If you think a six-page, full-color brochure of your people, the brand values, your premises, your services offered, and how many years you have been in business is going to work, then think again. Again, you'll feel good about the glossy brochure, but it won't work.

Everything you do in your marketing efforts must be about sales in a leveraged way. By leverage, I mean the medium you use (email, video, paper, seminar, etc.) and the number of people who see it.

The message you need to be selling is social proof and the results the clients get when they use you. In other words, by responding to your promotion how will the client be better off? It's all about the radio station that has been around since the dawn of the slate tablet—WIIFM—what's in it for me?

Q. Why should I inquire?

Q. Why should I respond?

Q. Why should I download?

Q. Why should I attend?

I don't care that you have been in business since 1973 and you are all CPA's. What I care about is the value to me!

With my definition as salesmanship multiplied, it is not a marketing function to make a sale. Few people buy professional services from a marketing message. They buy professional services from a person.

The job of the marketing message is to sell the idea that I should respond to find out more. .... Hmmm, that sounds good; I'll make an inquiry/click the button/attend the seminar/pick up the phone, and make contact.

Marketing is about selling a dream, hope, and just maybe. As I said, marketing is about invoking a response. In other words, marketing needs to be in the style of direct response. You send out a marketing message, and you get a response. Branding is important, and it must be done but it shouldn't be the primary focus.

> "To grow your numbers, you'll certainly need the right skills, the right tools, and the right people in place."

Direct response marketing has been around a long time, and any seasoned marketer will tell you that it is not an instant gratification process. It takes time. It doesn't work the first time. I hear so many partners of firms say, "We sent out one invite to my seminar and it didn't work." And then they give up. Paaalllleeeese!

Marketing needs to be a consistent approach that assists in the growing of revenue and profits. There is no point doing marketing when you are quiet. It takes a while to "crank it up." You need to be marketing all the time. That means every day!

Many firms start their marketing journey with no real objectives in mind. Now I know "build brand awareness" and "get our name out there" are objectives, but they are hard to measure (and ALL marketing must be measured) the real objective is to "get their name in here" while you build your brand.

Your marketing assists your sales function. It comes before sales. Marketing generates an inquiry, and then the sales function closes the inquiry into new business. A finely tuned marketing and sales machine can grow all sorts of numbers. To grow your numbers, you'll certainly need the right skills, the right tools, and the right people in place.

At the outset, you need to set your objectives. Which numbers do you want to grow? Take the following chart as an example. Your marketing and sales function combined can directly influence all 15 of these numbers. If you work out what your base is (and it is what it is), then set some targets and get active.

Marketing & Sales Objectives	Now	12 month goal
1. Number of client groups		
2. Number of projects each client buys from you each year		
3. Average project value - $		
4. Average fee per client (2 x 3) - $		
5. Percentage of total revenue in compliance - %		
6. Percentage of total revenue in advisory - %		
7. Average hourly rate / Realization margin in compliance - $		
8. Average hourly rate / Realization margin in advisory - $		
9. Number of new enquiries generated per year		
10. Conversion rate of enquiry to sale		
11. Number of new clients per year		
12. Each client visited / met with – times per year		
13. Number of clients on cloud accounting system		
14. Revenue - $		
15. Profit / EBIT before partner salaries - $		

> "Marketing needs to be a consistent approach that assists in the growing of revenue and profits."

I get asked all the time, "How much marketing should I do?" Or, "When should I hire a marketing person?"

My answer is always the same. It depends what your objectives are. You might think that even with a small growth target of 5 percent that you do not need to do any marketing. Think again. You cannot rely on some reactive referrals and a charge rate increase to grow anymore. I believe you'll need to do some marketing just to maintain your current revenue.

If you wanted to double your current revenue, then the following chart shows what your annual growth rate needs to be.

$1,000,000	Annual growth rate before your revenue doubles 12 month goal					
YEARS	7.5%	10%	12.5%	15%	20%	26%
1	$1,075,000	$1,100,000	$1,125,000	$1,150,000	$1,200,000	$1,260,000
2	$1,155,625	$1,210,000	$1,265,625	$1,322,500	$1,440,000	$1,587,600
3	$1,252,297	$1,331,000	$1,423,828	$1,520,875	$1,728,000	$2,000,376
4	$1,335,469	$1,464,100	$1,601,807	$1,749,006	$2,073,600	
5	$1,435,629	$1,610,510	$1,802,032	$2,011,357		
6	$1,543,302	$1,771,561	$2,027,287			
7	$1,659,049	$1,948,717				
8	$1,783,478	$2,143,589				
9	$1,917,239					
10	$2,061,032					

Growth is a good thing. It shows health, vitality, and innovation. You decide how fast you want to grow during what period of time. Whatever your growth targets are (even if it's a plodding 10 percent goal) you'll more than likely need to do some marketing.

Think of marketing like a wheelbarrow. It only works if you push it. The more marketing you do, the more choices you have.

Niche Markets—Your Best Buyer

"If you are everything to everyone, then you are nothing to nobody." That sums up my thoughts about who you should target as clients. I am a big fan of having clients in niche markets. I am a big fan of knowing who your best buyers are, what they look like, and where they hang out.

To help you determine your best buyers, the key questions to ask are as follows:

If there was a room full of my best buyers . . .

> ➤ What would they look like?
> ➤ Where would they come from?

"Once you understand the demographics of your target market, you can target better, you can become an expert in their industry, and you can command higher fees."

- ➢ What do they do?
- ➢ What are they interested in?
- ➢ What services do they need to buy?
- ➢ What size (revenue/wealth) are they?
- ➢ What age groups are included?
- ➢ What are their risk profiles?
- ➢ What are their ambition levels?

You are describing your ideal client, your best buyer. Once you understand the demographics of your target market, you can target better, you can become an expert in their industry, and you can command higher fees. Ultimately, you are more useful to your clients if you know more about them. Your services can be tailored to your niche. Your marketing can be tailored to your niche.

Your niche could be based on geography, service offering, behavior, industry type, or a mix.

- **Geographic niche**—we are the small business experts in Texas.
- **Services niche**—we help business owners to be financially retired.
- **Behavior niche**—we help entrepreneurs to start and then exit their businesses.
- **Industry niche**—we help restaurateurs to grow and develop their businesses.
- **Mixed niche**—we help entrepreneurial restaurant owners in Texas to start their businesses, develop their businesses, and get them to a point where the owners are financially retired from their businesses.

My niche market is clear to me and my team.

We help accounting firms of all sizes around the world build great businesses for themselves and their clients.

For me, it helps us get focused. We are global. We are servicing accounting firms (not accountants in commerce) of all sizes. We are interested in firms that want to grow and develop their businesses. And we are most interested in firms who want to take business advisory services to their clients.

> "You need to make a difference so they keep paying you and you can get case studies from them."

The articulation of our niche helps us make decisions on product development, marketing, sales, and support.

I have five questions when selecting a niche market to target.

1. **Are there lots of them?** You might like Mangalitsa pigs because they are wooly and a rare breed of animal. I am sure there are farmers who specialize in the growing and developing of said pig. However, I highly doubt there are that many farmers. I think your niche market needs at least 10,000 in your chosen geographical region.

2. **Do they have the ability to pay?** There might be thousands of lawn-mowing people (with the greatest respect to the people that mow our lawns), however, by and large, they don't earn much money and they might not have the ability to pay your fees. You need to select a niche that either has money now or has the ability to make money. You are not a charity!

3. **Can you make a difference to them?** The services you offer your niche need to be valuable services and the success of them (clients' improved conditions) needs to be measured. You need to make a difference so they keep paying you and you can get case studies from them. It also helps with your personal enjoyment.

4. **Are they enjoyable to work with?** You are going to spend a considerable amount of your professional life with these people. You need to at least like their company. Within any demographic, there are always miserable people who are negative whiners and complain about everything. Just cut them out of your list once you find them!

> "When picking your niche, you want to make sure they are going to be in existence in the future."

5. **Are they going to exist in the future?** So many industry/professional types are being marginalized (in some cases, eliminated) by technology. When picking your niche, you want to make sure they are going to be in existence in the future. Or, if they are going to be marginalized, can you help them change their business model so they thrive with your help?

Work out who your best buyers are, what they look like, where they hang out, and go and get them.

You . . . an Object of Interest

People don't buy professional services from "faceless" companies that have no personality. People buy from people they know, like, and trust.

I am about to choose an accounting firm to entrust my financial affairs with. We are about to get "intimate" on my finances, and I want to make sure that you are who you say you are and you are worthy of trusting.

The reason clients stay with accounting firms is not because of the service or the services (however, they will leave if the service or the services are bad); it's because of the financial intimacy that you have with me. You know things about my financial affairs that few people do. Clients are loyal to their accountants, and clients want accountants to be similar to them. Well, sort of like them.

If I am a boring person who likes beige (not to offend anyone who is a beige fan), then I will **not** choose a flamboyant accountant who wears floral, gold bling, and drives a Lamborghini. I would like to choose someone who is a bit more conservative. Maybe that is your target market. Not right, not wrong.

> "Your clients are a reflection of you. They are typically 10 years in age on either side of you, and they act in similar ways to you."

If I am an entrepreneur who likes to be creative, invent new things, and is tech savvy, then I will most certainly **not** pick an accountant who does wear beige, a woolen cardigan, and slip-on, soft sole shoes. I am looking for a bit more pizzazz and flair, some funky offices, and cool people in the workplace.

What if I am a professional and I run a professional services firm? Most are not overly entrepreneurial, and they will be interested in your "heritage." Which schools you went to, what qualifications you have, and which clubs you are part of and so on. They are **not** about to pick the racy, entrepreneurial-type accountant (with sometimes dubious qualifications) who likes to push the envelope.

What if I am a blue-collar worker—a contractor? I am a hard worker who likes to get dirty and who works hard. I might not have a university degree, so I don't want to be intimidated by those who have three degrees.

Your clients are a reflection of you. They are typically 10 years in age on either side of you, and they act in similar ways to you. If you know that, then you can do something about targeting them. You can design your office, your car, your dress sense, your mannerisms, your travel schedule, your service offerings, your team, and your marketing.

You can become an object of interest to your current and future clients.

Accountants are supposed to be the leaders of business. At least that's what the profession would like to think. I think accountants can be leaders of business, but if they are, they need to walk the walk. People like to look up to leaders. They like to put them on a pedestal and admire them.

There's a truth in leadership . . .

> **"In a pack of dogs, if you're not the lead dog,
> then the view is always the same."**

As a leader, you have an obligation to practice what you preach. So do not talk to me about wealth creation if you do not have the signs of wealth. Do not talk to me about business improvement if yours clearly needs improving.

If people like to follow interesting people, then why don't you become one? Why doesn't your firm become interesting?

It's a "sea of sameness" out there, and it doesn't take much to stand out from the crowd.

In many countries, the "tall poppy syndrome" exists. That means that in a field of poppies, the tall flowers get chopped down first. It is real and some people will attempt to "bring you down to size," but hey—are they your target clients? Probably not.

I believe I am an object of interest to a lot of people. I have designed it that way. In doing so **I get hate mail.** It's quite frequent and has been happening for a long period of time. I write and comment on matters in the accounting profession that upset some people. I tend to tell it the way it is, and I am not scared of doing so. The "hate mail" can be in the form of a letter, a fax, a feedback form, an email, and now on social media.

> "Being an object of interest gets you fans and it gets you detractors. Being an object of interest gets you a lot of business."

Sometimes it's a phone call or verbal abuse face to face. I am polite, but they ultimately get the standard response of "delete," and I never hear from them again. Bring on the hate mail, I say. Everyone is entitled to their opinion. And by all means, give me yours. I know I am right and the "hate mailer" is wrong. I know what I stand for and I am not afraid to say it.

Being an object of interest gets you fans and it gets you detractors. Being an object of interest gets you a lot of business.

Web Dominance

I am willing to bet that the vast majority of clients you currently have were referred to you by an existing client. A referral from a trusted source is a powerful marketing tool. That method of "lead source" will continue into the future. However, it's changing—and fast. There are still people involved and now so is the Internet.

The Internet is a massive connection tool. It connects people, devices, opinions, *thoughts, interests, hobbies, and information. It can be a platform for building a brand and destroying a brand—* sometimes in the same day. People (prospective team members, alliances, or vendors) can "check you out" before doing business with you. The Internet is where we go to search, explore, and generally get any information about anything we want. It's an awesome way to distribute content. It's an amazing way to promote your business. It is your "shop window" to the world.

> "The Internet is there to be leveraged. If you really want to grow your firm, then you need to **dominate the Web.**"

What does your Internet presence say about you and your firm?

If I search your name or your firm's name, what do I find? Do I find you at all? When I do find you? Do I see a website that is old, tired, and looks like it was a "template" site? Or do I find a modern site that encourages me to stay for a while and get engaged? Do you only have one site, or do you have multiple sites? Are you only on LinkedIn, or can I find you on other social media platforms? Can I experience some of your content (or your most recent speech) on YouTube, and can I see cases studies and testimonials of your clients somewhere?

The Internet is there to be leveraged. If you really want to grow your firm then you need to **dominate the Web.** You need to dominate your space that you want to operate in.

When I go on any popular platform and search for you, your business, or your product/service, then I find you. You're on the first page of your Internet browser, and you seem to be "everywhere." I can view a video, download an opinion paper, use a calculator on your website, or read an article or your most recent blog post.

I get accountants who say, "Do you think it is worthwhile having a presence on Facebook, Twitter, and LinkedIn?" Please do not ask me that question again. Yes, yes, and yes. It is not one platform—it is all platforms.

The following table shows a scoring system on each of the main areas you need to dominate. The first thing you need to do is mark in each box where you're currently at.

- Nonexistent—self-explanatory—you have nothing in this channel.

- Existent—you have a presence in this channel.

- Competitive—you are there and you are competitive against others in the same channel.

> "What does your Internet presence say about you and your firm?"

- Distinct—you are there and you are different from others in the same channel.

- Breakthrough—you are leading the charge and doing something different in this channel.

Web dominance					
Web strategy	Non-existent	Existent	Competitive	Distinct	Breakthrough
Main website					
Feeder sites					
Blog(s)					
Facebook					
Twitter					
Linkedin					
YouTube					
E-news					
Forum – connecting					
Search Engine Optimization					
Social advertising					
Other people's blog					
Content marketing					

Let's look at each one.

Main Website

The best main websites are those that have client case studies (video preferable), people (with photos) who can help me, content I can download/view, loads of testimonials/case studies, sign-up pages to newsletters, outcomes of buying services from you, and, most important, they are not boring. Make it fun, interactive, and remember it is your shop window and a sales tool.

Feeder Sites

Why limit yourself to just one website? Why not have other sites that are selling parts of what you do. You could have seminar sites, product sites, niche market sites, geographic sites, content specialty sites, etc. Think of what people might search for and create a website around that. They can all link together or feed into the main site. Each site is a mini sales tool, in its own right.

Blog(s)

Writing a blog post does not need to be a tiresome task. I started writing posts for my blog (www.robnixon.com) in 2010 to put my thoughts on my platform. I average a little more than one new post per week. Sometimes I do two or three posts in a week, sometimes I skip a week. What's important is that I am writing about current ideas, methods, celebrations, and the occasional promotion. If you want to be a thought leader you need to have a blog. If you want to dominate the Web, then you need something to say.

> "If you want to be a thought leader, you need to have a blog. If you want to dominate the Web, then you need something to say."

Facebook

It's free, easy, and it's another platform you should be on. Many people think that Facebook is only a "personal" platform. I disagree. It's a platform to bring out your personality. It's a platform to show that you "are living large." It's a platform to show travel and other interests. It's a platform to show off your family and your sporting prowess—or lack thereof. Remember people buy from people—real people. Get a funky company page setup. Email all your clients to "like it" and actively seek out your clients to "friend" with. But please, no pictures of your food.

Twitter

It's a 140-character blogging site that works—if you work it. Many of your clients might be on Twitter, but you'll never know unless you are too. A daily "tweet" can take less than 60 seconds. You can get a "social media enhancer" person working from home to do it for you. One of the cool things about Twitter is you can link from your short tweet to other websites—yours! You can connect with me on Twitter—@therobnixon.

LinkedIn

> "LinkedIn has a massive amount of content and you can also post your content."

The original intention of LinkedIn was to connect the world's professionals. That is one of the reasons so many accountants are on the platform. LinkedIn is a platform that has been disrupting the recruitment industry for a long time. It can also disrupt the accounting profession. LinkedIn has a massive amount of content, and you can also post your content. It's a sophisticated tool for finding people. It's a great tool for targeting companies you want as clients. Again, like all these platforms, you need to "work it, baby" and post regularly and add value to the reader. You can connect with me on LinkedIn—therobnixon.

YouTube

I love YouTube (in a professional sense), because with a standard smartphone I can create a video quickly, upload to YouTube, and then I can go to other platforms and tell the world about it. Making noise with video-based marketing is super cool because I can get to know you a bit before I decide to inquire or buy. Why not create your own channel and post updates and content? Add a bit of humor to it, make it graphically appealing, and you'll get more hits. Who knows, you might go viral one day!

E-news

First, we had paper newsletters (I even had a 20-page magazine at one point), then we had electronic newsletters. Now, a lot of people have forgotten about them. However, if done right, they are super useful. You can send a summary of the week/month to your database of content and happenings—maybe even some celebrations.

Forum—Connecting

You organize gatherings in boardrooms, town halls, seminar rooms, and the like. What about a gathering on the Internet? What if you created a private roster forum for your clients only? It could be a place for them to hang out, interact, ask questions, and get to know one another. You can do this for free on Facebook and LinkedIn by starting a secret group. Easy peasy to do. As humans, we like a place of belonging—a place of community. Why not have the accountant create that for us?

> "What if you created a private roster forum for your clients only?"

Search Engine Optimization

You can pay to get search engine optimization (SEO). It is not that expensive. Here's how it works. When someone searches for you, or what you do, or your location or specialty, you want to be on the first page of the search engine. It is pointless being on the second page of your browser, because statistics show (by the social media commentators) that if I have to go to the second page, then I don't. At least the vast majority of people do not. So, you want to engage a company to do this for you—to make sure that when someone searches under any permutation of searches that suit what you do, then you need to be there—in their face on the first page.

Social Advertising

One of the coolest things about social media advertising has got to be remarketing. This is where if you show an interest in a site or style of product, when you go elsewhere on the Internet these similar companies appear all the time. When you're on Facebook, amazingly on the side bar, ads appear of things you are interested in. It's because you have been to something similar before and a similar topic is "following

LET'S MAKE SOME TARGETED NOISE

you." Everywhere you go on the Internet a little "digital footprint" is left. That data is then used to target you and others to buy/visit more of the same. Accountants need to use this in their arsenal.

Other People's Blogs

As you are writing for yourself, why don't you also write for others? If you have a center of influence that has your target market as its clients, then why not offer to write for them? You could be a guest blogger for magazines (where your target market hangs out), and you could offer to write a blog post for industry associations. When you position yourself as an expert and you are writing extensively, people believe you!

Content Marketing

> "The real value in the content is not the content but the implementation of the content."

Accountants are scared to give away content/information for free. Why? Is that all you've got? The real value in the content is not the content but the **implementation of the content.** By giving your content away for free (using all the channels in this chapter), you tell me you are confident, you're not scared, and I can learn about you before I engage with you. Send me articles, videos, podcasts, white papers, research—anything that builds your credibility. People buy from people they know, like, and trust. I might know you by name, and I might like you when I meet you. I trust you when I can see what you can do for me. The Internet is rife with content from dubious sources. Why not give content on what I can do for free? Then sell the how to do it for a lot of money.

We learned our ABCs as a child. The new ABC is **always be contributing.** Not every now and again, but every day. The objective is to be seen as a thought leader. If you want to be a thought leader and be "everywhere," then you need to be everywhere!

Growing Your Database

If you want to grow your client base, then you'll need to massively grow the size of your prospective client database. It's all about getting the clients in your target market

263

to enter and "opt in" to your database. Once they have entered, the objective is to grow your prospective client database into a "clean" and "receptive" database. The size of your prospective client database will depend on your marketing capabilities and your growth targets.

Let's say you want to grow your active client base by 26 percent each year—which means you double the size of your client base every three years. It is commonly known in marketing circles that it takes nine times for a targeted prospect to hear or see a message before they act. The problem is that because of proliferation of marketing messages that we all receive, as consumers we only get to "see" every sixth message that is sent to us. I call this "Rob's rule of 54"—nine times to hear it and only every sixth message sent is seen. Before the turn of this decade, I used to call it "Rob's rule of 27"—nine times to hear it and three times to see it. Our attention spans have reduced by about 50 percent and we are getting more messaging than ever before. It takes more creativity, more discipline, and more patience to get people to respond these days. Based on my theory, you need to send up to 54 messages BEFORE you get a response!

> "I call this 'Rob's rule of 54'—nine times to hear it and only every sixth message sent is seen."

If that's the case, then the size of your prospective client database needs to be big. If you understand who your target market is (preferably a niche industry type), then why not make it your business to get a list of all of them! Every business in your target market and your chosen geographical location should be on your database.

Once you know who you are targeting, you can work out where they "hang out" and target them. You could find out which conferences they attend, what publications they read, which websites they frequent, and so on. With the objective of creating a large list of names that you can market to, your "appearance" (in a variety of forms) where they hang out is crucial to building your list.

Based on privacy act laws in your country, you might be able to buy a list of your target market or you can use a wide variety of techniques to attract your prospective market to your database. One of the best ways to grow your database is to find other non-competing companies (hosts) that have your target market as their current target market and arrange a beneficial marketing campaign. For example, you could write a white paper based on your expertise and have the host company email it, so their list of clients can get access to the paper. The prospects fill in their contact details and now you own the name. There are many other techniques, such as remarketing, social media usage, SEO, and nurture sequences to attract and create lists. There is so much detail in these, that I will save it for another book!

Marketing Must Generate Leads

The overall (and desired) objective of marketing functions in an accounting firm is to generate leads—lots of leads. The more marketing you do, the more leads you get, the more choices you have!

There are two types of marketing people—brand oriented or direct response. The brand-oriented people are vital to the "look and feel" of your corporate identity. They are vital in helping to build credibility. They will make you look great, and you'll feel really good about the work they do. However, they might not get you in front of your target market nor will they enable you to make much money—but you'll look good! My view is that you can outsource a lot of your brand development to contractors or offshore labor. You don't need to have branding types on your payroll. They are important, expensive, and do not help you make much money.

> "There are two types of marketing people—brand oriented or direct response."

The type of marketing people (and thus activity) you're looking for is a direct-response oriented person. These people are trained differently and your objective with them is to engage your target market and create inquiries for you to follow up. This is NOT the primary role of a partner. The primary role of a progressive partner is a sales role. Direct-response marketing needs to be done by professionals who know what they are doing. It's all about generating leads. The volume of leads you need is determined by your sales conversion rate and your new client (or new services per client) objectives. You can outsource your lead generation; however, if you want rapid growth it is far more effective to have the resource(s) in-house.

Your leads are going to come from two sources—existing clients or prospective clients. Both are rich sources of new business. The objective is to engage with your client or prospective client and have them respond to you. This is now a lead or an inquiry—someone who is interested to talk with you further.

If you want someone to respond, then you have to give them reasons to respond. And you need to give them a taste of what you have to offer. Just like you when you buy something, you like to "experience" it first. It's no different with professional services. How can your current or prospective client experience your smarts before they buy your smarts? Can they download a report, watch a video, listen to a podcast, read an article, attend a seminar, or all the above?

The following diagram is an example of eight of the best methods you could employ to get a response from someone. All of them work. Some of them cost more money, some more time. Some are a more effective use of your money and time, while some are more leveraged. All of them work in varying degrees.

> "There are two types of marketing people—brand oriented or direct response."

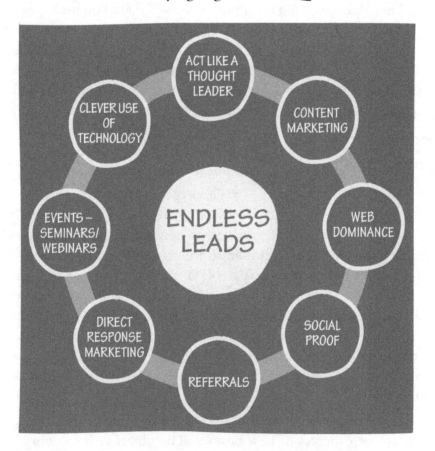

There is not just one way to get an inquiry any more. People respond in different ways to different mediums and methods.

Remember the objective is to generate leads (interested people who want to speak with you), and you need to employ all eight strategies.

Act like a thought leader. Who is the dominant educator in your niche market? Who is the company that your niche turns to for advice? If there is no one or there is limited education, then it could be you. You could take the primary position as the "go to firm or person" for all things about your niche and service sector. When someone in your niche market asks another person, "Who should I go to for the best business, accounting, and financial advice?" your new referral source says, "You MUST go to XYX firm—it has the best track record and produces the best results." Why would they say that? Because you told the market over and over and over again (in a subtle way through multiple channels) that you are. When you are the thought leader in your space, you get called on by the media for comments, and you are "cited" in other people's work. If you act like a thought leader, they'll believe you are a thought leader!

> "The most valuable intellectual property you have is how to do something. Not what to do—but how to do it."

Content marketing. The most valuable intellectual property you have is how to do something. Not **what** to do—but **how** to do it. Some advice you might give is, "You need to grow your revenue, reduce your expenses, and manage your cash flow better to thrive. That is what to do." Only a little implementation happens (and thus success) based on what to do. It seems valuable (and it is), but it is not as valuable as exactly how to do it. So give it away for free! It's content and it is moderately valuable, but to the recipient it is hugely valuable—because no one else is giving it away. People do not switch accountants that quickly, and unless you want a startup business, every prospect you want as a client is already serviced by another accounting firm. If you adopt a "try before you buy" strategy, then you can give away content and methodology so the clients can try you before they buy you. Prepare and distribute your content in a variety of forms—articles, papers, videos, social media, webinars, and seminars.

Web dominance. I have covered Web dominance previously in this chapter. If you skipped it or ignored it then here is a summary! The Internet is a rich source of new leads, if your site is interactive and interesting enough. It is common habit to search online for nearly everything before we buy it. What does your Web presence say about you and your firm? How can I interact with your website? Can I download your position papers? Can I view a video? Does it look modern, or is it stuck in the last decade? Is there an inquiry form? Can I fill in a calculator? Can I fill in an online questionnaire and get reports about how my business is doing? Can I buy a small product from the site so I can try you out? Is there an up-to-date blog on the site? These are all methods of engagement with your website. If you get engagement, you'll get leads.

Social proof. You're good, but who knows it? The great work you do with clients is like the best-kept secret in town. You need to tell your audience of your awesomeness. But promoting how good you are directly to your marketplace isn't the way to do it. You need to promote how good you are via the success of your clients. The best way to explain your content and methodology is with stories. Stories of your successful clients. I have found that telling the stories in the format of video or case studies instills belief in your market. The object of your interview or case study appeals to your prospect, who says, "That person is like me—I can relate to him." One of the best formats is an interview with a successful client. When you interview the client, use a three-part structure.

1. X years ago, when we met, **where** were you and what did your business situation look like? You want them to open up and explain their life before meeting or working with you.

2. **Now** what does it look like? You want to them to explain the current reality and how good it is.

3. **How** did you do it? You want them to tell the viewer of the great work you did for them.

If you can have your client tell your audience how great you are, then it is far more believable.

Referrals. Every accountant on the planet knows that a referral from an existing client is the gold standard of new business. An existing client who is happy with you and your firm is "putting his or her neck out" to refer someone they know. So, you know all this—but are you using it? How many clients do you ask to refer new clients to you? How often do you ask? The key is to start asking! Many firms put out the wrong vibe when it comes to referrals. Clients might ask, "How's business? The typical response is "flat out" or "busy." What have you just told your client? "We're too busy for any more business, so don't refer!"

> "Many firms put out the wrong vibe when it comes to referrals. Clients may ask you how's business and the typical response is "flat out" or busy."

Sometimes your clients can see that you're so busy by the amount of time it takes to get work done. Why would they jeopardize service standards by referring a new client? When you ask for referrals only ask your A-class and B-class clients.

Direct response marketing. Brand-oriented marketing does not generate leads. Or if it does, they are expensive leads. Not only is it expensive, it is hard to measure. On the other hand, direct-response marketing should earn you a direct return on investment. Direct-response marketing means you are sending out marketing messages and measuring the response. You spend $1,000 on a campaign; you measure every response, and relate it to an allowable acquisition cost. Every campaign should be measured, tweaked, and keep rolling out the good ones.

> "Many firms I know will run joint seminars with their referral sources and offer free reports and white papers to their client member base."

Events, seminars, and webinars. If you have a large database of clients, and they are educated to Web-based events (you can educate them), then you can run your own webinar. A webinar is simply a seminar conducted over the Web. You might schedule a webinar for 60 minutes at an appropriate time that suits your target market. You could prepare a PowerPoint presentation and talk to the presentation. You could interview two or three of your successful clients about your topic. You could offer a free consultation or report at the end. The reason I like webinars is because they are quick, cheap, and effective in generating leads. You get amazing leverage by sitting in your office talking to (possibly) hundreds of people at a time.

Without a doubt, the best way to introduce new services to your clients is by running seminars of some sort. However, they are expensive to run and time consuming. The event could be a large-scale business seminar, a private boardroom briefing, a small workshop, or similar. You can certainly meet with your clients one on one, but that is a slow process. When running seminars, you need to offer some value—not just selling. The best-attended seminars are where the business owner can take away ideas they can apply right away. That might include cash flow management, KPI reporting, profit improvement, or revenue growth. Start with a two-hour event that includes a demo of the new system (let's say a Cloud accounting program) and include a question and answer period. Give your event a snazzy title, like "How to Manage Cash Flow in a Crisis" and market it. If only a few register, then try something new

Clever Use of Technology

When I started my marketing career (in 1986), our chosen marketing technology was mail (lumpy, snail mail) and a telephone. Then one day a large box arrived. In it was a FAX machine. WOW! I thought—how cool. There was a problem though. None of our customers had a fax machine! We couldn't use it. So, we wrote (a letter) to our customers with a flyer of a fax machine and a deal we had struck, asking them to buy one so we could communicate with them better. They did—in droves. Fast forward a few decades and now look at the technology at your fingertips. The technology is inexpensive and plentiful. It can help you get names, source leads, qualify leads, nurture leads, book appointments, videoconference, and maybe even make the sales for you one day. Ahhh . . . nirvana—no humans needed for marketing and sales. Maybe one day! Understanding what technology is available now and how to use should be a priority.

> "Fast forward a few decades and now look at the technology at your fingertips. The technology is inexpensive and plentiful."

Measuring the Effectiveness of Marketing

No matter what methods you employ, you need to measure the effectiveness. Remember, this is direct-response marketing, so everything should be measured. If you do not measure the effectiveness of your marketing, then fairly quickly you will get despondent with the time and expense that goes into it.

An example of measuring is shown in this chart.

Measuring Marketing Effectiveness

Activity	Target	Quantity	Cost	Send date	Response %	Response	Gross Profit	ROI
Letter #1	Existing clients	463	$565	Dec 15	3.35%	15	$2,085	396%
Letter #2	Suspect clients	3,323	$4,500	Dec 15	1.25%	41	$5,699	126%
Email #1	Existing clients	463	$4.63	Dec 17	1%	5	$695	15000%
Webinar #1	Entire database	92	$50	Jan 15	12%	11	$1,529	3058%
Email #2	Suspect list	3,323	$33.23	Jan 18	0.5%	16	$2,224	6690%
Fax #1	Suspect list	3,323	$2,500	Feb 1	2.1%	67	$9,131	382%
Telemarketing test	Suspect sample	500	$3,500	Feb 5	4.5%	22	$3,058	87%

You can see that the campaigns are measured down to the decimal point. Everything should be based on a return on investment and any marketing and sales activity that you do should be treated as an investment.

> "If you do not measure the effectiveness of your marketing, then fairly quickly you will get despondent with the time and expense that goes into it."

Let's say you're looking to acquire new clients. If you were buying a database from another firm, then in most parts around the world you would gladly spend 75 cents to $1 for every dollar of new clients. You know that you will keep the client for 10 or more years, so you get your money back from year two on.

The same applies to marketing and sales. If you do a marketing campaign and it costs you $10,000 and you generate three hot leads that result in two new clients worth $7,500 each, then provided your cash flow can sustain it, you would keep doing the campaign.

I think every firm needs to have what's called an allowable acquisition cost and an allowable lead cost for new clients. It means you are prepared to spend up to $X to get the client for the first time. The way you work it out is based on your gross profit of your target client and when you want to get a return on your investment.

A simple example is this. Let's say your target client has an annual fee of $10,000 and the gross profit on every new client is $6,000 per annum. If you had an allowable acquisition cost of $3,000, then you make your money back in six months. Now, unless you are a sales superstar, you are not going to convert every lead. Let's say you meet with all leads and convert one in three. That means your allowable lead cost could be $1,000. So now you give a budget to your marketing team of no more than $1,000 spent per quality lead. Based on your current sales skills, it will take you three leads to get a sale and therefore the cost of acquisition is $3,000. Rinse and repeat.

Do not think of marketing and sales costs as a percentage of revenue or a fixed amount per year. You'll limit your potential. When you think of marketing and sales as an investment that is measured, then you have an almost endless budget—effectiveness, monitoring, and cash flow dependent.

ACCOUNTING IS SELLING

Sales Is a Confidence Game

There's an old saying that dogs can smell fear. It's the same theory for people who are in a sales role. If your "dog" (person in front of you) can sense that you are not confident, then you are not going to make the sale. You will get questions and objections from the prospects or clients who you don't want and ultimately not make the sale.

Just the thought of the word "sales" can put the heebie-jeebies into accountants. For some reason, accountants don't like the word. I am unsure why that is. Maybe they think it's a bit "grubby" and "we don't sell—we're professionals." Do you think new business will just come to you because you are a professional? Yes, you are a professional. You're a professional who needs to learn how to sell; otherwise, you're not going to thrive. To thrive in the future, you must learn the art of sales. Accountants

> "If you don't like the word sales, then how about changing your mindset to servicing your clients properly?"

are really good at sales (once they're taught) because they come from a position of trust and authority. The credibility is already there before you open your mouth and start talking.

If you don't like the word sales, then how about changing your mindset to servicing your clients properly? The duty of care that accountants have with their clients is that if you spot an issue or an opportunity, then you are obliged to let the client know about it. It's in your code of conduct. As you dig deeper into this, and if you are super interested in your clients, then you "provide every service to every client that helps them achieve their goals." That means you need to service them properly—also known as making SALES and helping them to buy.

Every accountant is involved in sales in every client interaction. Making a sale is a transfer of emotion and trust. Even when you are recommending a type of structure or a tax plan, you are selling. You are taking your idea and convincing the client that they need to use it or buy it. You do it every day when you meet with a client. You are selling every day. Accounting is selling.

Back to the dogs and the fear. No matter what techniques, processes, or questions you adopt in your sales role, it is all a waste of time unless you have confidence in what you are doing or promoting. To be good at sales and good at transferring trust, every accountant needs to work on their confidence levels. The more confidence you have, the more successful you'll be.

To increase your confidence levels, I think there are eight areas to work on.

1. Language
2. Tonality
3. Health
4. Dress
5. Knowledge
6. Success
7. Stories
8. Process

> "To be good at sales and good at transferring trust, every accountant needs to work on their confidence levels."

Language. What you say is so important while you are communicating with prospects and clients. It's the language of the sale.

Do you ask open-ended questions or closed-ended questions? Closed-ended questions get a yes/no/maybe answer—for example, "Do you have an estate plan?" Open-ended questions get a detailed response. For example, "What is your documented plan for your loved ones when you are gone?"

Are you telling your prospect/client what they need, or are you explaining why they need it? For example, "You need a budget and cash flow forecast" versus "Our best clients are freeing up new cash flow and creating more profit by having a detailed and real-time budget and cash flow forecast."

Are you giving statements or articulating your value and ending with a question? For example, "You need to apply our tax strategies so you can save some tax this year." Or "We've worked out that you'll save $40,000 per year for the next 10 years if you apply our tax strategies. That's a minimum of $400,000 that we can help you with. I'm curious, what would you do with $40,000 per year?"

Learning the language of the sale will give you more confidence and, more important, your prospect or client will see the confidence in you.

> "Learning the language of the sale will give you more confidence and, more important, your prospect or client."

Tonality. Not only is it what you say, it's also how you say it. When you are in a conversation are you boring and monotone, or do you have a bit of passion in your voice? Are you miserable looking, or do you smile? Do you sit still, or do you point and wave your hands? Do you alter your volume (higher and lower) during conversation, or do you remain flat? Do you talk faster sometimes and slower at other times to make a point?

You're supposed to be transferring passion in a sales environment. When I am in your presence, can I feel the passion and the excitement? If you want me to transfer funds to you, I need to know that you're excited by the idea that you're selling.

Whenever I design a seminar, I write a "running sheet," which is how the day will run. I have it timed in five-minute blocks so I am covering key content at certain times. I never rehearse, and I am always on time. I live by my running sheet. At the top of every running sheet, I have my ENERGY objective, my personal STATE, and by business OBJECTIVE. Here is the top of a recent running sheet.

Seminar Running Sheet

Energy . . . To create an inspiring, challenging, environment for accountants to realize their potential. The program will be full of energy, passion, excitement, and practical strategies.

State: Give it everything—excited, thankful, privilege, humble, sharing, fun, best ever, smiling all the time.

Objective: Influence the delegates to take action.

The top of the running sheet sets my tonality for the program. I have it on me at all times. My team also has a copy. Even if I am tired or if the audience is difficult, I want to set the tone and put on a great program.

The tonality of you will have a big impact on your confidence.

Health. It's a known fact that when you are fitter, stronger, and healthier, you feel better about yourself. Your poor health could mean your body weight, your bad teeth, your hair loss, your fitness level, or even your skin complexion. All can be fixed. I don't think accountants need to train excessively to run marathons or compete in triathlons to get more confidence. However, if that's your thing, then go for it.

You might only need to lose enough weight for people to notice and pay you a compliment. Or just getting your teeth professionally cleaned or adjusted might help you to smile more. You might need to see a dermatologist to get your skin clear or see a hair loss specialist to see what you can do with your receding hairline. Even training moderately a few times a week can improve your health and fitness.

I remember once talking to the partners of a three-partner firm. They were complaining that there was no energy in the office and everyone was "steady." They wanted a better culture with more energy in the office. They asked for my advice, so I gave it to them. I was in one of my "blunt" moods, so I simply said to them,

"Look, a fish rots from the head down. How will there ever be more energy in the business while the three of you are unfit and overweight?"

They got the message. They went on a health kick, lost some pounds, and led from the front. Your health makes a big difference to your confidence levels. Maybe it's time to sharpen up.

> "If you become a better conversationalist, you'll be more relatable and you'll get more confidence,"

Dress. Look sharp and be sharp. Most accountants (hopefully not you) I get to meet are "cheap," so they buy cheap shoes, wear cheap suits, and use cheap tools. The way you dress says so much about you and your style. If you look sloppy, then typically your work will be sloppy. If you use a cheap pen and paper, then I wonder about the quality of what you are telling me. If you wear ill-fitting cheap suits and out-of-date clothing, does that mean you are also out of date?

I am not saying that you need to spend $2,000 on a name brand suit. However, a decent suit that is properly adjusted to your body shape does make a difference. I am suggesting you ditch the cheap conference pen you got for free and the $2 notepad to something more upmarket. You are taking notes about my business and my future—please pay me some respect by using decent tools. You are offering me business advice and you look disheveled—it doesn't instill confidence in me.

If you are having problems with matching clothing, then hire a stylist for the day to take you shopping. For the sake of the fashion police, get rid of the "last decade" look and get up to date. Your confidence will improve as a result.

Knowledge. Knowledge is an interesting topic, and some accountants take it too far and want to know everything about a subject before they can talk about it. You don't need to know everything about a topic to know a lot. You just need to get good at asking questions and letting the other person talk. The idea of knowledge is to get more out of it and become more knowledgeable. It's about broadening your knowledge base so you are more interesting to talk to. The more interesting you are to talk with, the more sales you'll make.

I am amazed at how many accountants do not read the national financial newspapers at least three times per week. You're in the finance profession, yet you don't read the finance news. Bizarre! You don't have to read the newspaper from cover to cover, just scan the main headlines. You can store that content for later and if needed pull it out in conversation. The Internet is a wonderful tool for getting useful knowledge—sporting scores, political movements, the latest stock trades, trade news, etc.

It's all about becoming a better conversationalist. If you become a better conversationalist, you'll be more relatable and you'll get more confidence.

Success. The inner confidence of knowing that the work you do is really good shines though in your conversations. Every accountant I have ever met (more than 170,000 so far) has done some great work for clients. You have saved clients tax, improved their cash flow, kept them out of jail, been a shoulder to cry on, improved their profit, and even helped some to become wealthy.

> "Telling a relevant story can give me that social proof I am looking for."

What are you doing with all that success you have created? How many testimonials and case studies have you collected? In my business, we have the "wall of fame." As we meet a client for the first time, we take a photo of them, print it in black and white, and then get them to write something nice on it. I got the idea from the old-school restaurants where celebrities signed their photograph and wrote something nice to the restaurateur. We've filled one wall and have started two more. So far, there are about 1,200 photographs of happy clients and loads of positive words. The main wall of fame is in the hallway on the way to the restrooms. As you go to do your business, you feel better about business!

We also have a big focus on WHAMs—written happy accountant moments. When we interact with our clients, we ask them to put something in writing about what they are experiencing when using our services and tools. In 10 weeks, we collected 102 WHAMs. From there we go back and create proper case studies.

As the saying goes, "Success breeds success." Documenting the success of your clients gives you and your team more confidence.

Stories. Telling stories is so important in a sales conversation. It's all about instilling social proof in me. I am sitting in front of you, and you are espousing the fact that I need to do something different. I trust you and respect you, but deep down I am wondering if you can actually do what you say you can do. Telling a relevant story can give me that social proof I am looking for. Here are a couple of examples.

"The situation you are in is so close to another manufacturing client we helped last year. The company had rising costs, did about the same amount of revenue as you, and was faced with new competitors who drove the product price down. This caused a cash flow issue and pressure from the bank. What we did for the client was to put in place a budget and cash flow forecast, helped to refinance the debt, and we worked with the client every month to monitor the cash flow. After six months, the client could see the difference, and after 12 months the company had excess cash flow because we financially coached the client out of the problem."

> "Telling stories gives social proof and it instills confidence in the person you are sitting with that you know what you're talking about."

"I understand how you must be feeling right now. When we have had this conversation regarding restructuring company affairs, most clients felt exactly the same way you do right now—annoyed and anxious. One client in particular was annoyed with his previous accountant because he wasn't structured correctly. He was anxious as to how the family might take the new changes that we recommended. What he found was that when we showed him he was financially better off for making the changes, he jumped at the opportunity."

Telling stories gives social proof and it instills confidence in the person you are sitting with that you know what you're talking about.

Process. If you are like most modern firms, you will have an office procedures manual. That manual is all about how you do tasks in the office. They typically have guidelines, checklists, a process, and standard letters. Someone worked out the best way to file, scan, copy, collect the mail, lock the office, and pay the salaries. Then it was documented so others could follow the steps.

Sales is just like that. A sales process is like a workflow process. One thing triggers the next thing until a resolution happens. There is always someone in the office who is the best at sales. Hopefully they have been trained by my company! If they are good, then sit with them and document their process. What do they do at each step of the way? What do they say? How do they say it? What's their process flow? Once the process is worked out, it needs to be documented in a sales manual. The sales manual includes the sales process and the document is called a playbook. It's the game plan of how you want to play to win.

The objective is to create a repeatable sales process. A repeatable sales process will give you more confidence. More confidence leads to high self-belief. High self-belief leads to more sales. The dogs can smell it.

Sales Systems

I have been actively selling something since the age of 14. That's more than 30 years of selling. I have been formally trained in courses on how to sell. I have attended more sales seminars than I care to remember. I have read countless books and listened to audio programs on the science of sales. I have sold over the phone, on the shop floor in retail, from a seminar stage, one on one, one to many, and via webinars.

I have always been good at sales, because I use some simple systems that I have learned and fine-tuned to keep me on track.

I have never shared some of these systems before to anyone except my own sales team. Seeing this is a book of valuable content, I thought you might like some of the "secret sauce" of my selling systems.

Sales System 1—Getting through to the Owners

Owners of businesses are busy people. They are our buyer(s) and they are the people (and the only ones) you need to speak with. If you do a sales meeting with anyone but the ultimate decision maker(s), then expect to do the meeting again. But you have to get through to them to start the conversation and build the relationship.

I find that using the concept of a prebooked telephone meeting will help enormously. I remember sitting in an airport lounge once where I made 26 telephone meetings (via the reception of the prospect) in the space of one hour. I simply smashed the phone, booked the meetings, and then sent them individual confirmation notes later.

> "If you do a sales meeting with anyone but the ultimate decision maker(s), then expect to do the meeting again."

If your target owner has communicated with you somehow via a marketing report download, a seminar, or has made an inquiry of some sort, then it should be easy to get through. But you don't necessarily want to speak to the owner right away. You might need 15 minutes, and if you randomly call you might only get three minutes.

Your script goes like this.

"Hi, Mary (person who answers phone), it's John James calling from XYZ firm. Bob was on our website and downloaded a free report we offered, and I wanted to catch up with him to discuss it further—but not right now. What I'd like to do is find 15 minutes that works for both of us and I'll call him at that time. Do you have access to his calendar so we can schedule the phone appointment?"

OR if you get through to Bob right away.

"Hi, Bob, it's John James calling from XYZ firm. I wanted to catch up with you for 15 minutes on the phone—but not right now. What I would like to do is book a telephone meeting with you to discuss how we can help you improve your cash flow and grow your revenue. Have you got your calendar handy so we can book a time during the next week or so?"

Rob's rules of telephone meetings include the following:

1. Use an odd time—say 10:10, 9:15, 9:20, or 11:25.

2. Send an email to the prospect stating the meeting time.

3. Always call them—do not let them call you—EVER.

4. Always call PRECISELY on time—watch the second hand before you dial.

> "The really good salespeople I know are prepared for the meeting with a process flow of how the meeting will work."

5. Always announce yourself to reception, "Bob and I have a prebooked phone appointment at 9:15 a.m., which is now. Can you put me through, please?"

6. If Bob is not available, then **do not let him call you back**. Simply state, "That's OK. I have a fairly tight schedule, like Bob. Can we reschedule and I will call again?"

7. Never leave a message for someone to call you back. It's lazy sales and invariably if they do call you back, it'll be at the wrong time.

Sales System 2—Meeting Worksheet

Most accountants I have met use an interview pad of some sort in meetings. It'll have space for the client details at the top and then typically it will have blank ruled lines for note taking. The really good salespeople I know are prepared for the meeting with a process flow of how the meeting will work. The really, really good salespeople will take that process flow and make it the interview pad. That way you always remember your process flow and get to the conclusion you want faster. Here is an example of an interview pad that you could duplicate and use!

My state of mind	Sensational meeting, positive, listening, understanding		
Client name and business type			
Why here, set the scene	Always wanted to help, helping all clients achieve their goals		
Who are the buyers?—(decision making questions—DQs)			
Situation and background— (background related questions—BQs)	Revenue	$	
	Profit	$	
	Debt	$	
	Cash assets	$	
	Age		
	Kids + ages		
	Business progress		
	Goals when started business		
Objectives and motivation—The Awesome 8: growth, profit, cash flow, asset protection, tax minimization, succession, retirement, estate planning—(Motivation related questions—MQs)	3–5 years out		
	Earnings goal in retire	$	
	Retirement age		
	Lifestyle goals		
	Time and hobbies		
	Size of problem $ M	$	
Objectives and problems in the way— (problem related questions—PQs)	Overdraft / cash		$
	Time issues		
	People issues		
Measures—how will you know if achieved—(Measurement metrics questions MMQs)			
Value—assuming achieved, what would that mean to you and your family?— (Value related questions—VQs)			
Timing—assuming paid for out of new cash flow—(Consequence and timing questions CQs and TQs)	Consequences of not doing		
	Getting started—cyclical issues?		
Options	Go away and think about it—send implementation plan		
BAMFAM (book a meeting from a meeting)	Implementation plan send, read, meet questions, start date		

Sales System 3—Sales Nurturing System

Your prospects are busy people. They have demands on their time every day and most days they have salespeople attempt to sell to them. You are competing against a lot of noise, interruptions, and constant bombardment of information. Although the prospects might have met you, downloaded a report from your website, or even attended one of your seminars—**assume they have forgotten who you are**. To get them to remember you between calls, you need to be memorable. The way to do that is with a nurturing system that happens immediately after the first contact and does not end until they buy or die! Here's how it works.

What	When	Method
Find some personal information about the prospect.	On the first call	Phone
Send handwritten thank-you card with business card included.	Immediately after first contact	Mail
Confirm next meeting details with personal assistant and prospect.	Immediately after first contact	Email
Connect to prospect by LinkedIn, Facebook, and Twitter.	Immediately after first contact	Social tools
Confirm meeting details.	Two days before next meeting	Phone
Forward with personal note ("I'm not sure if you have seen this.") every newsletter you send to your existing clients.	Monthly	Email
Send a link to any new video on YouTube channel.	As new videos loaded	Email
Send a link to any new white paper or report ("I'm not sure if you have seen this.").	As new reports are loaded	Email
Send handwritten card with something of interest (magazine or article with what they are interested in).	One week after first contact	Mail
Send birthday card.	One week before birthday	Mail
Send case studies every time they are produced. ("I'm not sure if you have seen this. Give me a call if you need some help.")	As they are created	Email

Sales System 4—Return on Investment (ROI)-Based Selling

ROI-based selling is when you establish a starting point with a current financial model and then plan the future by altering the base numbers that are input-based numbers. Then your solution is the answer to helping them to achieve the result.

An example would be to use the growth equation to sell to them. Or you could simply use a whiteboard, flip chart, or a conversation.

> "ROI-based selling is when you establish a starting point with a current financial model and then plan the future by altering the base numbers that are input-based numbers."

You can use ROI-based selling in situations such as the following.

- Revenue improvement—key drivers being client numbers, transaction frequency, and average transaction value
- Profit improvement—key drivers being revenue, costs, and efficiency (AHR, write-ups)
- Cash flow improvement—key drivers being profit, inventory, and receivables

Example—Revenue and Cash Improvement

Key Area	Base Numbers Now	As Nominated by Your Prospect	New Numbers	Improvement
Number of customers	300	10 percent increase	330	
Number of transactions per customer per year	4	10 percent increase	4.4	
Average transaction value	$1,500	10 percent increase	$1,650	
Total revenue	$1,800,000		$2,395,800	$595,800 revenue improvement
Inventory balance	$225,000	40 percent decrease	$135,000	
Accounts receivable balance	$185,000	25 percent decrease	$138,750	
Total Lock-Up	$410,000		$273,750	$136,250 cash

The key to ROI-based selling is to get the prospect to volunteer the numbers now and the numbers of improvement.

Sales systems like these will help you enormously in your ultimate pursuit, which is to make sure to "provide every service to every client that helps them achieve their goals."

Sales Is Like Workflow Management

Most accountants have a workflow system of sorts. You get the information in, you check the information, you manipulate the information, you query it, and you then bind it up and file it. It's a process (simplified, I know) that is like a manufacturing line. The raw materials come in and after a series of steps and people touching the item, a finished product is created and shipped to the customer.

A sale to a prospect or client in an accounting firm is exactly like a manufacturing line. It's just like workflow management. First, branding occurs, then lead generation, then contact management, data collection, a series of meetings, a follow-up process, and finally after a sale is made, delivery of the sold service. Or to simplify, there are four core steps.

> "A sale to a prospect or client in an accounting firm is exactly like a manufacturing line. It's just like workflow management."

1. Lead generation
2. Lead management
3. Selling
4. Delivery

They happen in that order and there are many strategies, methods, and techniques that you could implement to improve each one. The following diagram highlights many of those strategies.

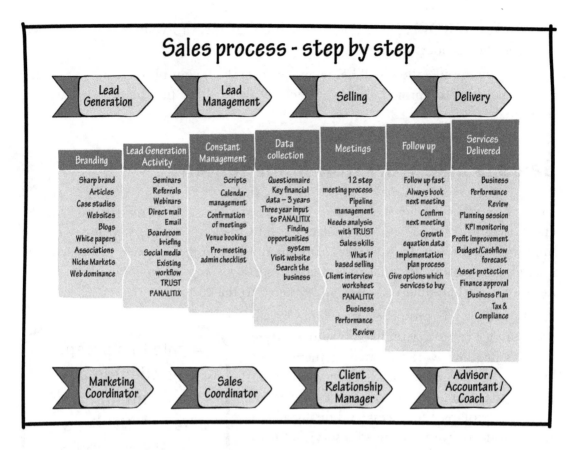

Just like you have different people in workflow scenarios "touching" the project, you also have different people in a sales process. Your marketing coordinator has different skills from your sales coordinator and your client relationship manager (typically partners or seniors) needs to allocate time to sales, otherwise it just won't happen. You need to look at this diagram and see where you can improve. If you have a sales machine in action, then you should be receiving new leads every day that you can sell to.

> "Your objective is to monitor the right numbers, make alterations to your methods, and ultimately optimize your sales process."

Just like you keep an eye on various indicators, such as utilization/productivity, turnaround time, and realization/write-downs for workflow management, you also measure different key performance indicators (KPIs) in your sales process. Following are some sales KPIs to monitor.

✓ Database size

✓ Open rate and click-through rate on campaigns

✓ Leads per week or month

✓ Follow-up time (hours) from lead created to first contact

✓ Number of sales meetings per month per partner

✓ Number of open opportunities per partner

✓ Probability and value of sale

✓ Close dates of sale

✓ Days to close a sale—from lead to resolution

✓ Conversion rate of meetings to sale

✓ Average hourly rate on the new sale

✓ Number of follow-up meetings needed per sale

✓ Total selling time per sale

Your objective is to monitor the right numbers, make alterations to your methods, and ultimately optimize your sales process. All this can be monitored and measured through Cloud-based customer relationship management (CRM) systems. Your CRM system can track your entire pipeline, all the probability, and all the sales stages. You should be able to create a sales funnel that looks something like the following image, so you can see where all prospects are at any given time in the sales cycle.

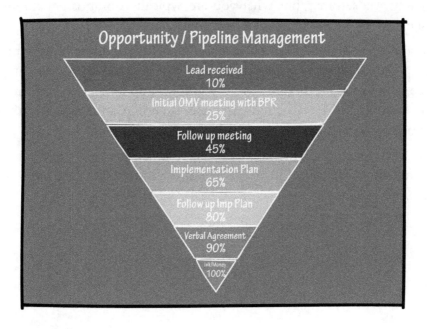

It's called pipeline management or opportunity management. With accurate stages and probability, you should be able to forecast your upcoming sales quite accurately.

Sales do not happen sitting behind a computer screen all day. You need to get out from behind the desk and meet some people. It's like a wheelbarrow. Unless you push it, it won't move.

Many accountants are employing marketing companies and internal people to generate leads. They're making noise in the marketplace. Without sales follow up, it's just noise and a complete waste of time.

> "Your objective is to monitor the right numbers, make alterations to your methods, and ultimately optimize your sales process."

Marketing Is Not Sales

Accountants are not good at marketing—marketing people are. My definition of marketing is **"salesmanship multiplied."** My definition of sales is **"finding out what the other person needs and then transferring emotion."** These definitions mean that marketing is a "one to many" strategy and sales is a "one on one" strategy.

Marketing is a leveraged activity—such as seminars. Writing emails, letters, and sales are typically not a leveraged activity. You can certainly "sell from stage" in a leveraged way at a seminar, but what you are typically doing is generating leads so you can speak with the prospects at a later date.

Every accounting firm that has serious growth plans needs to hire full-time marketing people. The job of the marketing team (or initially a singular person) is to enhance your company brand—make you look good—and to generate inquiries from your existing and future client database. Branding and leads—that's all. Make sure that your marketing people are capable of doing this.

Your marketing team might start with a marketing coordinator and you might end up with a full-time marketing manager and a small team that directs the marketing strategy of your business.

The role of your marketing team is to ...

- ✓ Manage your prospect database—add to it and keep it up to date with all contact details.
- ✓ Manage your client database—see above.
- ✓ Liaise with outside branding people to keep the image fresh.
- ✓ Coordinate your regular newsletter.
- ✓ Manage your website—freshness, words, etc.
- ✓ Liaise with your centers of influence and referral sources.
- ✓ Edit and prepare your articles for distribution.
- ✓ Manage your social media presence—blog, Facebook, Twitter, etc.
- ✓ Send out press releases, email blasts, mailers, etc.
- ✓ Organize and manage events—breakfast seminars, boardroom briefings, prospect luncheon meetings, cocktail receptions, seminars, webinars, teleseminars, conferences, etc.
- ✓ Book and manage nurturing visits (with existing clients) for the partners to attend.
- ✓ Generate X number of leads per month using the above strategies.

The entire list above is leveraged activities. Outside the administrative aspects of marketing, the best marketing people know how to sell. If your marketing people are good at selling, then the words they use (and how they use them) will have a great impact at generating leads.

Often an accounting practice will look around the team and see who has a flair for marketing—and put them in the role. NO! Accounting businesses will hire professionals for the roles who know what they are doing.

When hiring marketing people, make sure their primary focus is on generating leads. Marketing people are great at spending money on "awareness" and "image" type campaigns that do not generate any leads. They need measurement metrics (just like everyone else in

> "The firms that follow our material are hiring marketing people who are using our position descriptions all the time with great results."

your business does) to go by and the best one (key performance indicator) is number of leads generated each month.

The firms that follow our material are hiring marketing people who are using our position descriptions all the time with great results. Just like any position, you do not always get it right the first time. Persevere with the strategy, pay the right amount of money, and find the best people you can to market your business—you'll be glad you did.

This Sounds Like You

Salespeople typically have a bad image around the world. Even the word "sales" can make a lot of accountants cringe with distaste. The reason is often because you associate "salespeople" with words like dishonest, unethical, convincing, unprofessional, high pressure, and fast talker!

> "You find client issues and you solve them. Every day you are doing this. It's the same with being successful at sales."

There is no question—many salespeople are like that. However, they will not be that successful at sales if they stay like that.

After more than 30 years successfully selling all sorts of products and services, I think that being successful at sales is all about **"finding out what the other person needs and then transferring emotion."**

- ➢ You need to **ask the right questions.**
- ➢ You need to actively **listen.**
- ➢ You need to show **empathy.**
- ➢ You need to **solve problems.**
- ➢ You need to have **product knowledge.**
- ➢ You need to really **believe in your product.**
- ➢ You need to be **ethical.**
- ➢ You need to be **personable.**
- ➢ You need to **promote** your product so the other person gets excited by it.
- ➢ You need to be **persistent,** if you believe it is the right thing for the client.

It sounds a lot like being a good accountant!

What do you do every day as an accountant? You find client issues and you solve them. Every day you are doing this. It's the same with being successful at sales. You find what your clients need and then you convey the benefits of them buying what they need to buy.

To be successful at sales, you have to proactively speak with people. That means you have to get out from behind your desk and go and visit people or meet with people who would be classed as a qualified inquiry. To do that, you need to shake out of what I am calling "limiting sales beliefs." It's all the "mind chatter" that goes on when you are confronted with the reality that to serve your clients properly you need to make some sales.

> "As a professional accountant, you have lots to offer your clients—you have to believe that."

The following diagram is a great example of some of the "chatter" that goes on with most accountants. I am sure you can relate to some (or maybe all) of them.

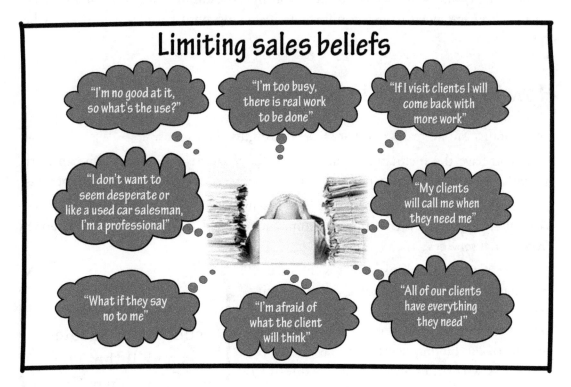

Remember these statements.

- ✓ You can be good at sales if you have the inclination.
- ✓ Yes, you are busy but there is nothing more important than properly serving your clients.
- ✓ You will come back with more work—more valuable work for your clients.
- ✓ Your clients do not know what they do not know—you are the finance expert, not them.
- ✓ Your clients do not have everything they need—they don't know what they need.
- ✓ What the clients think is none of your business—it's their business.
- ✓ They will say no from time to time—every no is closer to a yes.
- ✓ If you act ethically in the sales process, you will be seen as a professional.

As a professional accountant, you have lots to offer your clients—you have to believe that. Your job is to have relationships with your clients, to increase the average fee per client, and to win new business. You must ensure that all your clients' needs are met. You just need to get comfortable in talking with people to find out what they need.

How to Be a Guru in Sales

Accountants can be really good at sales—with guru-like status.

If you have the inclination, being successful at sales is a skill that you can learn. It involves scripts, dialogues, practice, asking questions, and following a sales process.

The first thing to remember with sales is why people buy professional services—particularly services over and above compliance-based services—your value-added professional services.

Most accountants think that it is the quality of the product, the methodology, the content, or the process of delivering the work that really turns the client on. Wrong! Only about 10 percent of the buying decision is based on this. And guess what most accountants (before they are professionally trained) spend most of their

> "If you have the inclination, being successful at sales is a skill that you can learn."

time discussing? You guessed it. They spend most of the conversation on product-related discussion. They seem to want to talk on and on about the quality of their products, the qualifications of their people, how unique their methods are, and how they will work with the client. Clients do not care about this as much as you do.

What clients are interested in (40 percent of the buying decision) is that you are likeable, trustworthy, you know what you are talking about, and that they can (or do have) a good relationship with you. Remember, people buy from people. Are your clients and prospects comfortable buying from you?

Even more important than your likeability (about 50 percent of the buying decision) your clients and prospects are most interested in what they get out of the transaction. They are wondering how your ideas will help them improve their results. They are wondering if your service will help them reach their objectives and what they are motivated to achieve.

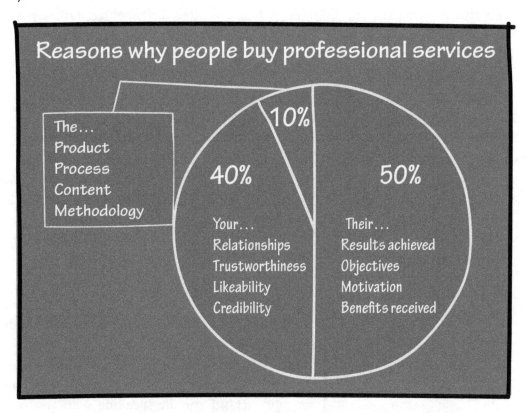

Ultimately what accountants sell is the same as what the cosmetics companies sell—**HOPE.** Clients hope that by buying your services you can help them achieve what they want to achieve. Your clients do not understand the intricacies of how you will do the work—nor do they need to.

Spend your discussion time getting your clients to talk about themselves—not you talking about you!

In addition to focusing on the right areas in your discussions, there are two key success factors in being successful at sales.

1. Your sales process
2. Your conversion rate process

Sales Process—You Need One!

A sales process is the sequential steps that happen one after another in a systematic and repeatable way. For example, what happens when an inquiry comes in? Do you send some information immediately? Do you book a meeting the same day? What is the script to book the meeting? What happens after the meeting? Do you send an engagement letter the same day or three days later? Do you meet again and how quickly after the first meeting? You need a sales process that each person in your business follows consistently.

The number one key performance indicator for salespeople is the **number of sales meetings** they conduct. You need to work out how many meetings your team can conduct. I call this your quality meeting capacity—your QMC. If a sales meeting takes on average two hours (with travel) and there are 1,600 hours per year available per person in sales, then each salesperson (at maximum productivity) can do about 800 quality meetings. Most of your salespeople (partners and client managers) will also be doing some delivery (doing the work), so you have to take that into consideration. You have an enormous amount of sales meeting capacity—how many sales meetings as a firm are you currently doing?

> "You need to work out how many meetings your team can conduct. I call this your quality meeting capacity—your QMC."

Many meetings are a waste of time, because you are not speaking with people who can make a decision (you MUST be speaking with all the decision makers at the same time, otherwise you are wasting your time) or your decision makers are just fishing for information. You must quickly qualify whom you are speaking with and what their time frame is for buying. You can do many sales meetings, however if the meetings are just "nice," then you'll have no traction—but you will be busy.

With the best of intentions, when accountants are in a sales role, they say things like, "It's an absolute certainty that this client will spend $X and the sale will close by [date]." The date comes around and you guessed it. No sale. They do not mean to tell lies—but they do. All salespeople tell lies. The reason is because there is no accurate forecasting and pipeline management system. The probability of a sale should be based on the stage (steps in the process) of the sale. So, an initial consultation might be 25 percent, a second meeting 50 percent, an implementation plan sent 75 percent, a verbal yes 90 percent, and money in the bank—100 percent. The date of closure should be based on when the client tells you it will close—which means you need to ask timing questions and let the client tell you when they want to do business. Never assume.

In your sales process, you need written meeting agendas, a question sequence to follow, and you need to record the major parts of the conversation. If you write the major points of the conversation, and you manage that through an online database management (often called CRM) system, you will be able to deal with more prospects at one time. When I have been in a full-time sales role selling professional services (average fee about $30K), I would typically manage about 100 prospects at any one time. Being organized enables you to do this.

Finally, whatever your sales process is, you need to set targets and monitor the success of the process and each person who follows it. Once you work out each person's QMC, get the salespeople to tell you how many meetings they will do. Some people will have a higher close rate (prospect to sale ratio) or the time to make a sale (number of days the opportunity is open) will be less. Others will have a higher average transaction per sale. Find out what these people are doing, have them train the rest, and replicate it over and over again.

> "You are looking for a higher conversion rate and fewer meetings per sale at a higher average transaction value per sale."

Conversion Rate Process

Just doing more meetings is a good start. Once you have people actually meeting prospects and clients, you will go a long way to making sales. As you monitor the conversion rate of each person (prospect to sale ratio), the number of meetings it takes to make a sale, and the average sale value, then you need to work on improving each area. You are looking for a higher conversion rate and fewer meetings per sale at a higher average transaction value per sale.

One of the key ingredients to sales success is the individuals' self-belief and conviction—it comes across as confidence and passion. You need to get more of it. Just like a dog can smell fear, so too can a prospect. If you have a speech impediment, this will affect your success. If you perspire a lot under your armpits or on the palms of your hands, this will affect your success. If you say "umm" before sentences, this will affect your success. If you look like an unkempt slob, this will affect your success. If you do not seem confident in your tone, this will affect your success.

You might need to "fake it until you make it" during your sales conversations. Take a deep breath before you get into the meeting. Wear dark clothing—and don't raise your arms. Wipe your hand on a cloth in your pocket before shaking hands. Invest in some new threads that make you feel better. Get some speech coaching. You need to think like a duck on a lake—cool and calm on top, but paddling like heck underneath. You need to get those butterflies flying in formation!

During your sales conversation, your number one goal should be to find your clients' motivations. You need to find out what their objectives are, what problems they are looking to solve, what their goals are, and what they want to achieve by using your services. You need to practice the types of questions you will ask. You need to role play with colleagues before you meet the client. You need to use words and sentences that are conducive to finding out what your clients objectives are (it's the "the language of the sale" that was previously discussed), and you need to do a "needs analysis" with each client.

> "You need to think like a duck on a lake—cool and calm on top, but paddling like heck underneath."

I love educating prospects during a sales process. That means they have learned something about their situation during the sales process. When you offer a "taster" of advice during the sales process, you are providing consulting to them while selling. An example is that you could tell your clients or prospect what to do, but not how to do it. During the process of selling, I like to use a strategy that I have perfected called "what if" selling. That means that you focus on **now** numbers (broken down by key performance indicators in the profit and loss and balance sheet) and based on you helping the clients (you tell them how you can help them), there is a hypothetical **where** result in each of the KPIs that the prospect nominates. Once extrapolated, the difference in profit, cash, and wealth is always massive. Makes your fees look insignificant and a great return on investment.

What you send to your clients or prospects during the process (you might have multiple meetings) will have an impact on your success. You should be citing case studies and testimonials of other successful clients you have worked with. You should be sending follow-up cards, emails, and other items of interest. Your implementation plans (you would typically call these proposals or engagement letters) should be a confirmation device that summarizes your conversation. They should follow the "language of the sale" process and cover no more than four pages.

There should not be an objection that you have not heard before. You should have a great answer for each objection. You should have a standard objection and answer list. Once you get an objection (and you will get plenty of them), the best way to handle them is to use the "feel, felt, found" technique. Here's an example: "I know how you **feel**, others that we have done this for **felt** exactly the same before we got started. What they **found** was that once we implemented this solution they . . . benefit, benefit, benefit.

So you have had a great meeting—now what? Most accountants in a sales role (and unsuccessful salespeople) say things like, "Come back to me when you are ready." or "Let me know if you are interested." Arrgh—you just poured cold water on the sale. You've had a good meeting, so always remember the true objective of the meeting—to book the next steps. You should always BAMFAM—**book a meeting from a meeting**. You need to progress the sale with the next step. The next step could be a follow-up meeting, an implementation plan sent, or a start

> "Once you get an objection (and you will get plenty of them), the best way to handle them is to use the 'feel, felt, found' technique."

date. Either way there is an event that happens after every sale. Systematically book it every single time after every single meeting.

If all else fails, simply ask for the business. Literally ask, "Do you want to achieve what we have outlined, and when do you want to achieve that?" They can only say no. If you have done the best job you can in the process, you have uncovered their objectives, and you have followed up in a timely manner, then remember they are only saying no to themselves and their objectives—not you. As a previous employee of mine used to say—"every no is closer to a yes." It's not your problem.

Twelve-Step Meeting Process

I am blessed to have been working with the accounting profession for more than 20 years. I love the influence that you can make and the difference to a client's financial position. You are loyal to your clients, your vendors, and your team. You are sometimes obstinate on parting with money, but that is not the most annoying thing. The most annoying thing in dealing with you is that you don't ask enough questions—sometimes none at all. It is so frustrating.

> "You have to remember to ZIP IT in a sales situation and not give the answer right away."

I am unsure why you don't ask questions. I am unsure why you are not more curious. I have a feeling that you think you need to know the answers and that asking questions is a sign of weakness. Quite the opposite. It's like you want to give the answers all the time rather than coax the answer out by asking quality questions.

The challenge with this behavior in a sales situation is that you jump to conclusions too fast, and you do not unearth the real issues or opportunities. You end up talking more than your client, and you are prescribing too fast without enough diagnosis. You have to remember to ZIP IT in a sales situation and not give the answer right away.

If you went to a sales training course a few decades ago, you would have been educated that "selling is telling." That might have been the case when product quality was the key differentiator to sell your product. You would follow the old formula of FAB—features, advantages, and benefits. You were taught to talk about the features of your product, talk about the advantages of the product, and finally (after more talking) you would tell the client the benefits of the product. You would talk yourself into the sale, and then out of the sale, and then into it again, until finally the prospects would buy so they could get rid of you! Or they would politely say, "I need to go away and think about it." That's a NO.

When I have a group of accountants who I am teaching to sell, I will initially (before the skills are taught) give them a role play. They have to pair up, with one as the client and the other plays the accountant (seller), and they are given a real client scenario to play out. When we do the debrief, the standard response was the accountant did all the talking and did not ask that many questions. And you guessed it, not too many made a sale.

Then I would demonstrate how it should be done. What I do is select any accountant from the audience and he or she plays the client—I play the accountant. The role play has to be about a real client who is a typical compliance-based client who has some potential. Most of the time, the client is paying the firm about $5K–$10K per year. I ask about 60 seconds of background questions (that I should know because I am the accountant), and then I set the scene. We are in a neutral place. I am visiting the client for the first time. The client knows the meeting is free. The audience has to observe the meeting and write any process, questions asked, etc. The audience also has to list potential additional services the client needs to buy to satisfy the client's needs. I tell the audience that this will be an amazing meeting, one of the best they have ever seen. They need to keep completely quiet, and it will be so good that we might start to levitate. Off we go, with me asking loads of leading questions in a **particular way.**

> "You would follow the old formula of FAB— features, advantages, and benefits."

I have done this interview (role playing the accountant) more than 100 times, and it always ends in the same way. The client buys with a substantial number of new services. Typically, the client will be paying five to ten times more per year with the additional services needed. The meeting format is predictable and teachable. You might never get to witness (or experience) this meeting with me, so instead of leaving you hanging, here is my 12-step meeting approach that I follow and teach.

Step 1. Make sure all the decision makers are at the meeting.

Step 2. Set the scene. Why we are having the meeting—the client is wondering.

Step 3. Frame the meeting purpose and time frame of the meeting.

Step 4. Understand the "now" by asking a series of background-related questions.

Step 5. Understand what the clients' goals and objectives are—what they want to achieve.

Step 6. Ask how they would know if they have achieved their objectives.

Step 7. Ask what it would mean to them if we helped them achieve their objectives.

Step 8. Ask what their current plans are to achieve their objectives.

Step 9. Ask what the consequences are of not doing something different.

Step 10. Ask timing-related questions—when they want to get started to achieve their objectives.

Step 11. Tell the client the next steps—write a plan to achieve objectives with options to take.

Step 12. Book the next steps—another meeting to clarify details or getting started date.

> "Being a sales success is not about telling. It's about asking open-ended questions and listening—really listening."

Leave a step out and the meeting is not predictable—it just does not work as well.

Being a sales success is not about telling. It's about asking open-ended questions and listening—really listening. The following model of great questions is about asking questions in a sequence. After years of testing, the sequence must be followed to the letter. You will see it follows my 12-step approach to the successful meeting.

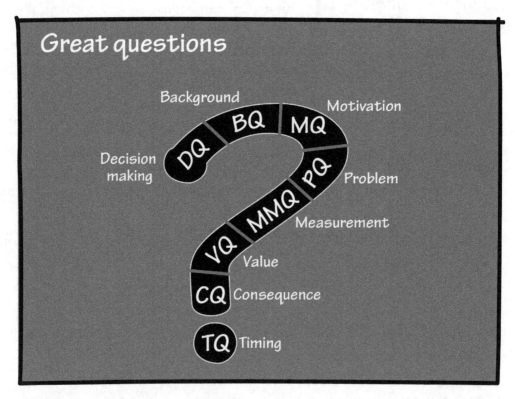

Under each of the categories there are a range of questions you could ask. Work out which questions you are comfortable with and ask them. Then listen, write the answer, and then ask the next one.

You have to ask quality questions in a structured way without giving away the answers. To simplify the types of questions to ask, you just need to remember BPOMVCT. You need to be asking questions to establish the situation and understand the **background.** You need to dig deep to find all of the **problems.** You need to understand the short- and long-term **objectives.** You need to establish the **measurement** metrics. Your prospect needs to tell you the **value** proposition when he or she implements your suggestions. Your prospect needs to understand the **consequences** of not doing something different. You both need to establish the **timing** of getting started.

> "Your prospect needs to tell you the value proposition when he or she implements your suggestions."

Asking questions with confidence and truly listening is the absolute best way to get sales. But it is absolutely pointless unless you LISTEN.

The way you ask questions is just as important as the questions. Here are some simple question-asking tips.

1. **Conversational, NOT interrogational**—not rapid fire, do pause and listen.
2. **Use question softeners.** A softener precedes the question—for example, "So that I can best help you" . . . "Could I just ask" . . . "That's interesting, have you."
3. **Answer a question with another question.** For example, "Yes, we can do that. What else are you looking for help in?"
4. **Give positive strokes.** It shows you are listening. For example, "Aha, I see" . . . "Really, I understand" . . . "Tell me more about that."
5. **Feedback what the client says.** For example, "So what you are saying is" . . . "So you said your objectives are."
6. **Always be confirming.** For example, "Just to confirm" . . . "OK, to confirm you are."

Let's dig into the detail of the questions to ask.

DQs—making sure you are speaking with your buyer. Often you are not speaking with all the people who can make a decision. You need to find the **decision makers** by asking direct questions.

1. Can you sign off on this plan without speaking with anyone else?
2. Who are the owners, directors, and shareholders of your business?

3. Who else is involved in making this decision?

4. Who are the key decision makers in your business?

BQs—understanding the **background** of the current situation. You cannot prescribe services until you diagnose the situation. You can ask questions, such as the following.

> "Often you are not speaking with all the people who can make a decision. You need to find the **decision makers** by asking direct questions."

1. So that I can understand your business fully—can you tell me what are the key things that make it work the way it does?

2. If you look back to when you first started or bought your business, where did you think it would be today?

3. So that I can understand your cash flow situation, can I just ask in what order do you pay the following: yourself, creditors, salaries, tax department?

4. What is your overdraft limit, and what is the typical cash balance?

5. How has the revenue and profit been during the past three years—increasing, flat, going backwards? And to what do you attribute that?

6. What are some of the best decisions you have made in the past three years?

7. What are some of the worst decisions you have made in the past three years?

8. If you had your time over again, what would you do differently?

9. I am curious. You started this business 10 years ago. When you started it, where did you think you would be today?

10. How many customers do you have?

11. How many times do they buy from you?

12. What is the approximate average transaction value?

13. If you could wave a magic wand, what would be some of the problems you have in business that you would like to go away?

MQs and PQs—you need to understand the clients' objectives. Where they want to go, what they want to achieve (**motivation**), and what they want to fix (**problems**). Ask questions such as these.

1. Over and above what you are planning to do—what would be your ideal world business objectives?

2. If you could crystal ball your business and your life, what would it look like?

3. Take the business out three years—what would you like it to look like?

4. Let's look at the next five years—where would you like to be with your wealth creation?

> "You need measurement metrics and the client must state what they are."

5. What would you like to achieve by us working together?

6. What help do you need from us—and why?

7. What has led us to having this meeting—what do you want to achieve?

8. What are the current issues you would like solved that you are grappling with?

9. What is getting in the way of you achieving your objectives right now?

10. What are the specific things you want to achieve?

11. Why are these objectives important to you?

12. How badly do you want to achieve these objectives?

13. How confident are you that you will achieve these objectives without our help?

14. What other objectives would you like to achieve?

MMQs—you and your client need to understand how the project that you are about to propose will be measured. You need **measurement metrics** and the client must state what they are. There is only one question to ask once you have determined the objectives.

1. We can certainly help you achieve those objectives. They are completely in line with what we do. We've helped many other clients achieve theirs; we enjoy it and we're good at it. So that you know if you have achieved your objectives, we will work with you to measure the success of every project. In line with measuring the success, how would **you** know if we have helped you achieve your objectives?

VQs—the **value** that the client receives by implementing your ideas. This is where you start to get emotional buy-in to your project.

1. We can help you achieve those objectives. As I said, we are good at it and we have done it before. If we could help you achieve them, what would be the impact on you and the business?

2. If we could help you achieve your objectives, what would it mean to you and your business?

3. If we could help you achieve your objectives, what are the main benefits you would realize?

4. If we could help you achieve your objectives, what significant difference would it make to you and your business?

CQs—having your client understand the consequences of not buying your services and doing something different. There are two key questions and a statement to make at the end.

> "VQs—the value that the client receives by implementing your ideas. This is where you start to get emotional buy-in to your project."

1. What are your current plans that you have in place to help you achieve your objectives?

2. What are the consequences if you do not do something different?

3. So what you are saying is you have to do something different to achieve your objectives!

TQs—**timing**-related questions that start to wrap up the meeting. You need to find out when this project is going to start.

1. What is going to happen from here is that I am going to go away and write a detailed implementation plan about how you can achieve your objectives and realize your potential. The plan will have an agreed-on start date, some different implementation options you can choose, and a set fee for each of the options. (If appropriate) Any fee charged will be funded out of new cash flow. So that I can set the start date, are there any scheduled cyclical dates or trips coming up that I need to be aware of?

2. OK—is this a later or a sooner project for you to get started?

3. What's stopping you from getting started right now?

4. What is your decision-making process?

5. I will check our workflow schedule and put a proposed start date during the week of (date)? How does suit you?

Finally, how to close the meeting and book the next steps—after the timing questions.

> "Do not ask dumb questions, such as 'What keeps you awake at night?' It is so stupid to ask that question."

1. I will send you the implementation plan by close of business (day). You'll have some questions when you read it, and we will more than likely need to meet again. When would you get a chance to read it?

2. So, could we meet again on (day) at (time) to answer questions and confirm the appropriate option and get started?

3. Just to confirm, I will send you the implementation plan by close of business (day), you'll read it (over the weekend), and then if we can meet again on (day) at (time), we'll go over everything, answer questions, and get started.

You will notice you are NOT talking about your firm, your people, how good you are, or your solutions. The entire conversation is about the client. His situation and what he wants to achieve by hiring you to help him and his business.

Do not ask dumb questions, such as "What keeps you awake at night?" It is so stupid to ask that question. You're going to get dumb answers, such as snoring, baby, the train, loud music, rather than what you are looking for.

You want to ask questions that invoke a response and help you move closer to a YES. When you look at human behavior, people buy professional services for only five (or a mix of) reasons.

1. To make money

2. To save money

3. To save time

4. To achieve pleasure

5. To fix pain

Your products and services can help in most of those areas. You just need to find out what is most important to the prospect right now.

For maximum success, here are a couple of sales tips that go with this meeting format.

1. Do not go armed with a long list of questions to ask—you'll get confused. Just remember the process and let it flow.

2. Make sure you have all the decision makers in the meeting—you are wasting your time otherwise. If you do not have all the decision makers in front of you, you will need to rebook the meeting.

3. It's a conversation—not an interrogation. Use question softeners before each question.

4. Your tonality will play a part in your success. If you have a weak tone or you mumble, then you will not make as many sales.

5. Your enthusiasm is important. Tell the clients if they have a good business and make sure you smile.

6. Spend most of your time on the BQs, MQs, and PQs.

7. Always, always book the next steps—book a meeting from a meeting—BAMFAM.

8. Remember to have fun. They can only say no. Every no you get is closer to yes.

If you get really stuck in your meetings, you could ask the following question to flush out the highest motivation right now.

"Our work with business owners like you is focused on five key areas. We are helping our clients to (1) grow revenue and wealth, (2) dramatically increase profit, (3) minimize tax, (4) protect assets, and (5) improve cash flow. Which of those are most important to you right now?"

> "When the level of 'pissedoffness' (technical term for really annoyed) is high, they will buy."

Then let them talk. You are flushing out the core objectives at the outset by asking questions like this. People typically buy additional services from accountants to move away from something (pain related) or move toward something (pleasure related).

It's human nature that people will tend to buy more to solve pain than to achieve pleasure. The pain in a business could be one or more of the following.

1. Cash-flow related
2. People related
3. Client service
4. Losing revenue
5. Profitability related
6. Competitor related

> "Asking quality, open-ended questions are at the heart of a sales conversation."

When the level of "pissedoffness" (technical term for really annoyed) is high, they will buy. You need to find that pain in the conversations you have with your clients or prospects. When you find the pain, you then exacerbate the pain (powerful sales technique here) by asking more questions about the painful area. You keep asking and probing and provoking the pain area. You "poke the bruise" until it hurts.

As you go through your sales meetings, you're ultimately looking for a resolution to the conversation. There are only three final answers in a sales process—YES, NO, or NOT NOW. You might get a MAYBE from time to time, but that is typically a smoke screen for an objection.

If you get a maybe, then you have not found out the pain points enough. You haven't found out the true objectives.

Asking quality, open-ended questions are at the heart of a sales conversation. To remain relevant in the future, you're going to need to get good at sales. Asking questions will help you get there.

Dealing with Objections

A game I play with accountants is "sales rugby." I gather the accountants in a circle and have one throw the rugby ball to someone who has to pick an objection card from the pack. On one side is the objection—the other side has the answer. I read the objection and then the accountant has to answer quickly and succinctly.

Here are three great objections, and ways in which you can deal with them.

Client: How much will this cost?

You: I don't know yet. I need to go away and think about it. I will come back to you with a detailed implementation plan, which will outline some implementation options you could take. Each option will have a set fee.

Client: I have no money to pay for it.

You: That's exactly why you need me/us! (in a serious and authoritative tone) I am serious about this, (name). We need to work with you to sort out your profit and cash-flow situation. If we do not help you, then you will always be in this situation. You will never be able to realize your potential, your family will not be properly supported, and any goals or dreams you have can be kissed goodbye. You will never succeed. We have currently helped (X) other clients (assuming you have) with exactly the same issue or opportunity. An example of that is (cite some examples), and they were in exactly the same situation as you are. They now are (give examples). Because a cash flow and profit plan is an ongoing project, we can structure the payment arrangements on a monthly basis. And typically, the fee we charge you will be funded out of new and additional cash flow. We're good at this sort of work. We've done it before, and we love doing it. But before we get into the specifics of how we can help you, I want to understand your objectives. Assuming we can help you in this area, and we can, what would you like your business to look like in the next three to five years?

Client: What is your hourly rate for this sort of work?

You: We do not use hourly rates. Our fees are based on our contribution to the value you receive as a result of the project. We will be fairly rewarded for our contribution, and you'll get a tremendous return on your investment.

> "We do not use hourly rates. Our fees are based on our contribution to the value you receive as a result of the project."

You've heard all the objections before. They should be documented. No objection should be a surprise. And when it's all said and done, and you've done the best you can do, remember this . . . .

I have been professionally speaking (getting paid to speak) since 1993, and I have been averaging about 80 presentations per year. I learned a long time ago that you always give three speeches, or you give three presentations, or give three meetings.

1. The one you intend on giving.
2. The one you actually give.
3. The one you should have given, that you give to yourself on the way home.

Your meetings, presentations, or speeches will never be exactly right. Get over yourself and go do some!

Sealing the Deal in Writing

You've just had a great meeting with your prospect or client. You made sure that 100 percent of the decision makers were in the meeting—you just wasted the meeting if they were not. You did your research about the client and the business, and you spent most of the meeting understanding the current situation and really understanding the objectives—the client told you these answers. About 80 percent of the meeting was understanding where the client is and where he or she wants to go. They told you what it meant to them (their value) to achieve their objectives, and they told you the consequences of their life if they did not do something different. They might have asked you how much it was going to cost, but you simply said,

"I'll go away and think about it. I'll put an implementation plan together during the next 48 hours as to how we can help you achieve your objectives. The implementation plan will reiterate our conversation today, and it will have three options of how we can work together. Every option will have a fixed price with no surprises."

You've basically followed my 12-step meeting process to the letter, and you're ready to put it in writing. The document you're about to write is not a sales document—it is a confirmation document. The document is not called a quote (that's for tradespeople or contractors), and it is not called a proposal. It is called an implementation plan. This is a document that is about how you are going to help your clients achieve their objectives and realize their value. It is what you are going to implement.

> "About 80 percent of the meeting was understanding where the client is and where he or she wants to go."

The format of the following implementation plan templates have originated from the excellent work of Alan Weiss. Alan has written more than 50 books for consultants on how to run a great consulting business. In many of his books, he references a nine-step system about how to document the meeting. You can find more details on these formats in Alan's book, *Million Dollar Proposals*. More detail on Alan Weiss can be found at www.alanweiss.com.

Template—Implementation Plan

Project Summary

A paragraph or two that explains why you are submitting the implementation plan. How did it come to pass? Why you are getting together?

Objectives

I see the objectives of our involvement as—

Include two to five objectives to be accomplished are stated as business outcomes.

Measurement Metrics

Measures for success will include the following metrics.

For example, weekly sales forecasts, exit interviews, customer surveys—whatever it is you have agreed to measure. You are providing more value to this client by putting measurement in place, and you are actually establishing the criteria for your own success.

Value

From what we have discussed, the value to your business of achieving these objectives, given the metrics above, will be as follows.

Timing

I am prepared to start this project within the next 30 days, and I accept that it would be completed sometime between three and five months from the date of beginning.

Joint Accountabilities

You are responsible for XXX. I am responsible for XXX. We are both responsible for XXX.

If either of us learns of something that will materially impact the success of this project, we agree to immediately inform the other.

Options

To deliver the proposed value to you, I see there are three potential options you could take.

Option	Deliverables
1	List deliverables in brief terms.
2	Everything in Option 1, plus the following List additional deliverables in brief terms.
3	Everything in Option 2, plus the following List additional deliverables in brief terms.

Terms and Conditions

Fees

    Option 1—$XXXX

    Option 2—$XXXX

    Option 3—$XXXX

Payment Terms

A deposit of 50 percent is required on acceptance of this implementation plan. The balance of 50 percent is required no less than 45 days from the date of acceptance of this implementation plan. As a professional courtesy, a 10 percent reduction is offered if the full amount is paid in full on acceptance of this implementation plan. Payments can be made by check, electronic funds transfer, or credit card, or a monthly payment option can be set up.

While this project might be postponed or rescheduled with our mutual agreement and without penalties, it is noncancelable and all fees are due as indicated in the schedule above.

Acceptance

This implementation plan has a 10-working day deadline. If the implementation plan is not accepted on or before (date), then the implementation plan will be deemed null and void.

Your signature below indicates acceptance of this implementation plan and the terms and conditions herein. If you accept the implementation plan, please sign and fax to (fax number). Upon receipt, a tax invoice will be forwarded to you for immediate payment.

Please check the option you prefer.

- ❑ Option 1—$XXXX
- ❑ Option 2—$XXXX
- ❑ Option 3—$XXXX

Please check the payment schedule you prefer.

- ❑ 50 percent deposit + 50 percent due in 45 days
- ❑ 10 percent discount with payment in full upon acceptance

Signed on behalf of

FIRM NAME   CLIENT NAME

By _____ By _____
Name _____ Name _____
Title _____ Title _____
Date _____ Date _____

To accept this implementation plan, please sign and fax back to (fax number) or scan and email to (email) on or before (date).

Real Implementation Plan—Cash-Flow Forecasting

The Directors

Company Name and Address

Dear Phil and Karen,

Further to our recent discussions and meeting on (date) I would like to outline a process for your business to achieve the goals you have set for yourselves and the business going forward.

You have indicated increased frustration in relation to the operating structure of the business and the level of reliance that is leveled at Phil personally to ensure the ongoing success of the business. You have advised that you are time poor and lacking motivation due to the demands being placed on you.

You have expressed an understanding that the business needs to introduce systems and procedures in order to deal with this situation. As reviewed at our meeting, you have confidence that the business has the financial resources and profit to underwrite a period of change, and as such you are prepared to move forward on an exciting journey of change during the next 12–24 months.

At our meeting, we discussed two immediate projects that are relevant to your situation. This implementation plan relates to the first of these projects, namely the profit and loss and cash-flow budgets for the business.

Per our discussions, I understand that you have set some goals that include the following.

- ✓ To have an understanding of the expected financial results of the business for the next 12 months
- ✓ To have an understanding of your working capital demands as the business undergoes a period of change
- ✓ To have the ability to review the actual trading performance of the business against an agreed benchmark
- ✓ To have financial management tools in place that can be used to educate key team members
- ✓ To have appropriate financial management tools in place that can be used to measure the performance of key segments of the business in addition to measuring the performance of and motivating key team members

✓ To have the ability to source additional funding for growth

✓ To generate sufficient cash reserves to release the bank security currently provided by XXX.

As you are aware, we have had numerous discussions regarding the fact that the business did not maintain an up-to-date financial budget. Financial budgets outline the targets that the business must achieve so that you can achieve your goals. They are used to monitor the operating performance and cash flow of the business, and as such are an essential financial management tool for any business. Budgets must be implemented, reviewed, and regularly updated to be effective.

Objectives

Based on what you told me, I see the objectives of our involvement as follows.

✓ You obtaining a clear understanding of the existing financial position of your business

✓ You obtaining a clear understanding of the financial impacts of the operational changes in your business

✓ You obtaining an understanding of the financial results that must be achieved to realize your goals

✓ You having the confidence to move forward with changes in the business

✓ To work closely with you to manage and improve the available cash flow from your business

✓ To work with you to effectively manage the growth of your business

✓ To work closely with you to manage the financial performance of your business

Measurement

Our measures for success will include the following.

✓ Implementation of financial budgets into your accounting system to be used as a financial management tool

✓ Improved working capital management systems within the business

✓ Improved working capital and cash flow

✓ Your ability to work more on the business rather than in it

✓ Your ability to step away from certain administrative business systems and have comfort that they will run effectively without your direct input

✓ Achievement of agreed actions in desired time frame

Value

From what we have discussed, the value to you will be as follows.

✓ Improved working capital and cash flow management

✓ Improved business operating systems

✓ Empowerment of key staff to step into more management-based roles

✓ Enhanced quality of life and less stress

✓ Ability to make better management decisions

✓ Ability to grow or manage the business without significant demands on your personal time

✓ Increase your ability to raise adequate finances to expand the business or to invest to create wealth

Methodology and Options

To deliver the proposed value to you, I see there are three potential options you could take.

Option 1

➢ Preparation of expected financial budgets for (company name) for the period 1 July XXXX to 30 June XXXX

➢ Preparation of best-case and worst-case financial budgets for (company name) for the period 1 July XXXX to 30 June XXXX

➢ Consultation with you to determine the assumptions and key drivers of the budgets

➢ Assistance with implementation of budgets into your accounting system to enable review and benchmarking of your financial performance.

Option 2

Everything in Option 1, plus the following

- ➤ Preparation of financial budgets for (company name) for the periods ending 30 June XXXX and 30 June XXXX (that is, two additional years)
- ➤ Review of your financial management systems and preparation of advice/strategy in relation to recommended system changes and/or improvements
- ➤ **Option 3**
- ➤ Everything in Option 2, plus the following
- ➤ Analysis of your actual results each quarter and make any adjustments to your budgets as a result of changed circumstances as required
- ➤ Detailed analysis and integrity check of your results on a quarterly basis and benchmarking them against the budget, including the preparation of a financial management report
- ➤ Establishment of financial key performance indicators for the business
- ➤ Training of key team members in relation to the generation of management reports and the interpretation of those reports for management purposes

Timing

I am prepared to start this project immediately on acceptance.

Joint Accountabilities

Our commitment to you is as follows.

- ✓ We will hold all details in confidence.
- ✓ We will meet all agreed-on project deadlines.
- ✓ We will respond to any communication within 24 hours.

Your commitment to us is as follows.

- ✓ You will meet payment terms as specified.
- ✓ You will not disclose any information provided to you (including this proposal) that is intellectual property in nature to any other business or individual.

✓ You will respond to inquiries, information requests, or communication promptly.

✓ You will inform me immediately if there are any internal/external changes that might affect the successful completion of this project.

Terms and Conditions

Your investment is one of these options.

✓ Option 1—$4,750

✓ Option 2—$8,750

✓ Option 3—$18,600

Year-end compliance work and other project work falling outside the scope of this proposal will continue to be carried out in accordance with our existing arrangement.

Payment Terms

A deposit of 50 percent of the initial payment is required on acceptance of this proposal. The balance of 50 percent is required no less than 30 days from the acceptance of this proposal. As a professional courtesy, a 10 percent reduction is offered if the full amount applicable to Option 3 is paid in full on acceptance of this proposal.

To enable you to better manage your cash flow, we also offer extended fee funding through (fee funding company) for a period of up to ten months. Please contact me for details if you wish to use this service.

Payments can be made by check, electronic funds transfer, or credit card.

Guarantee and Referral

We are committed to providing the highest quality of services. To reinforce this commitment, we promise to continue to work with you until you are completely satisfied with the services and products we have provided, within the scope of this project.

Upon completion of this project, if you are happy with our dedication to high quality service, the greatest compliment you can pay us is by referring family, friends, and others you feel would benefit from the use of our services, and our new value-based upfront pricing system. By establishing a referral expectation upfront, our clients have plenty of time to think of who they would like to introduce to our firm, helping us build a firm with quality clients such as you.

Acceptance

This proposal remains valid for 20 working days and expires on (date).

Your signature below indicates acceptance of the proposal and the terms and conditions herein. If you accept, please sign and fax to (fax number), or scan and email to (email address). Upon receipt, a tax invoice will be forwarded to you for immediate payment.

We would like to select Option _____ (enter 1, 2, or 3, based on your choice of options outlined above).

- ❏ Please check the payment schedule you prefer.
- ❏ 50 percent deposit + 50 percent due in 30 days
- ❏ 10 percent reduction with payment in full upon acceptance, applicable to Option 3
- ❏ Extended funding through (fee funding company)

Signed on behalf of

Firm Name

By _____

Name   _____

Title   _____

Date   _____

Signed on behalf of

XYZ PTY LTD

By _____

Name   _____

Title   _____

Date   _____

To accept this proposal by (date), please sign and fax to (fax number), or scan and email to (email address).

Real Implementation Plan—Cash Flow and Profit Improvement

Project Summary

From my discussions with (prospect or client) and my detailed knowledge of your financial position throughout many years, it is clear your business has a major problem with cash flow and profitability. I also understand your concern that you have lost control of your own business and are being thwarted by some staff in your attempts to drive the business into the more profitable area of commercial work.

You are seeking our assistance in turning this position around.

Objectives

I see the objectives of our involvement as follows.

Get you back in control of your own business.

Significantly improve profitability, cash flow, and personal wealth.

Get team buy-in about the changes that need to be put in place to achieve your goals.

Measurement Metrics

Your feedback will be the most important measure of your increased control over your business. Cash flow and profitability improvements can be accurately measured through monthly key performance indicators, profit and loss, budget, and cash-flow projection analysis. Meeting and preferably exceeding monthly sales targets for commercial work will evidence team commitment to this area of work.

Value

The major value to you will be a significant improvement in profitability of your business, ensuring its longevity. Cash flow is of prime importance, and your team members need to appreciate their roles and responsibilities in driving improvements in this area. An improved team culture will reduce stress in the workplace and promote commitment to your goals.

Timing

Option 1 is a one–week process.

Option 2 is a one–month process.

Option 3 is a seven–month process.

Methodology and Options

To deliver the proposed value to you, I see there are three potential options you could take.

Option	Methodology
1	Consultation with you, to fully identify all issues and problems and seek feedback on possible courses of action. Telephone discussions to seek further information and feedback during the following week, if necessary. Meeting to provide verbal recommendations of actions required to implement changes. Presentation of a one-page, dot-point summary of recommendations, including details of which financial reports need to be supplied to you on a weekly or monthly basis.
2	Everything in Option 1, plus the following Facilitation of a team meeting to evaluate team culture, commitment, and issues. Involve the team in developing hard and soft key performance indicators and encourage their buy-in to a monitoring and accountability process. An individual meeting with two or three key staff to clarify information and issues from the team meeting. A meeting with you to agree on organizational structure, reporting systems, targets, key performance indicators, and accountability processes. Develop an action plan for the implementation of the above changes.

Option	Methodology
3	Everything in Option 2, plus the following Every month, for the next six months, provide the following. Monthly review of your reporting systems data with particular focus on key performance indicators—this data must be provided by a specified date, to be agreed. Monthly accountability meetings with your key team members to review action plan and budget versus actual performance. Where key performance indicators and budget have not been met, conduct investigation into the reason and agree on measures for the rectification. This meeting would be held on specified dates within four working days of the provision of our reporting system data. One-on-one meeting with you each month to discuss results and confidential matters. Phone access to me or (professional partner) who would assist with this project to discuss any issues in relation to implementation of your action plan and profitability turnaround.

Acceptance

This proposal has a 10-working day deadline. If the proposal is not accepted on or before (date), then the proposal will be deemed to be null and void.

Your signature below indicates acceptance of this proposal and the terms and conditions herein. If you accept the proposal, please sign and fax to (fax number) or email to (email address). Upon receipt, a tax invoice will be forwarded to you for immediate payment.

Please check the option you prefer.

- ❏ Option 1—$3,600
- ❏ Option 2—$15,900
- ❏ Option 3—$29,900

Please check the payment schedule you prefer.

❑ 50 percent deposit + 50 percent due in 45 days

❑ 10 percent discount with payment in full upon acceptance for Option 3 only

❑ $4,600 deposit + $4,600 per month for six months payable with five days of invoice

Signed on behalf of

Firm Name

By _____

Name   _____

Title   _____

Date   _____

Signed on behalf of

XYZ PTY LTD

By _____

Name   _____

Title   _____

Date   _____

To accept the implementation plan, please sign and fax to (fax number) or scan and email to (email address) on or before (date).

Real Implementation Plan—Business Development Project

Project Summary

ABC Co. is at a crossroads. Having established itself as a significant business in the (anytown) area, the business is too reliant on the founder, David Jones. To move forward, changes need to be made so that valued senior team members are able to take on higher profiles and play driving roles in the next stage of the business.

Consequently, ABC Co. is seeking the most effective way of reaching a situation whereby reliance on David is reduced while the business can still progress, allowing all team members to grow and develop new skills.

Objectives

The objectives of this project are as follows.

- ✓ To position Bob, Martha, and George to be considered for partnership by 30 June XXXX
- ✓ To ensure that workflow management and business operations are enhanced so that efficiencies are found, hence increasing average hourly rate recovered
- ✓ To control work in progress (WIP) and maneuver WIP management away from David
- ✓ To reduce dependency on David in winning and delivering high-value work through skills development of other senior team members (including Ann) so as to share the load, create a culture of learning and, as a team, add more value to clients
- ✓ To win new work as a result of targeted marketing activities that are designed to contribute to the team's development needs
- ✓ To better serve existing key clients by freeing up David's time to nurture and develop those relationships

Measurement Metrics

The measures that will tell us we are on track are as follows.

- ✓ David will work fewer hours per week, with predominance of chargeable time on high-value work for profitable clients.
- ✓ The senior team will win the high-level work and delegate to more junior people.
- ✓ Bob, Martha, and George will be in a position where they are ready to be considered as partners.
- ✓ A marketing plan is in place and implemented.
- ✓ Improved client satisfaction is demonstrated.

Value

The value to the organization of implementing this project is agreed to be more life-balance than monetary-related and can be summarized as follows.

- ✓ The business will be less reliant on the partners and able to grow through other means rather than exclusively David selling and delivering high-value work.
- ✓ Enhanced team satisfaction seen through focused career development plans.
- ✓ Increased profitability and business value will be demonstrated through better efficiencies, creating more high-value work to be performed. Based on a conservative estimate of 5 percent productivity gains and an average hourly rate of $250 on new services sold in the time freed up by such gains, fees would increase by at least $200,000, virtually all of which would drop to the bottom line.
- ✓ Increased ability for David to invest time with the team members to help them achieve their goals.
- ✓ David having more time with his wife, to exercise, and to undertake study.
- ✓ Business under control and management reporting done in a timely manner.

Methodology and Options

There are three ways in which we can achieve these objectives.

Option 1

- ✓ We will facilitate an evaluation meeting with your team members to understand development needs from their perspective and ensure buy-in to the personal development program. This will be done either at your office or at a venue selected by you close to your office.
- ✓ We will attend, by phone, a senior management meeting as required, to review key business numbers and hold you accountable to short-term targets and projects.
- ✓ We will design and deliver a coaching program for the management team and (if required) David and Ann, involving individual short- and medium-term goals, guidance in designing the projects required to achieve those goals, and the provision of accountability to drive implementation.

✓ We will design and deliver a training workshop focused on identifying, selling, and delivering high-value work. This too will be done either at your office or at a venue selected by you close to your office.

Option 2

We will implement Option 1, and also the following.

✓ Conduct a client focus group to raise awareness of the services your firm can provide and gather feedback on client perception of your ability to provide services.

✓ Develop the format for a monthly marketing workshop to be held by your management team, the aim being to provide a regular forum for discussing opportunities, provide feedback on individual marketing activities and results, and ensure each member of the senior team engages in activities aimed at developing themselves and the business.

✓ Provision of agendas and workshop materials for the first three meetings.

Option 3

We will implement Options 1 and 2, and also the following.

✓ Facilitate the initial marketing workshop to transfer the skills of running such meetings to your team.

✓ Run a second evaluation meeting with your team at the end of the project to gauge progress and, as a result, suggest any changes required to keep the momentum going.

✓ Run a second focus group with clients at the end of the project to measure their changes in perception in the firm and the management team.

Timing

Option 1 includes a coaching program (we expect an initial term of six months would be adequate to achieve the objectives) and can be scheduled around Ann's holiday commitments. We are ready to start as soon as you give the go-ahead and have tentatively scheduled June 2 as the commencement date.

The additional work in Option 2 should be completed within 30–45 days of the inception of the project.

The additional work in Option 3 should be completed within 60–75 days of the inception of the project.

Joint Accountabilities

ABC Co. will be responsible for making team members available for interviews, focus groups, and workshops; informing them of the project; and providing a private area to hold interviews. ABC Co. will be responsible for providing information about the business, as requested; for adhering to the payment schedules established for this project; for organizing and inviting clients to client focus groups; for providing venues for client focus groups; for reasonable access to senior team members for ongoing progress reports, discussions, and problems; for organizing offsite venues for training, if required; and for coordinating workflow and priorities to allow for the project to meet its time frames.

We are responsible for all focus groups, workshops, and other interventions called for this in this proposal; we will ensure minimal disruption in work procedures and adhere to all schedules; we will provide updates and progress reports at your request; we will schedule all coaching conference calls; we will immediately inform you of any peripheral issues that emerge that we think merit your attention.

Each of us will inform the other immediately of any unforeseen changes, new developments, or other issues that impact and influence this project, so that we can both adjust accordingly. Each of us will accommodate the other's unexpected scheduling conflicts. We each agree to err on the side of over-communication to keep each other abreast of all aspects of the project.

Terms and Conditions

Fees

Option 1—$19,000

Option 2—$26,000

Option 3—$34,000

An amount equal to 50 percent is due upon acceptance of this proposal, and the balance is due 45 days following that payment. As a professional courtesy, we offer a 10 percent discount if the full fee is paid on commencement. Payment may be made by direct bank transfer, check, or credit card.

Expenses

Expenses will be billed as actually accrued on a monthly basis and are due on receipt of our invoice. Reasonable travel expenses include economy airfare, train, taxi, car rental, hotel, and meals. We do not bill for fax, courier, administrative work, telephone, photocopying, or related office expenses. Any offsite venue hire costs associated with focus groups and team workshops will be borne by ABC Co.

Conditions

The quality of our work is guaranteed. Once accepted, this offer is non-cancellable for any reason and payments are to be made at the times specified. However, you may reschedule, postpone, or delay this project, as your business needs might unexpectedly dictate, without penalty and without time limit, subject only to mutually agreeable time frames in the future.

Acceptance

The signatures below indicate acceptance of the details, terms, and conditions in this proposal, and provide approval to begin work as specified. Alternatively, your deposit indicates full acceptance and also will signify approval to begin.

Option selected (please indicate) Option 1   Option 2   Option 3

For (firm name)	For ABC Co.
Signature	Signature
Name	Name
Director	Title
Date	Date

SOME PEOPLE ARE NEEDED

The Current Team Might Be Short Lived

Around the world, technology is disrupting many jobs in many industries. Among jobs in the firing line include those that involve repetition, problem solving, information dissemination, and data processing. If there is any type of human algorithm involved, it can now be done by a computer or a robot. If there is manual data entry, then much of that can be done by supercomputers with barcoding. If there is consistent repetition in the job in the future, it can be done by software and supercomputers. If there is information dissemination involved, then that can be done by the Internet and clever algorithms.

> "What's happened with all this technology? I think it has dumbed down the value of an accountant."

Sound like anyone we know? Yes—you!

The current team members might be short lived, if technology takes hold the way I think it will. Due to technology, there has been significant progress in how clients interact with their accountants.

Here is a rudimentary summary of how clients interact with their accountants.

1. Client has problem or opportunity or requirement to interact with an accountant.

2. Client contacts accountant (or vice versa) and accountant tells client what information is required.

3. Client sends in relevant information.

4. Accountant checks that information is complete.

5. Accountant processes the information.

6. Accountant creates report/letter/study/meeting/structure and presents to client.

7. Accountant files the information with relevant parties.

8. Client says well done and pays the bill.

It's been the same process since before the days that accountants have been tracking time!

What's changed? The only thing that has changed is the technology and tools so the job could be done more efficiently. Here is a timeline of technology usage in accounting firms throughout the years. Paper receipts were delivered by horse, by oxen, or on foot, in an old shoe box, then . . .

> Paper receipts were entered into a handwritten cashbook, then . . .

> Handwritten equations and a lot of thinking worked out the client's situation, then . . .

> The postal service enabled distribution of information, then . . .

> The handwritten cashbook was turned into a spreadsheet, then . . .

"Due to technology, there has been significant progress in how clients interact with their accountants."

> There was one computer in the office and it had its own charge code, then . . .

> The spreadsheet was saved to a floppy disk, then . . .

> There was a paper-based "working paper" and paper filing in big filing cabinets, then . . .

> A calculator replaced the pencil and paper equation, then . . .

> There was a thing called a fax machine and clients faxed in information, then . . .

> The spreadsheet turned into software and it was saved to a floppy disk, then . . .

> There was a pool of computers in the office administered by experts, then . . .

> The software on a floppy disk got too big so it was saved to a CD-ROM, then . . .

- ➤ The firm had one email address only and a slow (dial-up) Internet connection, then . . .
- ➤ The software on the CD-ROM got too big so it was saved to a USB stick, then . . .
- ➤ There was a computer on every desk with one screen, then . . .
- ➤ Electronic work papers appeared and paper filing still existed, then . . .
- ➤ Scanners started appearing on each accountant's desk, then . . .
- ➤ Everyone had an email address and they now had two computer screens per person, then . . .
- ➤ The paperless office is now a reality, then . . .
- ➤ The Internet speed increased dramatically, then . . .
- ➤ Powerful searching could now take place on the Internet—no need for books, then . . .
- ➤ Accountants started to get three screens on every desk, then . . .
- ➤ Accountants got good at using the software in front of them, then . . .
- ➤ Cloud-based software appeared and the accounting world changed forever!

> "I think a whole new market can be created by accountants where the profession looks nothing like what it does today."

Any of this bringing back memories?

What's happened with all this technology? I think it has dumbed down the value of an accountant. These days, accountants need to know which keys (on the keyboard) to hit in which order and how to use the software. What happened to the thinking behind accounting? I think the thinking has gone. The technology has taken away the smarts of an accountant.

Cloud-based accounting software has found its feet and by the year 2020, I think it will be commonplace in the majority of small to medium businesses. Because the Cloud-based accounting software is driven by smart supercomputers, the accountants that we have today are not needed. You can get computing power to do most of that work. There's an app for that!

What the profession needs is the accountant of yesteryear. **Before technology, the "yesteryear accountant"** used basic technology, like a pencil and paper to solve client problems. They had to think about what was going on and manually work it out. They gave real advice based on wisdom and experience.

These days, the computer is working out the clients' problems and the Internet is giving the advice. Soon it will all blend into one and the "app" will work it out and give the advice. If you have an iPhone, think Siri for business.

To thrive, accountants must add value to what is in front of them. If they don't, they might go the way of the dinosaur. I am not saying that accountants will be 100 percent redundant. Not at all. I think a whole new market can be created by accountants where the profession looks nothing like what it does today.

That new market is where the entire profession is giving an experience to the human that the computer cannot. That new market is financial coaching, business counseling, and business advising.

We'll still need people in the profession, but not as many redundant-data accountants. If that's you, then get out now or change.

If you're not adding value to the data in front of you, then your days are numbered!

A Virtual Team

Having a team offshore can sometimes be a touchy subject with some people, but it's not going to go away. Clothing has been manufactured overseas for years, and now it's office jobs. When the labor costs are one-fifth to a tenth of what is paid in Western countries, it is a compelling opportunity for businesses to consider. There is also an abundance of people who are educated and keen to work.

"With an up to 80 percent cost reduction on labor costs those who are using offshore teams can hire more people and give a better service."

Although many Asian countries are offering outsourcing resources, I am most familiar with the Philippines market. There are approximately 1.2M people currently hired (in the offshoring/outsourcing space), and it is growing at 20 percent annually. Office facilities can't be built fast enough to house the workers. To become a qualified CPA, it takes five years after university, and you can hire these CPAs for about $5–$10 per hour. This is considered a good salary.

When I first visited on an outsourcing study tour, the following line got me, "Any job that is done over the phone or behind a computer, we can do for a one-fifth to a tenth of the cost." So basically, any non-customer facing role can be done cheaper and often better.

The use of Cloud technology is critical to making this happen in accounting firms. Instead of sending large data files back and forth, the offshore accountants are working on the same file you are. Here's something quite blunt . . . if accountants locally are not adding value to the work they are doing, then their days are numbered.

The accounting firm of the future will have local team members who are customer facing and adding value. Everything else will be done somewhere else. This is happening right now.

Many accountants I have spoken with reject this reality, because they still want to hire locally. Hiring local people is a noble thing to do. I do it, but I do it mainly for customer-facing roles. Many accountants are worried what will happen to the profession if they don't hire local graduates and train them. This is a good concern to have. It's also a real one. If you are going to shift your processing team offshore, then how are you going to train local talent to "come through the ranks"? The entire training model might also need to be turned on its head.

The challenge you have is that other firms are doing this, and they are using the significant cost savings as an advantage and reducing their prices. With an up to 80 percent cost reduction on labor costs, the clients who are using offshore teams can hire more people and give better service. They can do more marketing, create more products, and give a better experience to their clients.

> "Many people come over here with their current business or product in mind. Then they see the machine in action. When they leave, they have invented new businesses and new product ideas."

The biggest challenge you will have with this strategy is "selling it" to your existing team members. They will feel their jobs are threatened. If you take the view that it is a business-growth strategy and not a redundancy strategy, then that will help a lot.

You don't have to go all in and create your own full-time team from day one. You could start by hiring contractors on the various contractor websites to do one-off special projects.

In the not too distant future, here's what your offshore team could look like.

- ✓ Administration
- ✓ Your internal finance team
- ✓ Marketing team—all functions
- ✓ Sales coordinators
- ✓ Client services assistants
- ✓ Technology creation and support
- ✓ Accounting processing team
- ✓ Bookkeepers
- ✓ Para-planners
- ✓ Product and systems developers

If you are interested in this space, then I strongly suggest you hop on a plane and go on a study tour so you can see it for yourself. As a tour operator (Mike) said to me,

"Many people come over here with their current business or product in mind. Then they see the machine in action. When they leave, they have invented new businesses and new product ideas."

The machine is full of gas and is waiting to be started.

Team Engagement

It's hard to grow and develop an accounting firm on your own. You need the support of your team. You might want to implement a lot of the ideas from this book; however, your team might have other ideas. Unless you have a super flexible team, who is used to change, then the reality is you might struggle with team engagement or buy-in. You might struggle to get the change you're looking for.

Everything in this book is about change management. It's all about doing something different to get a different result. With that comes behavior challenges. If someone has been successfully (in their eyes) doing the same thing for 15 or 20 years and all of a sudden you want them to take a sharp right turn and do something different, sometimes they resist.

One of the most important lessons I have learned with change is the following.

"People like change; they just don't want to be changed.
If you want to change the behavior, then you need to change the system."

Team engagement is not a singular event. It seems some partners think that sending the team to a seminar will do the trick. They'll get all enthused, learn some new skills, and hey, presto, it all changes. Sadly this is not the case. Team engagement is a process.

Here is an eight-point summary of how you get team engagement—assuming you have the right people to start with.

> "Unless you have a super flexible team, who is used to change, then the reality is you might struggle with team engagement or buy-in."

1. **Vision.** For a team to be on the same page, there first must be a page to be on. Do you have a one-page plan (not a lengthy business plan) and a painted picture of your vision? Do you know what it looks like when it is done? Does the team?

2. **Leadership.** If you settle on an idea, plan, strategy, and process, then the leadership team members must practice what they preach. So many times I hear that well-intentioned plans go astray because one of the leadership team members went back to the old ways.

3. **Culture standards.** Have you documented your culture so everyone knows how they are to behave while interacting with one another? Every firm I meet wants to improve the culture. What does an improved culture look like? Send me an email, and I'll send you some examples.

4. **Quarterly themes.** These really rock! You work out your biggest challenge or opportunity for the quarter and you wrap a theme around it. You dress the office up. You get everyone involved and have fun with it. Some examples might be "home run," "buzz," "round up," "growing the grass," and "delivering happiness." Each quarterly theme has a daily metric that you can measure and track progress, such as the number of clients, number of new opportunities, number of testimonials, etc.

5. **Meetings.** More meetings and less time per meeting is the mantra. Make them short, stand up, and directive. Make them regular with no waffle (give me the baby, not the delivery) and make them at odd times like 7:47, 8:08, 10:10,

or 12:51. Only ask three questions: (1) What's up today? (2) What's your daily metric? (3) Where are you stuck?

> "More meetings and less time per meeting is the mantra. Make them short, stand up, and directive."

6. **Reporting systems.** Why do accountants hide the profit, the cash flow, and the revenue? Remember that your team members are accountants, and they can probably work it out. What's there to hide anyway? If you let the team know the KPIs and the results of those KPIs, then you've got a better than good chance of achieving the results. It's a popular management technique called "open-book management."

7. **Daily sprints.** Sitting behind a keyboard all day with limited human interaction can be a bit boring. Why not have some fun and create a competitive spirit every day? You could introduce the concept of "sprints," where there are daily prizes for the activities done. The first person to get a completed project out the door gets $10. The first person to find another project within a project gets a voucher of some sort. Mix it up and have fun, and you'll be amazed the buzz that you'll create. While you're at it, get a bell (a big ships' bell) to celebrate. We have one in every office and above it says *"every time this bell rings, an accountant get's their wings."*

8. **Accountability.** How often do you "call people" on their commitments? How often do you publicly remind people of what they committed to? You said you would do it—why didn't you? You don't have to say much to hold people accountable. Being embarrassed in front of their peers is often enough. Someone once said to me, "If you want someone to be accountable, they must be in control of what they are accountable to." It's great to hold people accountable to their actions, but they need to be able to implement. They need to be in control of whatever they are accountable to.

If all this fails, then the last resort is to "coach, then fire." What do you do if the plan is solid, the explanation of the change is articulated well, the partners endorse it, regular coaching and training has happened, and they still don't get it? Simple . . .

Fire them.

Free their future and let them go and work at another traditional accounting firm. Let them go and ruin someone else's firm. Sometimes you have to take a hard line and put FIFO in place—fit in or f#@* off!

Rewarding Your Team

I have a view that for a fair day's work, a fair day's salary should be given. I do not believe you should overpay people (base salary) just to keep them or get them in the first place. If you create a great culture where people are challenged, they are learning a lot, and they are having fun, then they will stay with you regardless (within reason) of the base salary.

Rewards come in many formats.

On the first day (or as close to it) of a new team member starting, I have five minutes with them. They have already been through many hoops just to get a job and they are now in the induction process. They have been allocated to a team and they typically report to someone else other than me. They are sometimes a bit nervous for that first week as they are settling in. Here's how my important speech goes.

> "I do not believe you should overpay people (base salary) just to keep them or get them in the first place."

I call it the leaving speech.

"[insert newbie name], welcome to the team. We're thrilled you're here. I am sure you're the right person for the job and I know there is a lot going on this week. I just wanted to talk to you for a few minutes about the day you leave. You will leave one day, everyone does. I know this is your first day and I know you'll leave sometime in the future, so I figured we should talk about it now. I have a number of hopes and desires for that inevitable day. First, I hope we part on good company. I don't want someone to fire you because you didn't work out or make you redundant because of a business downturn. Second, I hope that you learn a lot, contribute a lot, and have a lot of fun. Third, I hope that you live by our values, service and culture standards, and the standards we set become part of your life. And last, when you look back at this block of time, no matter how long it is, you look back on it fondly as an amazing part of your career. Welcome to the team. That's all I wanted to say."

It's an interesting meeting to have, because who gets to talk about leaving the job they just started. Often they gasp and look at me weird. I like to think it sets the scene for the future. Learn a lot, contribute a lot, have fun, live by our values and standards, and look at this time fondly as an important time in your career. To give the gift of learning, contributing, having fun, and giving great service is an awesome reward.

I think a reward is having a snappy office environment. Most offices are not that nice, and your team is going to spend more than 40 hours a week in this location. It needs to be uplifting and inspiring. I think the reward of recognition is a powerful one. To recognize people publicly for a job well done is a powerful motivator. A clap, a mention, or a card goes a long way.

> "To recognize people publicly for a job well done is a powerful motivator. A clap, a mention, or a card goes a long way."

I think the reward of positivity and laughter in the office is powerful. The team members' home life might not be that great, but when they come to work they enjoy themselves. The reward of formal learning with a "book of the month" program or many seminars is both helpful and useful. It is amazing to see how a team will pull together to reach a target when a day off or a week of extra leave is offered. Team dinners and dress-up occasions are always fun and add to the culture.

I once encouraged my team to write their personal goals at an annual business planning session. I provided inspirational magazines, special writing paper, and a motivating environment. They were charged with writing 100 or more life goals in a two-hour time frame. Most did. When they finished the exercise, I collected the papers, made a copy, and told them I wanted to help them achieve their goals. The goals went into my safe at home. What they didn't know was I went through the goals and bought something special for each person for that upcoming Christmas. It was a magical Christmas party with my "Santa sack" full of goodies that they all wanted. We had tears, laughter, and excitement as Santa handed out the gifts. Then we all partied!

After much debate and researching, I have worked out that profit-share systems and commissions do not work for anyone other than salespeople.

It's not about the money. The money is important, but it's more than that. It's about the experience.

Together Everyone Achieves More

When it comes to sporting success, what is better—a team of champions or a championship team? You know the answer. A championship team will beat a team of champions every single time. The sporting arena is littered with successes where a team that works well together outperforms the team that has the superstars and big names in the team.

The same with business success. You need a single team working together with the one vision, one plan, and the shared passion to achieve your success.

So how do you get everyone on the same page with complete buy-in, working together, and implementing?

There are five areas to focus on when building a high-performing team in an accounting business.

1. Do you have the right people?
2. Are they motivated, excited, and passionate?
3. Do they know what to do?
4. Do they know how to do it?
5. Is the environment conducive to a high-achieving culture?

The Right People

You know if you have the wrong people on your team and to get rid of them would be a great benefit to your business. You know this, but you do nothing about it. Why is that? You will always make some mistakes in hiring people and you will always have problems with people—hire one person and you start to have problems! But putting up with the wrong people for so long in your business—that's inexcusable.

With so many people available to be hired, there is no excuse to not have the best people on your team. If you change your business model, you can create additional profitability and afford to have the best people available.

A great litmus test is to ask this question, "Would you enthusiastically rehire them?" If there is a hint of doubt, then action your gut.

Get rid of the wrong people. The leopards will never change their spots, and they will drag your business down. If you have to fire them, performance manage them out, or even make the position redundant, then do it.

The right team members need to be selected on attitude first and skills second. You can train the skills—hard to change the attitude.

> "A great litmus test is to ask this question, 'Would you enthusiastically rehire them?' If there is a hint of doubt, then action your gut."

Motivated, Excited, and Passionate

Assuming you have the wrong people off your bus and the right people are on it, then you need to make sure they want to be there. Are they motivated to help clients? Are they excited to be doing what they love? Are they passionate about their work?

Last time I looked there were 168 hours in a week. How many hours do you think are associated with each of the following?

1. Getting ready for work.
2. Getting to work.
3. Actually being at work.
4. Coming home from work.
5. Thinking about work!

My guess is that about 50 percent of your waking life is associated with work. Half of your (and your team members) adult working, waking life is associated with work. Half your life! I sincerely hope that for the benefit of your clients, your loved ones, your fellow teammates, and particularly yourself, that you are motivated doing what you do and you enjoy it.

If you do not enjoy what you do, then do something else. You're going to spend half your life doing what you're currently doing.

I was in a coachingclub meeting once, talking about doing what you love and an accountant (a sole practitioner, Janice) said, "I do not enjoy this business. I loathe it. My husband and I have other business interests. I am going to sell it." The next day she sold the firm to her second in command for $750K in cash.

> "My guess is that about 50 percent of your waking life is associated with work. Half of your (and your team members) adult working, waking life is associated with work."

Knowing What to Do

Do your team members have clear job descriptions, implementation tasks, and workflow projects to keep them busy? Do they know what to do on a daily basis? Is it crystal clear what they are working on, what their priorities are, and whom they are working with?

Many accountants I meet run out of work to do—yet the partners are always busy. If the business is well run, from a workflow point of view, then it should be properly resourced and the team should be kept busy all of the time.

Knowing How to Do It

Let's say you hire a new accountant. She has eight years of experience working for two other firms. You are excited to get this fully qualified superstar accountant on your team. You have loads of work to do, so the induction process might go like this.

"Hi Robert, welcome to the firm. You'll be working on Susan's team. Here is your desk, your computer, your chair, your login, and here is a heap of unfinished work to get into. You have eight years of experience, so you must know what to do. Let me know your progress on Friday afternoon. Good luck."

> "Just like you can change your business model to be more profitable, you can also redesign how your team works. It's your choice."

Just because this superstar accountant has eight years of experience at two other firms, it does not mean she knows how your business works. Have a good look at your induction process and ongoing training process. When someone joins your business, what happens in the first week? Are they properly inducted into your business? What is the ongoing soft-skills (not just technical-based) training program?

Are your teams enjoying a healthy mix of internal and external training programs?

The Right Environment

If you and your team are going to spend 50 percent of your working waking life at work, then shouldn't the workplace be a great place to be at?

I visit many accounting offices and I mostly find the environment is not that great. Often I find the furniture is tired, the office is closed and dark, the computer equipment is not up to date, the meeting rooms are untidy, the colors are dated, and there is a limited choice of food and beverage available.

You know you have the right environment, if your team members bring their friends to work to show off the premises. Let your team members decide what sort of workplace they want. Have a brainstorming session, get them involved, and do not put the "financial editor" on during this process. Do the cost justification and all the ideas come out.

With a coat of paint, some fresh plants, a variety of beverages, some new furniture, and some fresh ideas, you can make any environment look great.

As I observe high-performing teams in the business and sporting arena, they have a few things in common.

1. Common purpose—they are striving for the same purpose.
2. Values and standards—they have clear performance standards and shared values.
3. Goal alignment—everyone is shooting for the same goal.
4. Roles, responsibilities, and priorities—they all know what and when to do things.
5. Open communication—there is a channel of consistent communication.
6. Participation and support—they get involved and support each other.
7. Plan of action—there is a plan of action that is followed.
8. Risk taking and innovation—calculated and innovative risks are taken.
9. Celebration—there is constant celebration, such as sales bells, recognition, and plenty of parties!

Just like you can change your business model to be more profitable, you can also redesign how your team works. It's your choice.

A Growth Culture

What is a culture? Think back to your school science days. A culture is a growth. It's a living organism—just like a business culture. If your culture is not a growing-based culture, then it is a dying culture.

Most accounting firms have a culture, but it was not created—it just happened. And what it is today is what it is. If you want to have a high-performing business, then you need a culture that matches your objectives.

> "Your performance standards should be everywhere, and everyone should have a copy of them with them at all times."

Whatever culture you decide to create, it will take a while to create it. Your culture might be fun based, success based, financial-achievement based, client-service based, team based—or all the above. To change your culture will mean changing some of your people (who do not buy-in to the new culture), and it will mean summarizing it into written performance standards.

Your performance standards are how you want to people to act and behave. Your performance standards should be everywhere, and everyone should have a copy of them with them at all times. You can incorporate your performance standards into your daily or weekly training or meeting programs, and you can incorporate them into career development and performance management.

My business is not perfect by any means (which business is?), however, the consistent and positive comments we receive from clients regarding my team and team culture indicate that we do it better than most.

To give you an insight into my service and success-oriented culture, here is an in-depth look at my business, where my team operates under 15 service standards (external standards), 15 culture standards (internal standards), and five core values.

We use these performance standards in training, performance management, induction, team meetings, and, of course, client or prospect interactions.

Client Service Performance Standards

1. I lead by example.
2. I constantly raise the bar, as we lead the accounting profession.
3. Clients will be completely delighted with what I do, and how I do it.
4. I always maintain positive relationships.
5. I greet and say farewell to everyone by name with eye contact and a smile.
6. If at fault, I will apologize and make restitution—right away.
7. I demonstrate a positive can-do attitude at all times.
8. I focus on solutions to clients' objectives.

"You can incorporate your performance standards into your daily or weekly training or meeting programs, and you can incorporate them into career development and performance management."

9. I am creative and innovative in my approach to helping our clients succeed.

10. I always act with integrity, I respect others, and I use empowering conversation.

11. I always reply to all communication by the end of the same day that it was received.

12. I will own any queries or complaints that I receive, and ensure they are addressed within the same business day that I receive them.

13. I always answer the telephone within two rings and, with a smile, I always say "Welcome to XXX, this is [first name] [last name]."

14. I am always "on the stage" and act accordingly.

15. I always live and demonstrate the company values.

Team Culture Standards

1. We work in a positive environment, full of excellent people, who are focused on solutions at all times.

2. Personal responsibility and integrity exist at all times, at all levels.

3. Personal accountability is core to our beliefs—doing what we say we will do.

4. While we respect the individual, the team is more important than any single person.

5. Everyone adds value to the company and contributes to its performance.

6. Everyone knows their roles and respects the roles of others.

7. Everyone chooses to be here; there is no victim mentality.

8. The work environment is relaxed, healthy, comfortable, and creative, but professional and appropriately urgent at the same time. It is a fun environment that elicits creativity and supports camaraderie.

9. Our team members are committed to personal development. They show initiative in seeking out personal growth opportunities, making them well rounded and whole, outside our company.

10. We do not operate as a consensus company to move the company forward. We operate on a functional model, based on the vision of leadership.

11. We speak politely using a person's name—and we say "please," "thank you," "It'll be my pleasure," and "certainly," as a minimum.

12. If we talk about a person who is not present, we speak as if he or she is listening to our conversation.

13. If we have a problem with someone, we talk about the problem only with him or her in private.

14. If something goes wrong, we first blame a system, not a person.

15. To be part of our team, you MUST live our values and follow our client and culture performance standards to the letter. Every team member is empowered to correct any other team member who is not living and adhering to them.

Values

➢ Outlaw—push boundaries, be bold, step up

➢ Honor—code, culture, standards, clients, self

➢ Outrageous fun—don't be square

➢ Kaizen—continuous improvement

➢ Influencing lives—make a massive difference

You need to develop your own performance standards and values that suit your culture—or you can just use ours.

> "To be part of our team, you MUST live our values and follow our client and culture performance standards to the letter."

WHERE THE RUBBER MEETS THE ROAD

You've gotten this far with mindset, tactics, and strategies. The only thing left to do it implement. There's an old Zen saying, "to know and not to do is not yet to know."

What is the point of reading this far, nodding, getting frustrated, and realizing your potential if you're not going to implement? This chapter is all about implementation.

It starts with a scorecard of how well developed your firm is and then we dig into strategy of how you actually get things done.

Measuring a Well-Developed Firm

My definition of a well-developed firm is the following.

> "A firm that has implemented a whole host of strategies that make a positive difference to the firms' performance."

How well developed is your firm? How well do you implement anything? With what you implement, do the strategies produce a positive result to your financial performance? If you want to change the performance of your firm, then you need to change the actions and strategies—or implement those you know you should!

> "What is the point of reading this far, nodding, getting frustrated, and realizing your potential if you're not going to implement?"

As we coach firms, we have them focused on key strategies that make a difference to their performance in 90 days or less. If they are the right strategies, then you'll produce an exceptional **profit;** create excess **capacity;** and have solid, predictable, annual revenue **growth.**

The outputs of **profit, capacity,** and **growth** need inputs. The inputs are the key strategies that need to be implemented. To quantify how well developed your firm is, I created a scorecard with key strategies. I selected 30 of the best strategies that produce awesome profit, excess capacity, and exceptional growth. There are 11 strategies for profit, 8 for capacity, and 11 for revenue growth.

If you're looking for suggested and achievable benchmarks on profit, capacity, and growth, then the following would apply.

Outcome	Commentary	Benchmark
Profit	It's easy to prop up profits in an accounting "practice"—just get the partners to do more chargeable work. They have the biggest charge rates and anything they do goes to the top and bottom line. If you're wanting to run a peak performance accounting "business," then you increase profits with less partner chargeable time! Partners should follow the 30:60:10 rule and only be doing three things. High-end chargeable work based on value-based fees for less than 30 percent of their time Sales activity to win new clients or new work from existing clients for about 60 percent of their time Leadership activity—driving performance of the business for about 10 percent of time There are 11 strategies in the scorecard to drive your profits through the roof.	More than 50 percent before partner salaries with average partner chargeable time less than 30 percent

| Capacity | The old way of creating capacity is to hire more accountants. Yes, you can certainly do that. However, the issue is (a) finding and training accountants and then (b) the sheer cost of the exercise. What if you could do it by being more efficient? What if you could create capacity by "taking time out of client work" by focusing on technology and process?

Most firms I have met have about 50 percent capacity, but they don't know it. When they really focus on reengineering the way that they do client work and focus on reducing time, 50 percent can be achieved.

That means doing double the revenue with the same headcount. Most of the new revenue is pure profit!

There are eight strategies in the scorecard to drive capacity without hiring more expensive accountants. | Ability to do more than 35 percent new work each month |
| Growth | Most firms grow by being reactive. They put their charge rates up a little bit each year and get 5–7 percent new clients each year by referral. Yawn, yawn, and bigger yawn! Or they go on the acquisition trail and buy firms and proclaim they have grown by 18 percent per annum for the past five years!

True growth is organic growth. Which means new clients, higher prices, new services, and making sure to "provide every service to every client that helps them achieve their goals." Organic growth more than 10 percent per annum means focused marketing and sales activity.

For organic growth, you need to know who your ideal clients are, how you find them, how they find you, what you're selling them, and how you price what they're buying.

There are 11 strategies in the scorecard that drive organic growth. | Growing revenue more than 25 percent per annum organically |

As you go through the scorecard and rate your firm, remember these four rules of the scorecard.

1. You are scoring for your firm—not you personally.
2. You need to be brutally honest—it is what it is.
3. Score based on the exact description.
4. You need to follow the scoring rating scale at the bottom.

Firm Development Scorecard

	Strategy	Objective and detail of strategy	Score
	Profit	**>50% before Partner salaries with Partner productivity <30%**	
1	Upfront pricing	All clients know the price & scope of all projects before starting – in writing	
2	WIP and Receivables	Strict system in place for reduction of each – lockup <30 days of revenue	
3	Write off / ons	Process for write ons / net $ write ups every month	
4	Services Mix	Low profit services identified & eliminated - focus on high profit services only	
5	Value Pricing	Education / systems in place, entire team trained, represents >30% of revenue	
6	Average Hourly Rate (AHR)	It's known, measured on every invoice, it grows monthly, >$350 AHR	
7	Productivity	Accountants at a healthy 1,350 hours (no more) Partners 500 hours (no more)	
8	People Development	Structured Education process in place to get team more profitable faster	
9	Client selection	Low profit / high hassle clients and moved up or on	
10	Client Service	Structure service program – all team deliver exceptional levels of service	
11	Communications Program	Structured process – face, phone, events, >12 communications / year	
	Capacity	**Ability to do >35% of new work each month**	
12	Policies / Processes	Documented systems for everything – best way of 'how we do it here'	
13	Workflow management	18 step workflow system fully operational <10 days average turnaround time	
14	Efficiency model	All projects under hours' budget <80% of allocated hours' budget	
15	Firm on the cloud	All of your internal technology systems are cloud based	
16	Clients on the cloud	More than 80% of clients are pure cloud accounting – not hosted	
17	Team performance	You'd enthusiastically re-hire them all + team are focused on innovation	
18	Administration team	Administration team to do administration work associated with accounting work	
19	People mix / location	Offshore / contractor team in place and working well	
	Growth	**Growing revenue >25% per annum organically**	
20	Niche markets	You concentrate on target sectors (industry type) and own that niche(s)	
21	Best buyer strategy	Clearly identified best buyers, database owned and strategy to get them	
22	Brand development	Thought leaders in your space – known as the 'go to' firm for 'X'	
23	Web dominance	You are everywhere on the web – all possible channels & platforms	
24	Lead Generation program	Consistent weekly marketing process that generates leads and positive ROI	
25	Sales process	Documented Systematic process that works for all client facing team members	
26	Sales skills	Sales education process in place to enhance client facing team	
27	Retention system	Documented 'Client Success' process that works	
28	Average project value	It's known, measured, focused and increases monthly	
29	No. projects / clients / year	All clients buying all services they need to help achieve goals	
30	Business Advisory Services	Currently represents >30% fee base and growing monthly	
		Total score / 300	

Implementation Rating Scale

1	2	3	4	5	6	7	8	9	10
Not even close		Toe in the water		Sort of done		Oh, so close			Nailed it!

When you're done, add up your score. All 10s will equal 300. Thousands of firms have done this test and the range is from 30 to 254. Approximately 5 percent score more than 200 on their first go. There is a direct correlation between a high score and high profitability, capacity, and revenue growth.

This is a guide of what you have to do to improve your business, based on your score.

Score Range	Comments and Actions
30–100	You're just getting started, or you've implemented only a little that makes a difference. It's time to decide—do you really want to be in this business? If so, then get serious about your goals, rethink your business model, allocate some resources, and get busy.
101–150	You're approaching halfway. You've seen some early wins. Now it's time to nail the low scores. Set some realistic goals during the next two years and work through each strategy. Look at those that are below a five and get committed to sorting them out once and for all.
151–200	You're just above halfway. Congratulations on what you have implemented so far. Don't get complacent. You've still got a long way to go to achieve your potential. Get disciplines, focus, and increase your "working ON" time by double and smash through 200 this year.
200–250	You've implemented a lot. Congratulations. Your core numbers should reflect your implementation. If you are motivated, then it's time to turn on the burners. Invest heavily in marketing, product development, and niche markets. Time to grow the revenue by double or triple in the next few years.
250+	You are in the elite of the elite implementers. You've implemented many projects throughout many years. Extremely well done. If you haven't already done so, create a corporate model so the business can work without you. Partner chargeable time should be approaching zero, and now you can enjoy a passive income business. You've now got a serious asset that performs.

Getting Buy-In

One of the most common questions in relation to team members is getting them to buy-in to your new ideas. You want to have your team right behind you, as you conquer the world! Team buy-in is all about change management. The more aligned you are as a business, the faster and easier you will be able to reach your goals.

For a traditional accounting practice that has been operating the same way for a long period of time, then (unless you change your entire team) change will take some time—but not as long as you think. However, what you will find is that many of your team members are just waiting for something exciting to happen.

With change and buy-in, you have to remember a few things.

> "The more aligned you are as a business, the faster and easier you will be able reach your goals."

1. Your team (and your business) have been doing the "old way" for many years.

2. The new way might seem to make sense, but some of the team think the old way is not really broken—you are getting by, doing what you are doing.

3. Change management is not a singular event—you constantly have to drive it

So with that in mind, here are some ideas you can do to change behavior and get constant buy-in.

1. From a leadership level, search for the reasons **why** you want to change. You need to have the leadership team (other partners and/or key stakeholders) buy-in to the change first; otherwise, you have little hope of success. Alignment at the shareholder level is crucial to your success. The shareholders must have objectives that they are motivated by. If your shareholders are comfortable, not ambitious, have no goals, and are happy with the status quo (and you are the opposite), then you will have some major difficulties. You might need to leave your current business or get some new shareholders! If you need to bring in some outside help to guide you through this, then do it.

2. Decide **what** it is you want to change. Do you want to change the entire business or just some tactical aspects, such as pricing upfront instead of pricing in arrears? Make a list of the critical strategies that need attention and prioritize them. Get the list to be as short and succinct as possible. In my business, we focus on five key priorities each quarter, and then we have the number one priority that when implemented the rest follow. We have quarterly business priorities, CEO priorities, team priorities, and individual priorities.

3. Decide **who** needs to change. Is the entire team involved or just a critical few? My advice is that the entire team should be involved with doing something.

4. Decide **when** you want to change. Too much change too fast can cause disruption. Spread the change out over a few years. Have a ten-year, three-year, one-year, and 90-day plan.

5. Decide what the nonnegotiable **rules** (for example, all jobs priced upfront, value pricing, proactive focus, client communication strategy) are from a leadership level. It's your business. You might not tell the team the rules just yet—you might need to have the team buy-in to the new rules.

> "You might not tell the team the rules just yet—you might need to have the team buy-in to the new rules."

6. Conduct **events** that show your team members why they need to change. This could include regular training, seminars, client case studies, industry facts, internal testing, and social proof of other firms that have been successful.

7. Always bring it back to **WIIFM**—what's in it for me! Your team members are interested in a better-working environment, their enjoyment, salary and benefits, fulfilling work, clients' success, and career development.

8. Promote, promote, promote, and don't give up. If you believe that change needs to happen, and it is in the best interests of your business, then be like a dog with a bone. If after constant coaching of your team they do not buy-in, then coach them out.

In response to a recent forum post by a new member on "getting team buy-in," one of our most successful clients (David) wrote this excellent response.

"This is by far the biggest challenge that you will face on your journey. We have been around coachingclub since day one and with up to 100 people on our team to keep engaged, I have constantly been challenged with this question. I am sure that you have heard the word chunking. Well, we take the list of things to be done, break them down into chunks, and then allocate the responsibility for implementation to accountants within the business—not partners or managers, but everyday accountants who are on the floor and at the coal face. They would report their progress to me monthly, and I would give them all the support they needed to implement the change.

I always found that getting the partners and managers to commit was the easy part, because I dealt with them regularly. The best way to get everyone else involved was then to charge them with the responsibility of making it happen. Partners and managers have enough responsibility. I would run a competition to see who could implement things the best. At the end of a period (could be six months or whatever was appropriate), I would award a prize for the most successful person (and their group). This always ensured that things were happening, as the drive was from the staff and the prize was always well sought after."

Buy-in is not a singular event. If you want to change the behavior, then you have to change the system.

Implementing Anything

What's the point of coming up with an idea unless it is implemented? If the idea is worthy of the research, thinking, brainstorming, and effort needed to crystallize it, then don't you think it deserves to be implemented? Yet many good ideas are not implemented.

> "Implementation is relatively easy, if you know how to implement anything."

Implementation is relatively easy, if you know how to implement anything. I learned how to implement projects through necessity.

In a former life, I was asked to be the general manager (GM) at a small company that was in trouble. It had just come out of a disastrous merger and was making losses (a loss of $340K where normally it had a $1M profit), it had mounting debt ($1M cash debt instead of cash in the bank), and sales had declined by 50 percent to $3.4M. Technically, it was insolvent, however, the overseas parent company was propping it up with cash so it could pay its bills. Team morale was low and the clients were not happy either. My job as the new GM was to fix it and rebuild it. I gathered the team members (what was left of them), told them the brutal facts, and between us we brainstormed 149 key projects that needed to be implemented. After 15 months, we implemented 134 of the projects, and the business looked completely different. Profit went from a loss of $340K to a profit of $2.5M. The $1M debt was paid back in full, and sales went from $3.4M to $6.7M. The business was fixed up, rebuilt, and sold for many millions of dollars.

To grow a business or to turn one around, it takes focus and discipline. I used a nine-step process that I developed while turning that business around. Since then I have fine-tuned it and used it over and over again with many businesses and with many clients. I call it **lasercution™**—execution with laser focus. Note: I made that word up and the "TM" is fake.

1—Motivation. As the GM, I was motivated. I had a 5 percent bonus riding on profit improvement over a certain figure. You must find your personal motivation and your team motivation. During the course of the turnaround, I gave away about $100K in bonuses to the team, in addition to trips, vouchers, and other rewards as an incentive for a job well done.

2—Buy-in. Once the brutal facts were uncovered (all of them), I asked who was in and who was out. I had some resignations—five in one day from a total team of 12! That was OK because the new people I hired didn't know any different. The balance of the team was committed to making the business happen. I conducted "team advance" sessions every quarter to replan, report, and have fun. For more detail, review the getting buy-in information in the preceding pages.

3—Planning. I asked the team what needed to be done to fix and rebuild the business. We had an initial planning session and it was the team members who came up with the project list of 149—not me as the chief. These days, I keep my business plan to one page (albeit larger than a regular sheet of paper in size) that covers every aspect of my business.

4—Key projects. Once we had the project list, we put each entry into categories. For example, marketing, sales, logistics, finance, client service, products, etc. Each project was categorized, prioritized, date bound, and each one had a project leader who would be responsible for reporting on the success of the project.

5—ON time. Every week working ON time should be in your schedule. This is the time that you are not interrupted so you can focus on important business development projects. The writing of this book is a great example. I estimate that it will take about 100 hours to write and edit. I spread that time over a three-month period with blocked-out time in my schedule. Each project leader needs ON time in their schedule, so they can focus on projects that are not associated with client delivery.

6—Themes. Each quarter, a theme needs to be developed and rolled out to your team members. The theme for the quarter could be internal and/or external. An internal theme might be clean up, buzz, blast off, or systems. An external theme might be client cash flow, client profit, client assets, or client wealth. Have some fun with this and promote the themes to team members in addition to clients.

7—Visual management. Once you have your projects, your themes, goals, and plans, do not just hide them in a written report, file, or spreadsheet. Get them out there in a visual format. Use whiteboards, colorful props, large thermometers for targets, ships bells, flip charts that stick to walls, and even sticky notes on your computer to keep you reminded. My main team meeting room is called "the situation room," where most people would normally call it a boardroom. Is it a boardroom or a bored room? I love the use of whiteboards for planning and visual management. It's powerful to be constantly reminded, when you see it every day.

8—Accountability. If each person has set his or her own targets and time frames, then they can be held accountable to those targets and time frames. If you want someone to be accountable, you have to give them control of what they are accountable of. I like to keep people accountable on a daily basis. We have a short (no more than 45 seconds per person) daily stand up meeting at 8:38 every morning. We call it our 8@838. Each person has to answer three questions: (1) What's up—what are you specifically doing today? (2) Daily metrics—what are your numbers or outcomes that you are focused on today? (3) Where are you stuck—do you need any help to keep you on track? On a weekly basis, I run a full management meeting for management accountability (50 minutes) and then also a monthly, quarterly, and annual planning session. If people are consistently missing their targets, then alternative solutions and coaching is provided, or we find people who can meet their targets.

> "Every week working ON time should be in your schedule. This is the time that you are not interrupted so you can focus on important business development projects."

9—Coaching. Ever since I turned the above-mentioned business around, I have been a big believer in coaching. I had a business coach to help me do it. The best athletes have a coach. The best businesspeople have a coach. It is lonely in business, and I believe every businessperson needs outside support to guide, focus, encourage, and motivate them. I have used many forms of coaching throughout the years. I have used mastermind groups, where you informally meet with likeminded businesspeople and keep one another accountable. I have hired personal coaches who just help me, and I have been in group coaching. For implementation, the most effective form of coaching is group-based coaching. The reason is, with a one-on-one coach, you can still get away with not implementing. Think of group coaching like a formal board of directors with a chairperson. When you have to turn up to seven (or more) other businesspeople AND a coach and report in, it becomes embarrassing if you have not implemented what you said you were going to do. You are more motivated to achieve more, when there is more accountability.

When you spend the time developing a plan, make sure you spend the time to implement it.

It's All about You

As a business owner, I am a big fan of business by design, meaning you should design your business by your rules and the way you want it to be. You're taking all the risk, so you should have all the spoils. Many partners of accounting firms get the concept and they agree with the theory. What I find is that they often lack the personal development to pull it off.

I have been fortunate to have been involved in the personal-development space since 1987—two years after I left school at age 16. I have attended dozens of seminars, read hundreds of books, listened to hundreds of hours of audio, viewed hundreds of hours of video, and devoured countless manuals, websites, articles, and papers on a quest to become a better me.

I have always believed that if you want to run a better business, then you must become a better businessperson. I also believe that the development of the business will never outpace the development of its leader.

So to round out the last chapter of this book, I am going to focus on 12 critical traits on you becoming a better you. They are 12 traits that when implemented fully will serve you well on your quest to become the best business leader you can be.

Here's how this chapter works. I will explain the critical area and you are to score between 1 and 10 how you are on each of the critical areas. Here is the scoring guide.

> "I have always believed that if you want to run a better business, then you must become a better businessperson."

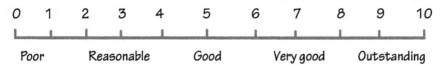

After you've read the trait description, put a mark where you fit on each trait on my spider wheel. In the middle is 0 and the outer point is 10.

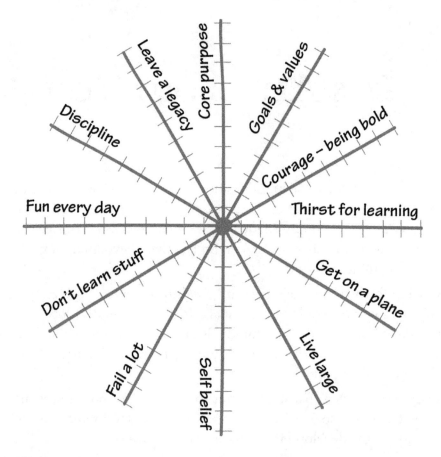

I've got 12 key traits to cover. Do not score on the spider wheel until you have read the trait. Of course, the more honest you are with yourself, the more success you'll have.

Core Purpose

Why do you do what you do every day? What is your reason for being on this Earth for this short amount of time? Some people call this your why and others your core purpose or your mission in life.

> "What is your reason for being on this Earth for this short amount of time?"

I found my core purpose in 2006 in Bali, Indonesia. I was attending an entrepreneurs conference, and I was asked to sit with one of the speakers and do an "exercise." We'd just finished playing golf and he (Thomas) ordered from the barman 20 pieces of paper and one beer for each or us. Thomas said at the end of the exercise, I would have my core purpose and I would cry like a baby. For the next three hours, Thomas asked me question after question about me and at the end, two words popped out: **influencing lives**

Not changing lives, but influencing lives—this is what I am all about. I like to influence. I like to make a difference. I can't change someone's life, but I can influence it. I like to write, speak, and develop products and services that influence. I like to get feedback on how people have used my ideas and concepts. I love case studies and success stories. One of my core values in business is to influence lives. I align my business decisions to my values. As a business, I want to make sure that I am influencing lives every day.

Thomas was right. I did cry like a baby when I discovered my core purpose in life. What's yours?

If you know your core purpose and you live by it, then score yourself a 10. If not, score what you feel is right for you.

Goals and Values

There have been countless studies done on the fact that if you physically write your goals, then you have a good chance of achieving them. Most people plan their holidays better than they plan their lives. There is a lot of talk about goal setting, but little on the process of achieving the goals. So I thought I would give you in detail **my goal achievement process.**

> "I want to make sure that I am living my short life in line with my values, while checking off my goals in life."

Let me just start by saying that I have been setting and achieving goals for more than 30 years. My first major goal achieved was to be the Under 15 Australian Archery Champion. I achieved the gold medal in 1984. Then I had a goal to be the Under 18 Australian Archery Champion. I achieved that in 1987. It was the same year I got into personal and business development material.

Throughout the years, I have fine-tuned my goal setting and goal achievement into a process that works for me. Here it is . . .

1. I **handwrite** everything into a special annual journal. I buy it from a UK luxury stationer, Smythson of Bond Street, London. I have the journal customized with my name and the current year.

2. At the back of the journal, I have all my **life goals listed**—currently 135 of them. I update this every year before the start of the new year.

3. In the journal, I also have my **personal values,** my overarching **purpose in life,** my constant **energy and focus state, what's important to me,** and a list of my **beliefs**—all handwritten.

4. Throughout the year, I will collect as many pictures as I can (from magazines) of my life goals and put them onto my **vision board.** I will also have a visual management process, so I can see how I am doing in achieving these goals.

5. I write at the front of my journal a **list of goals for this year.** There are typically twenty listed for each year—however five are the most important. The top five are highlighted. Most of the goals for the year are from my full list—either moving toward achieving them or completing them.

6. Once all the goals are listed, I reflect on the past year and work out why I did not achieve all my stated goals. Something has to be done differently. I write what I am going to **start doing** differently, **stop doing,** and **continue doing.** Each one covers a page in the journal.

7. For goals that take time to achieve, I **block out time in my schedule for the entire year for each one.** I block out . . . family day trips, board meetings (monthly), accountability meetings (monthly) management meetings (weekly), seminars to attend (typically 12–16 days per year), known seminars to deliver, gym sessions (3 per week), bike riding (2–3 per week), blog post writing (2–3 per week), date nights (monthly), dinner parties to host, holidays (8–10 weeks), golf lessons (many), golf practice (not enough), golf playing (1–2 per week—not enough), me weeks, camping trips, school holidays, etc. Everything is blocked out and then I work with what is left. It's amazing how much time is actually left for random stuff or extra work, if needed, when the year is blocked out. I have a view that **if it's not in the schedule, it won't get done.**

8. I write **action plans** for each of the goals on my annual list, including fun, business, personal, health, family, relationship, etc. I add bullet-point action plans for those that need it.

9. **I only divulge my goal list to people who are going to help me get them.** It's private. So that includes my wife, my accountability group, and some goals for my management team and employees.

10. **I keep myself accountable** to my goals each month by my accountability forum.

11. **I review and read my goals** every week.

12. While achieving my goals, I live by all my core values, especially **finishing what I start and doing what I say I am going to do.**

To make all this happen, I still sleep seven to eight hours per night, and I wake up at 4:45 six days per week. I want to get everything out of this life and be the best I can be. I love living up to my core purpose and having great stories to tell of my experiences. As I said, this works for me—it might even work for you.

My personal values are interwoven with my goals. I want to make sure that I am living my short life in line with my values, while checking off my goals in life.

If you have your goals written and you have a process for achieving them, then score yourself a 10 on the spider wheel. If you have no written goals (typed or handwritten) then that's a "0" score for you!

Courage—Being Bold

I find the fear of failure stops a lot of people. There is an acronym for FEAR—false evidence appearing real. It does take courage to do something different. The lack of courage causes the dreaded "P" word—procrastination. As the late Zig Ziglar, a motivational speaker and salesperson, used to say with considerable gusto—"Procrastination is the assassination of motivation." I always look at the issue/ challenge/target or whatever it is as "what's the worst that can happen?" If it's only losing a bit of money as the worst that can happen, then I'll typically give the go ahead. If the data stacks up and we believe in our abilities, then we do it. Sometimes we win; often we fail. But at least we had a go.

> "As the late Zig Ziglar . . . used to say with considerable gusto— 'Procrastination is the assassination of motivation.'"

The challenge the accounting profession has is that it is too comfortable. The business of accounting is changing; however, it's still a comfortable business to be in. Here's my view of what being comfortable does to a business . . .

Comfort breeds apathy.

Apathy breeds procrastination.

Procrastination breeds lack of innovation.

Lack of innovation breads stagnation.

Stagnation breeds death!

To succeed in business, I think leadership needs a healthy discontent with the present.

I have had the privilege of several times meeting one of this world's great entrepreneurs, Sir Richard Branson. He is known for his business acumen and his "just do it" attitude to life. However, as I discovered on a number of occasions, he does not jump into projects or businesses without research, data, and careful consideration. He told me once that he always "protect the downside" when he starts or gets involved in a business. As he described to me, "if the planes go down, the trains can't." He has the courage to try different things and push the boundaries, but he does it with a calculated view.

How are your courage levels? If they are outstanding, give yourself a 10. If not, then mark a score that reflects your current courage and boldness for trying new things.

Thirst for Learning

How curious are you? How many questions do you ask? How many nontechnical books do you read? How many webinars or audio/video sessions do you attend? How often do you read your national financial newspaper? How many business visits do you go on to learn how you can do it better?

These are questions that indicate your ongoing thirst for learning. I meet a lot of accountants who only do the required hours of continuing professional education per year. Typically these events are technical related, which is great if you want to be a better accountant. What about being a better person? What about being a better businessperson? What about being a better communicator, leader, mentor, and marketer?

> "I think there is too much time spent on 'technical' learning, rather than on what might be called 'soft skills.' It's the soft skills that define us."

I think there is too much time spent on "technical" learning, rather than on what might be called "soft skills." It's the soft skills that define us. It's the soft skills that will propel us forward. I am fortunate to associate with many high-profile entrepreneurs and leaders. The value they all have in common is their thirst for learning. They tend to have a systematic learning program of reading, viewing, and attending.

This book is about accountants, and one characteristic I find bizarre is how accountants do not ask that many questions. I often wonder if asking a question is seen as a weakness with accountants. I think the opposite—asking questions is a sign of curiosity, interest, and intelligence. I know some people are naturally shy and reserved. Maybe that's the problem—not enough confidence and low self-esteem.

What is going to be your annual learning plan?

- ✓ Number of books to read
- ✓ Number of courses to attend—locally and internationally
- ✓ New skills to learn
- ✓ Businesses to visit

Maybe you need to hire a mentor or a coach. Whatever you decide, make sure you are learning something new. If you're not learning, you're not growing. If you're not growing, don't expect your business to grow beyond the development of you.

If you are outstanding at learning, give yourself a 10 on the rating scale. If not, maybe there is something in this trait you can work on.

Get on a Plane

I have the view that someone, somewhere, has done what I want to do. They could be in another city, state, or even another country. Wherever they are, I want to find them. And I do find them. Often that means getting on a plane to go meet with them. I will respect their time, and I will listen intently. The biggest compliment I can give is to implement what they told me and then write them a thank-you note with what I have done.

Most people I meet are not prepared to jump on a plan. They complain about the cost, the time, and the hassle. Yes, quality air travel in a good seat near the front of the plane can be costly! However, the benefits outweigh the costs. The person or company you are about to meet might be a world leader in your field. He or she might have some insights that could save you years of work and millions of dollars in mistakes.

I am a keen golfer and often random people say to me, "Can I give you a tip?" My standard answer is NO. Unless you are a teaching professional who has runs on the board, I am not going to listen to you. I want to learn and follow someone who has done it before, not a "15 handicapper" who has read some magazines!

The person or company you seek might not be within driving distance of where you live. Sometimes you need to get on a plane to seek them out.

> "The person or company you seek might not be within driving distance of where you live. Sometimes you need to jump on a plane to seek them out."

Live Large

My personal success mantra is "doing what I want, when I want, with whom I want, in a manner I want." The last point (manner I want) is all about me living my life the way I want to live it. That means I like to live large!

Life is for enjoying, and there are many things that make life a little bit more enjoyable. I like to fly business or first class on every flight. I like to sleep in five-star hotels. I like a driver to pick me up wherever I travel. I like good clothes, food, and wine. I like to drive quality cars. I like to donate money to charity. I like to have a cool office in a cool street in town. I even like to go glamping, glamour camping! I have a camping wine rack among other cool camping gadgets. That's an example of the manner I like to live.

When it comes to accountants living large, they might desire to live better, but they have a big concern. The concern is "What will my clients think?" Many accountants have moved offices and had the customary office opening party. A client will make a smart remark that your fees are likely to go up now. Or you'll buy a new car and a client will comment that they now know why their bills are so high.

The vast majority of clients will not say anything, yet most will remember the client who made the smart comment. I think of it this way. What someone thinks of me is their business, and it's none of my business—it's their business.

Why not be proud of the fact that you are successful? I think people in the advisory space should be more successful than those they advise.

I came back from Las Vegas, Nevada, once after buying three pairs of really cool cowboy boots. I wore them out one night to a client function. One of my clients quipped, "Oh, that's where our fees are going." I said, "Yes, and thank you!"

If you are living the life you want to live, then score yourself a 10. If you are too afraid of your clients, mark a 1. It's not about flaunting it. It's about being proud of what you have achieved.

Self-Belief

As I mentioned previously, my favorite Māori (New Zealand indigenous people) word is "mana," pronounced **mah**-nah. According to the online Māori dictionary, it means

> "(noun) prestige, authority, control, power, influence, status, spiritual power, charisma—*mana* is a supernatural force in a person, place, or object."

I love this word. That person over there has mana. When they walk in the room, they have presence, they command the room, and they are in control. When they speak, they speak with authority and charisma. They are influential in everything they do.

> "I meet many partners who are overpaid client managers—just doing the job they did before they became a partner."

Do you have mana? Who do you know that has mana? I think mana is what self-belief and self-esteem are all about. To succeed in business, you need mana. You need to have self-belief and a high self-esteem.

I have a view that there are too many partners of accounting firms in the accounting profession. Many partners are there for retention reasons, not good business reasons. I meet many partners who are overpaid accountants—just doing the job they did before they became a partner. They have not stepped out of their comfort zone; they are not creating new business and new opportunities. Even when they try to create some new business, they are unsuccessful compared to others.

They are not doing this because they do not have the personal development, self-belief, and confidence to be a super-success.

Most don't have much mana!

Here are my top 10 tips for increasing your mana. Geez, I love that word!

1. **People you hang around with.** If you want to be successful, hang around with successful people. It will rub off. It's not about hanging around with the "loud" people. Sometimes people who are overly talkative and loud are masking their own self-esteem.

> "My favorite Māori (New Zealand indigenous people) word is 'mana,' pronounced **mah**-nah."

2. **Material you absorb.** What content are you reading, watching, and listening to? There is a rich source of self-development material for free on the Internet or, if you're like me, you can buy copious amounts of books and attend seminars every day.

3. **Client successes.** Take a look at what you have done for your clients in the past. What have you helped them with? How have you made them successful? Realize that without you, they wouldn't be what they are. You are amazing!

4. **Team successes.** How have you helped your team members grow and develop? How are they better off since joining your firm? Take the successful stories and relish in them!

5. **The way you dress.** The saying "Clothes make the man" is true. How do you dress? You don't have to be in $2,000 suits, but a wardrobe makeover can make a world of difference.

6. **Looking at your accomplishments.** Your career is littered with great successes. From awards to certificates to stories, letters, and testimonials. How often do you reflect on what you have done? Be proud of yourself for what you have accomplished to date.

7. **Be happy in your own skin.** The health and fitness industry is booming by telling people they are fat, unfit, and about to die, if they don't do something about themselves—TODAY. OK, if you are obese and a health risk, then do something about it. But why not be happy just the way you are and live life well now?

8. **Goals and affirmations.** I have four pages of written beliefs, affirmations, and energy states. I read it constantly to keep myself "up."

9. **Positive exterior.** Do you carry a smile or a scowl on your face? When someone asks you how you are, how do you reply? "Not bad. Pretty good. OK"—all negatives. Why not reply with "Great. Booming. Enjoying myself— something more positive? Remember, sometimes you have to fake it until you make it.

10. **Self-talk.** This is the big one. What do you say to yourself when there is no one around? Is the chatter so negative that it stymies your development? Does it make you fearful of the world? STOP IT.

Self-belief is such a critical key to success. It's not about being arrogant; it's just being sure of yourself. It's time to get some more mana. Wimps need not apply!

Go ahead and score based on where you believe you are now versus where you want to be.

Fail a Lot

If you're failing, you're not growing! Who knows where I got that from, but it is true. To fail means you are "having a go" and you are trying new things. I have tried so many things, ideas, processes, strategies, business models and I must say most have not worked. However, a few of them worked really well.

But I keep trying and never give up. I keep reading and learning and implementing. I have a healthy discontent for the present, which means I am always looking for the next idea. This drives my team members crazy sometimes, but they're used to it by now.

One of my most recent "epic fails" of my business career was a few years ago when I had this idea that I could leverage my successful coaching business around the world. I was looking for 100 licensees who could coach accountants in a geographical area. Those coaches would each have 100 accountants as clients, and in turn each accountant would have

> "If you're failing, you're not growing! Who knows where I got that from, but it is true."

100 small-business clients signed up to our online software platform. We called it 100 cubed. It was a flawless plan on the spreadsheet and the slide deck. It was a $100M

business opportunity (on paper) waiting to happen. We marketed the program and got 650 inquiries from around the world in a matter of weeks. We only needed 12 to validate and get going. We built a team to support it and spent a fortune on IT platforms.

How could we fail? Well, it did.

The reason it failed was because we were looking for the perfect type of person. Someone who could hit the ground running with minimal training. If we lowered our standards, then we could have found hundreds (as many franchise coaching companies have) who could potentially do the role. We weren't prepared to do that. Instead we canceled the program and moved on.

As a small business at the time (circa $5M in revenue), it ended up costing $1.5M, with no borrowings in the business—that came out of cash flow. Ouch, ouch, and more ouch! We licked our wounds for a couple of years on that one. We had a go.

> "I choose to do tasks I like doing and that I am good at. If I like doing a task, I learn how to use the tools to do the task."

We failed and we learned. Out of the exercise, we ended up with an awesome IT platform that is now used by thousands of accountants around the world.

So from failure there is sometimes a silver lining.

I find accountants do not fail enough, because they do not do enough. They are too comfortable doing what they are doing. Maybe if technology (software and machines—not kidding here) replaced accountants in the future, they would be more active in trying new ideas.

Where are you on my annoying rating scale? If you are trying a lot and failing a lot (as long as you learn), then rate it a 10. Otherwise score it lower.

Don't Learn Stuff

I choose to do tasks I like doing and that I am good at. If I like doing a task, I learn how to use the tools to do the task. If you look at office equipment, there are many tools that make life easier that I don't want to learn how to use.

Take the scanner. It's a useful tool, but I'm not going to learn how to use it. If I do, I might have to use it. Or what about that contraption with sharp teeth called the binding machine? That thing can hurt you. There are trained professionals who know how to use the binding machine. I don't want to be one of them.

I like to get focused on the "three highest-dollar, productive activities" that I can do in my business life. I am brutal with my time on this, and I don't do what is not a "top three" activity. I delegate it to someone else.

In the year 2005, I started my accountants coaching business from home. Within a couple of weeks of my new startup, I wrote in permanent ink on my whiteboard the following. I will only do three things in this business.

1. Marketing
2. Selling
3. Delivery

I will not work for anything less than $750 per hour.

Remember this was 2005. My self-esteem was not as high as it now, and that's why I priced my time at $750 per hour. Fairly quickly, I took that to $1,000, then $2,000, then $3,000, and then I moved to value-based fees and it didn't matter anymore.

> "If I can spend 80 percent of my time on my top three, then the business is better off for it and so am I."

These days my top three activities have changed. My business has grown, and I have a team of people around me who are professionals in what they do and I am a professional in three things only.

1. **Leveraged marketing.** Writing this book is a good example.
2. **Strategic thinking.** Basically coming up with ideas.
3. **Leadership.** Inspiring the team to greatness.

If I can spend 80 percent of my time on my top three, then the business is better off for it and so am I.

This chapter is all about you. You are the primary risk taker in your life and you should get the spoils. Go ahead and rate yourself where you are about learning "stuff" versus what you would not like to know!

Fun Every Day

In 2001, I started my first software business. It was exciting at the start (as all startups typically are) and super busy. We raised quite a lot of capital to get it going, and we were away. As the cofounder, one of my roles was sales. I was selling every day to my target market. It was tough work, but the product was working, the clients liked it, and we were making a difference. However, I was not enjoying it. In 2005, we decided we should chase some big fish and that meant looking for distribution in the United States. I went for a visit, met with the key people in the target company, and they also liked what we had. It was all going great and they verbally said they wanted to distribute the product throughout the United States. I was excited.

A few weeks after returning home, I had a 4:30 a.m. phone call with the key people in Chicago. I got a "not now" answer from them. It turned out to be a big fat "no." At 4:45, I put my head in my hands and I actually beat my head against my desk. Why is this so hard? Why is this not working for me? Why am I not enjoying it? The day prior to this call (October 25, 2005), I had received my test results of my wealth profile—which path I should follow to create wealth and enjoyment in business.

> "I had received my test results of my wealth profile—which path I should follow to create wealth and enjoyment in business."

I looked at the test results, and I instantly realized I was in the wrong business—for me. I could not be "me" in the business, and I felt the business was boring. Something had to change. I waited until 7:30 and I called my then business partner. I told him I needed to see him. He asked what it was all about. I said, "I'll tell you when I see you."

A couple of hours later, I was at his home and I told him that I was not enjoying the business and I wanted to leave. He asked, "When?" "Today," was my answer. He said, "You can't leave today. What are you going to do?" I replied that I didn't know what I was going to do, but I was going to follow this "star" thing and see where it takes me. My mind was made up and I ended up leaving two weeks later. The company gave me a nice sendoff and I was out of there.

I had no money, no method of making money, no assets, kids in private schools, car leases, and a mortgage. I had the whole thing going on. That weekend I was at a barbecue at a friend's house and he too asked me what was I going to do? I had no idea. He gave me three ideas, which I followed through on. One of them (coachingclub) turned out to be a $35M (and counting) idea.

So I started a new business from home. The first month I did $2,000 in revenue. The second month I did $22,000. The third month I did $24,000, and by the time the first 12 months finished, I did $975K in revenue. I made a profit of $450K in my first year and in the second year, I had more than $1M in profit and have never looked back. Since that day (October 26, 2005), when I decided to take massive action, I have been in my flame (not in the wax) and enjoying business and having fun literally every day.

The business of business should not be a drag. If you have designed it your way, then surely that involves having fun and enjoying the journey.

How much fun are you having? Are you passionate about what you are doing? If it is "off the charts" fun every day, then score a 10. If it's a drag, not working, and you're not passionate about it, then score lower. And do something about it. It's a business, and we're only here once!

> "The business of business should not be a drag. If you have designed it your way, then surely that involves having fun and enjoying the journey."

Discipline

All top performers have immense discipline. The top-performing person could be an athlete, a musician, a politician, a spiritual leader, a salesperson, a doctor, or a business owner. It doesn't matter what field the person is in, successful people all have a disciplined approach to success.

So how does discipline make its way into an accounting firm? Here are seven examples that require discipline.

1. **Workflow processes.** Do you have a process? If you do, is it followed every time? I bet not. My guess is sometimes you do it, sometimes you don't. We created an 18-step workflow process, which works with every accounting job, no matter what source of software you use. Every accountant we teach it to loves it, and when they implement it, they get amazing results of efficiency, customer service, and margin improvement. One of the steps is to do a business performance review once per year with each client. Every single accountant

agrees it is the right thing to do. The accountants agree they should do it at least once per year with every business client. Do they? Not likely. It takes discipline to follow a workflow process.

2. **Meeting rhythm.** We endorse and teach regular (and short) stand up meetings, which are designed for quick communication. Every accountant we teach it to loves the idea. They're supposed to start at an odd time (9:09, 10:10) and go for a short amount of time. There are three questions asked of each team member: (1) What's up? (2) What's your daily metric? (3) Where are you stuck? Those who follow this idea get amazing results of communication and problem solving. Do they always follow it? Not a chance.

> "It doesn't matter what field the person is in, the successful people all have a disciplined approach to success."

3. **Systematic growth.** If you want to double the revenue of your firm in three years, then you need 26 percent revenue growth per annum or 2 percent per month—month in and month out. If you want to double the revenue in five years then you need 15 percent per annum growth or 1.2 percent growth per month—month in and month out. To grow a business, you need a systematic approach to marketing, sales, and service. Each month builds on the last month. It takes discipline and focus.

4. **Sales meetings.** I strongly endorse that partners should do a minimum of 20 client visits per month with existing clients. The objective to see where the clients are with their businesses, understand their objectives, and then see if they need any help (new services) to achieve their objectives. Let's call it what it is. It's a sales meeting. They take about 90 minutes per meeting and then with some follow up (write a document and maybe meet again), it might take another 90 minutes. So three hours per client times 20 clients equals 60 hours per month. If you did this (and you were really bad at sales), then you'd get at least five new projects per month. Those who have been trained in our sales methods are getting 15 projects from 20 clients. Let's be conservative and work on five projects per month from 20 clients. If each project has a value of say $7,500 (based on value-based fees) that's $37,500 of new business. That's a $625 per hour return. It's a fairly good use of time and the client is better off

for it. It takes discipline to do 20 meetings per month. Most accountants don't, but all should.

5. **Meeting times.** I like to schedule meeting times at odd times during the day. I'll call you at 10:15. Let's meet at 8:08. How about we catch up for coffee at 9:40 on Tuesday? Then I like to play games with time. I like to watch the second hand on the clock get to the 12 and then start calling. I have exactly 60 seconds to connect with the person and most people look at the clock on their computer or their phone. I am calling precisely as agreed. I am meeting with you precisely as agreed. We are starting the meeting at precisely the time we agreed, and we are not going over time in any way, shape, or form. I like to call the person, and I rarely let anyone call me. I do that because I know I will be on time with my meeting or calling schedule. It takes discipline to do this. Most people are sloppy with meeting times, and many will say, "We'll get started as soon as such and such is here." Not on my watch. I am not going to punish those who are on time because a few people are late. Incompetent people are late. Competent people are sometimes behind schedule.

6. **One thing at a time.** I think multitasking is a crock. How can you do three things at once really well? The human attention span is dropping every decade, as our lives are flooded with more and more content and data every day. It's coming from all angles, all the time. To deal with all that life and business throws at us, the answer is not getting good at multitasking. The answer is to get focused on the one thing you have to do right now. Do it properly and once only. Do only one project at a time. Have one uninterrupted conversation at a time. Deal with emails when you deal with them—not emails, Facebook, phone calls, and Twitter all at the same time. Have one open client job at a time and stay focused until it is done. If you attempt multitasking, you'll enter into "job pick up, put down" syndrome, which leads to inefficiencies and mistakes.

7. **Saying no.** If you know who your target market is and what services you offer, then you need to stay true to that and say NO to potential clients, services, and projects. If you have a business plan and you set the objectives, priorities, and projects at the start of the year, then make sure you stick to them. Say NO to shiny new things that might look good but might divert your course. It takes more discipline to say NO than to say YES.

At the end of the day, it's about being true to your values, doing what you say you're going to do, and finishing what you start. If you start something, then take it through to the finish line. Sometimes you might not finish exactly in the time frame you intended, but at least you finished.

You know you better than anyone, so score yourself honestly on this one.

Leave a Legacy

When you're gone from this Earth, what will others say about you? What are you building or doing that is making a difference? Have you written your own eulogy?

As the saying goes—we're only here for a short time, not a long time. My life coach is an ex-monk and he introduced me to my "death" clock. I thought death was a bit harsh, so I renamed it to be my "time to die" clock. It counts down every second on my smartphone, and it is quite sobering to realize that I don't have much time left.

I set my clock to exactly 100 years old. I am going to checkout on (or thereabouts) August 28, 2069. I figured that 100 years is long enough.

In that time I want to live by my core purpose, have goals and values, have courage and be bold, learn a lot, get on planes, live large, improve my self-belief, fail many times, don't learn stuff I don't need to, have fun every day, be super disciplined, and leave a legacy!

For the last time, score where you sit on the legacy scale.

So, how did you do on your scores? Like most people you'll have some high and some low points. It's time to join the dots. When you join the dots does it look something like this?

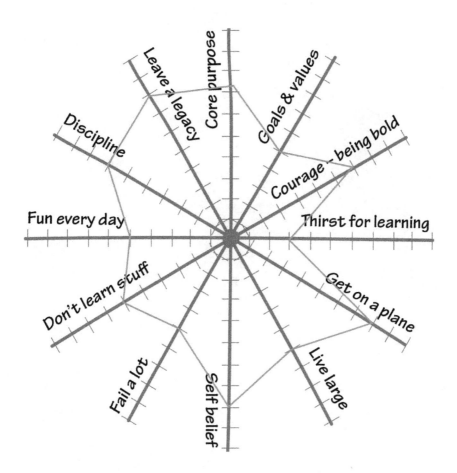

It is what it is.

The 12 traits are all about making a wheel. This is the wheel that will get you from A to B in your business life. This is the wheel that will keep you sharp, as you strive to succeed.

What does your wheel look like? How is your wheel going to roll? Wheels are supposed to be round, aren't they? If you have a small round wheel (all 2s and 3s), then your journey to success will be tiresome with a lot of effort and you'll feel every bump in the road.

If you have a large round wheel (all 7s and 8s), then the journey will take effort and you'll cruise over the bumps.

How do you want your wheel to look? Maybe it's time to pump up the tires!

MAKING AN IMPACT

I get asked all the time why I chose accountants to work with. I think as I look back on how I got started, I have come to the realization that accountants actually chose me. You should by now know that I am not an accountant (nor will I ever be one), and you now know that I have forged a unique niche in the worldwide profession as a thought leader and entrepreneur.

After years of working with accountants, I have come to understand my true purpose as to why I work with accountants. Here it is . . .

If I, and the people on my team(s), can help accounting practices to become accounting businesses and during the process we help them to sort out their operations, client service, people, workflow management, marketing, sales, profit, and cash flow, then we can make a significant difference—to that one firm and the people in it.

However, if we can also show those same accounting businesses how to offer value-added services to their clients that help their clients with growth, profit, cash flow improvement, asset protection, and wealth creation, then we can make a significant difference. You can make a significant **impact** to those business clients, their shareholders, and employees.

Think of the massive and long lasting **impact** you could have. Let's say you have 200 business clients. You can choose to positively impact them or negatively impact them—in four distinct areas.

1. Revenue
2. Profit
3. Wealth
4. Happiness

Revenue Impact

Let's say the average revenue of your 200 clients is $1M each. That's $200M of revenue in your client base that you could positively impact by being proactive and adding value or negatively impact by doing nothing.

Profit Impact

Let's say that your clients make an average of 15 percent profit. That's $30M of profit in your client base that you could positively impact by being proactive and adding value or negatively impact by doing nothing!

Wealth Impact

Let's say each business averaged a five times profit multiple to get a valuation. That's $150M of business wealth in your client base that you could positively impact by being proactive and adding value or negatively impact by doing nothing!

Happiness Impact

Let's say each of your 200 business clients employed an average of 10 people. That's 2,000 people in your client base that you could positively impact by being proactive and adding value or negatively impact by doing nothing!

Your impact is huge when you can be proactive and add value. If we can find enough accounting firms that want to help their clients build great businesses, then **we can change the world**—one accounting business at a time.

Get involved. Make an **impact**. Come with me, as we change the world.

THE FINAL WORD

Thank you for reading my book. I hope you enjoyed it. Now what? Are you going to just read it and then file it (do nothing) with the rest of the books you have read? Or are you going to take some action and implement the relevant ideas?

I learned this simple formula a long time ago . . . . **goals + vehicle + decisions + action = results.** If you liked what you have read, then from here it's all about making decisions and implementing them. You are only going to make some decisions and take some action if the goals you gave are strong enough. Why do you want to do this? Is it revenue, profit, cash flow, wealth, happiness, client delight, or lifestyle? Or maybe it's everything.

If you're just looking for a few tweaks here and there, then you've probably wasted your time reading the book. Give the book to a colleague. Assuming you liked the book, here are some action points.

1. Buy a copy for your team members—get them involved.
2. Connect with me on social media platforms (details below).
3. Subscribe to and read my blog (details below).
4. Create a list of all the possible projects you could implement.
5. Implement two to five projects from the list every month.
6. Let me know of your progress—what's working and what's not.

If you're looking to thrive, then maybe it's time to step up and make some significant changes. I have held nothing back in the book and provided a lot of my best content with significant details so you can implement it.

It's my hope that I have provided a good business case where you are influenced enough to take action.

All the best with your success!

Rob Nixon
April 2017, Brisbane, Australia

Contact details
Email—rob@robnixon.com
Blog—www.robnixon.com
Twitter—@therobnixon
LinkedIn—therobnixon

ABOUT ROB

Rob has forged a niche to be the world's foremost authority on how Accounting firms can achieve peak performance. Rob believes that Accountants are the natural trusted advisor to business. He believes that accountants can make a massive difference to their client's condition. He also believes that unless accountants change their business model then a big part of their current revenue will go the way of the dinosaur.

Since 1994 he has been running businesses that specialise in helping accountants run better, more profitable businesses. Accountants intrigue Rob and over the years he has trained them, consulted to them, coached them, researched them and visited thousands of them. His speaking work has taken him around the world where he has spoken to in excess of 170,000 accountants.

In 2005 he created the revolutionary coaching model called coachingclub. The coachingclub model enabled firms to be accountable, to consistently learn and to share ideas amongst their peers. Over 800 Accounting firms have graduated from his coachingclub program. The vast majority of firms have doubled or tripled profits because of the program.

In 2014 he released a groundbreaking cloud software solution called PANALITIX. Accountancy firms around the world use PANALITIX to engage their clients and build a great business.

He is the author of 2 bestselling books *"Accounting Practices Don't Add Up – why they don't and what to do about it"* AND *"Remaining Relevant – the future of the Accounting profession"*. Both have received rave reviews from accountants and industry professionals from around the world.

Rob is a keen golfer (single figures) and adventurer (he is ticket holder 293 on Virgin Galactic to go into space). He lives in sunny Brisbane, Australia with his lovely wife Natalie and 3 children.

CPSIA information can be obtained
at www.ICGtesting.com
Printed in the USA
LVHW101120010720
659454LV00024B/311